The Autobiography of a Beggar Boy

James Dawson Burn

Edited with an introduction by
David Vincent

London
Europa Publications Limited

Europa Publications Limited
18 Bedford Square, London WC1B 3JN

© David Vincent, 1978

ISBN: 0 905118 26 X

Printed and bound in England by
Staples Printers Rochester Limited
at The Stanhope Press.

The Autobiography of a Beggar Boy

Contents

Preface

The Autobiography of a Beggar Boy is the second in a series of republications of working men's autobiographies from the nineteenth century. The complete text of the first edition is reprinted together with an introduction which examines some of the themes and implications of the autobiography and outlines Burn's career and publications in the years following its composition. The comparative historical neglect of the subculture of beggars and pedlars within which Burn was raised, of the family life of the working class, and of the main areas of Burn's adult life—hatting, Scottish radicalism in the 1830s, and the Oddfellows movement in the north—enhances the value of the work, but equally such neglect has made necessary the inclusion of notes to the text to clarify and provide some context for the events in the narrative. The unnumbered notes are Burn's, the remainder are the editor's. As with *Testaments of Radicalism*, the text has been reprinted with the original spelling and punctuation in the interests of authenticity, although obvious printer's errors have been removed. I should like to thank Mr. Charles Hill of the Manchester Unity of Oddfellows, Dr. Bernard Sharratt, the staff of the Mitchell Library, Glasgow, and my wife for their help in the preparation of this volume, and Adele Biagi for typing the manuscript.

DAVID VINCENT
University of Keele

Introduction

The Autobiography of a Beggar Boy was one of the few working men's auto-biographies in the nineteenth century to become a popular commercial success.[1] Between 1855 and 1859, it went through four editions and was republished in a revised edition in 1882, but thereafter fell into neglect and is now scarcely known, even by historians working in the fields covered by Burn's life.[2] The illegitimate son of itinerant beggars, Burn led a life of constant geographical, social and economic mobility, and his account of his restless search to secure a place as a respectable member of society is told with a skill which matches the drama of the events he is describing. His mobility, together with the energy of his actions and observations, made him an unusually wide-ranging and perceptive witness of the transformation which his society was undergoing and the work provides important contributions to many areas of the social, economic and labour history of the period. Burn is one of the few working men to face up to the real task of the autobiographer and through his intense exploration of the changing relationship between his inner self and the world in which he lived he provides the modern reader with a rare and valuable insight into the consciousness of a working man as he struggles to make sense of his experience in an industrializing society.

I

The title page of the first edition of the autobiography raised the question of the identity of the author, and indeed the very status of the work. None of the first four editions carried any reference to the name of the author, and the reviews of the first edition indicate that there was initially some doubt as to whether the work was a true autobiography at all.[3] *The Times* thought it

[1] The few comparable successes were Robert Butler's *Narrative of the Life and Travels of Sergeant B, written by himself* (Edinburgh, 1823) which went through at least three editions; Samuel Bamford's *Passages in the Life of a Radical* (1839–41, 3rd ed., 1844) and *Early Days* (1848–49) which were republished in 1857 and 1859 and together in 1893; and Thomas Cooper's *The Life of Thomas Cooper written by himself* (London, 1872) which went through four editions in two years. At the end of the century the radical journalist W. E. Adams looked back to Burn's reception as encouragement for his own attempts at autobiography. See *Memoirs of a Social Atom* (London, 1903), vol. 1, p. xvi.

[2] The only serious exploitation of the work is to be found in Bernard Sharratt, *Autobiography and Class Consciousness. An attempt to characterise nineteenth century working class autobiography in the light of the writer's class* (unpublished Cambridge Ph.D. thesis, 1974). I am grateful to Dr. Sharratt for allowing me to make use of his excellent study.

1

necessary to discuss the authenticity of the work before proceeding to a more detailed assessment of its contents but, after noting that doubts existed, came to a firm if ponderous conclusion: "It unquestionably abounds with circumstantial notices of persons and places, and where our previous acquaintance with such particulars affords a superficial test of its accuracy, we must admit that it sustains this test satisfactorily. So far, then, we can consistently acquiesce in its confiding reception by its numerous readers."[4] Thereafter the work became accepted as genuine, but its author, James Dawson Burn, successfully kept his name a secret. He sustained his desire for anonymity throughout almost the whole of his publishing life. Only his first two works, a lecture and then a book on the Oddfellows movement published in 1840 and 1845, and his last, a revised and extended version of his autobiography published at the very end of his life, bore his name.[5] The books he wrote following the favourable reception of the autobiography are merely signed "by the author of The Autobiography of a Beggar Boy".

The decision to publish the autobiography anonymously may have been based on a perception that such a work by a man who was otherwise wholly unknown would gain little in popularity from the author's name and might, to the contrary, gain much from the mystery surrounding its concealment. Further, the deliberate anonymity would enhance one of the main justifications for publishing an autobiography of a beggar boy, that the section of society from which the author sprang, and of which he was, in a sense, a representative, was itself hidden from the readership. However, the refusal to attach a name to the author also reflected a central characteristic of the life which the book described. At every turn, beginning with the date of his birth and the person of his natural father, whom he does not meet until his early teens and whose name he subsequently rejects, and extending into the whole area of his social, occupational and class position, Burn was deeply uncertain about his own identity; as he wrote at one point, "Amid the universal transformations of things in the moral and physical world, my own condition has been like a dissolving view, and I have been so tossed in the rough blanket of fate, that my identity, if at any time a reality, must have been one which few could venture to swear to." (p. 56). If the central theme of the book is that of a man in search of his identity, it is appropriate that he should have omitted the most basic label of all from the book.

But if the subject of the autobiography is a man fragmented and adrift, a man who had led what the title page properly describes as a "strangely

---

[3] In the final 1882 edition Burn wrote that, "When I published the first part of my Autobiography I had no idea that such a plain and simple tale would have been taken otherwise than the narrative of a real life. I found however that many people were sceptical of its truth. The publisher was interrogated upon the matter both by letter and otherwise; and one gentleman, having learned my name and address, wrote to me to satisfy himself that the book was not a fiction." (p. 403).

[4] *The Times*, 28 December 1855, p. 4.

[5] The 1882 edition also listed all his earlier anonymous publications.

chequered life", then the form of the autobiography, as of all true autobiographies, is that of an attempt, from the point at which the autobiography
was written, to find some order in the mass of remembered experiences. As
Roy Pascal puts it, ". . . an autobiography is a shaping of the past. It imposes
a pattern on a life, constructs out of it a coherent story. It establishes certain
stages in an individual life, makes links between them and defines, implicitly
or explicitly, a certain consistency of relationship between the self and the
outside world."[6] It is clear from the preface and the opening pages that at
least in his intention and ambition Burn had recognized the task of the
autobiographer. For "self" Burn uses the term "character", for the outside
world, "circumstances". The book is to trace the survival and development
of his character in the face of the pressures of the circumstances of his life.

In one sense the conceptual structure is an extension of the puritan tradition of autobiography which was the main literary antecedent of the
nineteenth century working men's autobiographies.[7] Burn is deeply concerned with the history of his spiritual being and the extent to which he
succeeded in avoiding the "temptations" which the outside world placed
before him. But in a number of respects the autobiography marks a sharp
departure from the seventeenth and eighteenth century tradition. Most
obviously it is a fundamentally secular work. Although Burn probably con-
siders himself a Christian, he is not a churchgoer and we are given no
information as to which denomination, if any, he belongs. His comments
on organized religion are confined to attacks on the religious extremism, both
Catholic and Protestant, which he witnessed in his youth. The moral values
with which the book is concerned are Christian only in the very broadest
sense, and unlike the puritan autobiographies the meaning of the outside
world is not confined to its impact on his private spiritual being. He is very
much concerned with a particular society at a particular point in time, and
one of the main purposes of the account is to cast light on the changing state
of a section of society which lay outside the written history of the period.
Indeed it is a very public autobiography. The epistolary structure adopted
by Burn, in which his memories are addressed to his eldest son, Thomas, "in
the hope that my numerous trials and difficulties, and the experience of my
chequered life, may be of service to you in guiding your steps in the path of
duty" (p. 39), ought, if seriously carried through, to result in a private communication. It is, however, soon obvious that the device is largely superficial.
Thomas remains little more than a name;[8] we are given no indication of his
personality or of Burn's relationship with him, and none of the recounted
incidents assumes prior knowledge or shared experience on the part of the

[6] Roy Pascal, *Design and Truth in Autobiography* (London, 1960), p. 9.
[7] See Owen C. Watkins, *The Puritan Experience* (London, 1972), *passim*; Paul Delaney, *British
Autobiography in the Seventeenth Century* (London, 1969), pp. 6–104; John C. Morris, *Versions
of the Self* (New York, 1966), chapters II and III.
[8] We are not even told that he is Burn's son until p. 132, over half way through the autobiography.

recipient. In the revised 1882 edition the device is dropped altogether, presumably because Thomas had died in the meantime, and little reorganization is required. The main purpose of the form in this instance is to facilitate the didactic function of the book. He is speaking from one generation to another, and also from one class to another. In this sense the book belongs to the diverse and voluminous contemporary genre of improving literature, which frequently adopted the fictional autobiography as a means of instruction, and which may in turn explain why there was initially some doubt as to its authenticity.[9]

One problem Burn had to face was how to communicate his general conclusions without moving the focus away from his personal development, but before he could begin to instruct, he had to impose a pattern on his life, and construct a coherent story. We can gain a hint of the difficulty Burn is going to have in this respect from the preface. It appears at first sight as if Burn has not only recognized, but successfully met the challenge. The pattern has been found, and his life divided into three firm divisions. The first of these is to be organized around his life as a vagrant; the second is to be concerned with the "misdirected energies of an uneducated man whose ambition was fettered by a want of early training," but when we get to the third, in which the overall pattern should be finally revealed, all we find is an epoch in which "the Author's life may be said to be ruled by a series of conflicting circumstances . . ." which is an admission of a failure to establish a coherence both in his life and in his autobiography.

Another indication of the problem is to be found in the ambivalent way in which he uses the term "character". In one sense the term seems interchangeable with the moral inner man, whose battle with "circumstances" is to be at the centre of the book. The rather defensive tone of the "third epoch", in which his "character" just enables him to "weather the storms of adversity" is an indication that the import of the book may be less affirmative than at first appears. However, he also uses the term character in the sense of an acted role: "The first division of the book will introduce the Author in the character of a wandering vagrant." His enthusiasm for Dickens, manifested in the Dedication, may have tempted him to display himself as a "character" and certainly one of the main appeals of the book to its readership must have been the series of strongly drawn "characters" which fill its pages. But by distancing himself from the "wandering vagrant" in this way, the authorial Burn implies that there is a different "real" self. The confusion in the way he uses the word is symptomatic of the difficulties which lie ahead. Both in his life and in his autobiography the great problem is to discover the identity of that real self.

[9] A popular recent example had been Charles Kingsley's Chartist novel, *Alton Locke*, first published in 1850, the title page of which simply announced "An autobiography" of "Alton Locke, Tailor and Poet" and gave no indication that it was fiction or in any way connected to Kingsley.

II

The first two sections of the book are concerned with the life of a wandering vagrant, the "beggar boy" of the book's title, and with his adventures between his separation from his parents at the age of about fourteen and the beginning of his apprenticeship about five years later. Although he underwent a deep personal crisis when he rejected his natural father and was in turn rejected by his mother, the two periods of his life, which roughly correspond to his childhood and adolescence, are thematically linked at a number of levels and can be read as one unit. The first six letters, just over half the autobiography, are devoted to this period which was spent almost continuously on the move, mainly around Northumberland and the Scottish lowlands, but including journeys as far afield as Ireland and London. Until he was about thirteen he lived with his mother and his step-father, William McNamee, an alcoholic ex-soldier who supported his growing family by whatever means were open to a man with no roots and no trade, peddling when he could afford the outlay on stock and possibly a pack animal, begging when drink or some other misfortune had once more rendered the family destitute. In 1815, while on a visit to Ireland, Burn was deposited with his real father, a corduroy weaver and smallholder, who had parted from his mother at around the time of his birth, and now had a family of his own. He worked with his father's family for the best part of a year, but eventually the physical and emotional hardship of his life became unbearable and he fled back to his mother's family, where he found that his step-father had died in the meantime. Thereafter he occasionally travelled with his mother, but increasingly wandered by himself, taking a variety of casual labouring jobs until he reached what he hoped would be the major turning point in his life when he settled down to learn the trade of a felt-hatmaker.

Whatever the private motives for composing his autobiography, Burn is faced, in the opening pages, with the task of justifying the value of such an account to a readership whose ignorance of the section of society in which his youth and childhood were spent would often be reinforced by a contempt for its mores and behaviour. His answer is twofold. Firstly, this section of society exists, it is real and connected to the rest of society and those who would refuse to recognize this fact stand condemned for their spiritual poverty. As with all the working class autobiographies, the work is in part an attempt to redefine the standards of social significance, to attack the obsession with the histories of statesmen, whose lives Burn would prefer to see "consigned to oblivion" (p. 39) and to assert the intrinsic value of the lives of the working class. Secondly, he makes the basic point that only by living in a section of society can you properly understand it. "Like a large number of my own class," he writes, "I was born in poverty, nursed in sorrow and reared in difficulties, hardships and privations. It is only such as have passed through the various substrata of civilised society who can justly appreciate the feelings and sufferings of the thousands who continually live as it were by chance" (p. 40). In this respect his life is to be seen if not typical, then in an important sense representative of the world in which he was brought up.

There were a number of levels at which the account of Burn's wanderings might enable the readership to "appreciate" or understand the feelings and sufferings of the substrata. The reader is drawn into the world by the sheer excitement of the narrative. By any standards Burn's life was highly eventful, and he took great pleasure in the deceptively simple act of telling a good story. His childhood is presented as a picaresque novel come to life. Having dealt with his earliest memories, the first of these being, typically, a public execution by which he attempts to date his own birth, he previews the remainder of the chapter: "In the course of a few years after this I had passed through a life full of hardships and romantic adventures" (p. 43). The reader is not disappointed. The narrative moves at great pace, and Burn reveals a genuine talent for recreating events and people. The account of the winter night's journey from Wark to Hexham with his father, in the grip of d.ts., conjuring up blue devils before his freezing and terrified child (pp. 48–9) lives in the memory, as do many of the characters he meets, such as Peters, the gentlemanly but dissolute man of colour, or the "consummate vagabond" John Rooney, the whole of whose conduct "tended to three points in the compass of human action, namely, fighting, whoring and roguery" (p. 98). At times, particularly later in the book as the tension of the narrative slackens, Burn is recounting anecdotes merely for their own sake—there is little ulterior meaning, for instance, in the series of smuggling stories with which he concludes Letter IV (pp. 88–91). It is at such points that we most easily recognize the roots all working men's autobiographies have in the age-old tradition of oral story-telling.

But in attempting to recreate the vitality of the world of beggars and pedlars Burn does have a number of more serious intentions. In the first instance he is anxious to establish that this substratum or subculture is real in the sense that not only is it full of very colourful individuals, but also that it constitutes a highly organized and complicated social structure. During the preceding three decades the London publishers had discovered a highly profitable vein of low-life reporting in which the more bizarre and seamy areas of metropolitan society were visited by journalists and writers, mostly middle class but including some working class writers and autobiographers, particularly Thomas Cooper and Charles Manby Smith, who wrote up their impressions in entertaining and at times sensational terms. The stream of books and pamphlets titillated the curiosity of a more respectable readership but did little to alter their assumption that beyond the boundary of respectable society all was anarchy and moral chaos. Only Henry Mayhew in his *London Labour and the London Poor*, first issued in 1851 and 1852, attempted to make a more serious study of the structure and mores of the urban subcultures, borrowing some of the terminology of the nascent discipline of anthropology,[10]

---

[10] The best discussion of his approach is to be found in E. P. Thompson and Eileen Yeo (eds.) *The Unkown Mayhew* (Penguin, 1973).

and though we have no evidence as to whether Burn had actually read his work, he does make a similarly serious attempt to transmit the complexity as well as the humanity of his particular world. "People who look down from the comfortable eminence of social life", he writes, "will necessarily imagine that all class distinctions will cease to exist among the wandering *nomads* who live upon the charity of the well-disposed. In this they are very much mistaken." (p. 45). He goes on to describe the culture of begging with an accuracy and eye for detail which anticipates any academic work on the subject by half a century.[11]

The second point he wishes to make is that if every section of society has its own organization, it also has its own system of morals: "I have found", he writes, "that nearly every class of people in the kingdom have a moral code of their own, and every body of men has its own standard of perfection" (p. 52). Such a discovery leads him to mount a search for the moral quality in groups and individuals which in its persistence and objectivity runs directly counter to the vast majority of contemporary investigations into the moral state of the poor. Burn himself is not without his own moral values. In most respects he displays the characteristic outlook of a self-consciously "respectable" working man. However, he examines his own career and experience and comes to a twofold conclusion which leads him to treat the failings of those about him with a sympathy which is at times quite remarkable given the threat to his very existence that some of these failings presented, and to attack any tendencies to moral complacency among his readership: "It is the simplest thing in the world", he writes, "for men in comfortable circumstances to moralize upon the sins and weaknesses of human nature" (p. 137). On the one hand he asserts that moral degradation is to a considerable extent dependent upon the social and physical environment, and on the other that individuals cannot help where they are born and that fate, or chance, can often prevent the most virtuous man from rising and can conversely cast down those who have risen. He does not carry his analysis of the relationship between environment and morals to the full Owenite conclusion of regarding character as entirely the product of circumstances—it would scarcely be possible to explain his own rise, which he puts down in part to his own inherent "species of manly independence" (p. 115), if he did so—but in the concluding paragraphs of letter VI, he retains an acute sense of the vulnerability of moral virtue to "the merest accident", which, in his own case, "might very well have made me a vagabond without redemption" (p. 121).

The third question Burn wishes to discuss in his examination of his life as a vagrant is the extent and cause of historical change. Unlike Mayhew, his main concern is with the past, or rather with the relationship between his present self and his past self, and, by extension, between the past and present state of society in general. In a literal sense he had a little over fifty years of

[11] The first serious social history of this area was H. G. Graham's classic, *The Social Life of Scotland in the Eighteenth Century* (1st ed., London, 1899).

time to study, but the journey he had made from the remote rural areas of the Borders to Glasgow, London, and the northern textile towns in the vanguard of the industrial revolution, meant that the period of change which he had witnessed was in many respects much longer than the half-century which had elapsed since his birth. Looking back he saw a world which seemed very distant from that which he now inhabited. There were many areas of his experience which he might have chosen to illustrate the scope of change, and it is interesting that, in common with many other working class autobiographers, he was particularly fascinated by the prevalence of super-stition. All the autobiographers were bound together by their high degree of literacy, and in this period it seems to have been the case that the more literate a working man became, the more he became dependent upon the written word to know himself and his world, the more interested he became in pre-literate, non-rational forms of behaviour that were slowly disappearing from his culture. The destruction of their influence demonstrated with particular clarity both the justification for the pursuit of knowledge and its achievement. Burn differed from the other autobiographers in that his child-hood was furthest of all from "civilized" society, and consequently the discussion of superstitions is the most elaborate.[12] He dwelt at length upon them, partly because they had exerted such an influence over his childhood that the shadow of their impression was with him still, and partly because above all else they illustrated the "otherness" of the past.

The twin agents of change were communication and movement. There were a number of reasons why Burn should have been particularly conscious of the significance of the penetration of regional, social and intellectual isolation. In the first instance his family had itself been one of the main instruments of communication in the inaccessible valleys in which it travelled as beggars and pedlars. During the eighteenth and early nineteenth centuries the goods and services which the inhabitants of the scattered farms and villages could not provide for themselves were supplied by a variety of travelling craftsmen and traders. There were few permanent shops, and tailors and cobblers moved from place to place carrying out their work on the spot.[13] In a period in which travelling was still extremely difficult and newspapers were few and far between, these itinerants and craftsmen were looked upon

[12] See pp. 66–8. For accounts of superstitions and customs in other working men's auto-biographies, see W. E. Adams, *Memoirs of a Social Atom* (2 vols., London, 1903), vol. 1, chapter VI; Benjamin Brierley, *Home Memories and Recollections of a Life* (Manchester, 1886), pp. 3–5, 6–7, 15–16; Samuel Bamford, *Early Days* (London, 1849), chapters XIV–XVI; John Clare, "The Autobiography, 1793–1824", in J. W. and Anne Tibble (eds.), *The Prose of John Clare* (London, 1951), pp. 23, 27 and 29; William Lovett, *Life and Struggles of William Lovett* (London, 1967 ed.), pp. 9–11; John Harris, *My Autobiography* (London, 1882), p. 39; Thomas Wood, *The Autobiography of Thomas Wood 1822–1880* (privately published 1956), pp. 1–2; John Younger, *Autobiography* (Kelso, 1881), p. 195.

[13] See Marjorie Plant, *The Domestic Life of Scotland in the Eighteenth Century* (Edinburgh, 1952), pp. 132–44; George Robertson, *Rural Recollections* (Irvine, 1829), p. 39; Thomas Somerville, *My Own Life and Times 1741–1814* (Edinburgh, 1861), p. 351.

as the major sources of news, and this was particularly the case with the beggars who otherwise had nothing else to offer the households from whom they demanded a meal and a night's rest. Burn's account of his father's activities as a news vendor (pp. 44 and 65–6) is of particular interest for the insight it gives into the degree of interest and involvement in the Napoleonic Wars in these rural areas and for the way in which it illustrates the crucial role of pedlars and beggars in connecting the people to national and international politics. It is a topic which would repay more serious research.

Even after he had left his family, Burn never stopped travelling. His life was one of constant mobility, in every sense of the term. He was physically on the move, in this period almost always on foot, apart from one sea voyage, sometimes covering huge distances in a day.[14] At this most practical level he would be more conscious than most of the transformation wrought firstly by the turnpikes and then by the railways which were well established by the time he came to write. Socially and occupationally he was equally mobile, never holding a job for any length of time, even after he had served his apprenticeship, painfully climbing the economic and social ladder, and until the last few years covered by the autobiography, being forever cast down; no place lived in, no post held without the imminent possibility of change, for better or for worse. In an intellectual sense his mind had been transformed by his belated introduction to literature in his mid-twenties, when a whole new world was opened out before him. Finally, of course, it was the distance he had travelled since his childhood that made it possible to discuss his life with some attempt at objectivity. In his experience of the impact of communication and movement[15] he saw himself as a representative figure of his age. Nobody had felt the changes more profoundly, nobody had been more profoundly changed by them. He writes at one point that "Our growing commercial relations, and the consequent fusion of the people have effected a revolution . . ." (p. 58) and it was the fusion of the people, the connecting of isolated groups and the breaking down of every sort of barrier which he had seen, which he represented, and which his autobiography was in turn designed to promote.

[14] See for instance the day's walk of 62 miles he made in search of harvesting work in his late teens (p. 107).

[15] It was a common concern of the autobiographers. Alexander Somerville, who grew up at the same time and in the same area as Burn, wrote in similar terms of the interconnection of improvements in communication and more general progress: "Universal enfranchisement, railways, electric telegraphs, public schools . . . these are some of the elements of a moral faith, believing in the universal brotherhood of mankind, which I daily hold, and never doubt upon; which I believe will as certainly be realised, as I believe that *good* and not *evil*, was the object of all creation and is the end of all existence" (*The Autobiography of a Working Man*, London, 1848, p. 361). Lovett wrote of "the progress of knowledge among our people, by means of the press, the school, and the rail . . ." (op. cit., p. 11). See also, Thomas Frost, *Forty Years' Recollections* (London, 1880), p. 28. Brian Harrison noted a similar enthusiasm among teetotallers ". . . for industrial progress, for science, for the railway (in which many of them invested) . . ." (*Drink and the Victorians*, London, 1971, p. 98).

Although Burn has occasional doubts about the quality of modern architecture, and also, more interestingly, about the effect the loss of superstition would have on the quality of poetry, change, for him, represents progress. At virtually every level, in the physical environment, in the customs and habits of the people, in their material well-being, in the spread of reason, and in politics, the world had moved forward over his lifetime. But if the agents of progress were to be discovered within his own experience, there remained the ultimate cause of change. Here the elements which are missing from his account become relevant. In many respects he had an extremely acute eye for the most significant areas of change, but we get little indication in the autobiography that the Borders at the time of his childhood and youth were well advanced into a profound agricultural revolution that was transforming not only communications but the whole fabric of social relations. Farming was becoming more capital intensive, new standards of entrepreneurial efficiency were being applied to the management of land, and as a result the gulf between those who owned or managed land, and the propertyless labourers was rapidly widening. Many were forced off the land into the towns, where it was certainly the case that economic mobility, upward or more probably downwards, was far more likely than it had been on the land, but for those who stayed, the classes were moving apart.[16] Worst hit of all were the beggars, who failed even to share in the slight rise in overall prosperity in the first three decades of the nineteenth century.[17] Burn's inability to comprehend how increased mobility and increased class conflict can go hand in hand largely explains, or is explained by, his conclusion as to the underlying cause of change and progress. It is the middle class: as he writes on page 103, "whatever social advantages we now enjoy over the preceding age are, in great measure due to the well-timed exertions of this now powerful class". His location of the motor of history in a section of society to which he at best aspired to belong made his failure to investigate the problem of increasing class antagonism in his world almost inevitable. A closer examination of the bitterness aroused by "progress" within the agricultural communities would have seriously endangered his attempt to reconcile his admiration of the middle class achievement with his claim to be in some way a representative of those communities.

In his discussion of the world of pedlars and beggars Burn's conclusions are generally affirmative. He has clear and confident statements to make about the complexity and morality of his subculture, and about the nature of historical change. But there is another side to his recollections of this

---

[16] For an account of the agricultural revolution in the Lowlands, see L. J. Saunders, *Scottish Democracy 1815–1840* (Edinburgh, 1950), pp. 7–75; H. G. Graham, op. cit., *passim*; T. C. Smout, *A History of the Scottish People 1560–1830* (London, 1969), pp. 302–25.

[17] "Of all the ranks in society," wrote George Robertson, "the beggars of modern times have fallen the lowest; or rather, they are the only class whose circumstances have not improved." (op. cit., p. 109).

period which is best brought out in his treatment of his family experience. Most working class autobiographers in this period are comparatively reticent about their emotional life, a reflection less of a lack of affection than of an acceptance of the prevailing conventions of polite literature. The historian is left to piece together a somewhat shadowy picture from stray references and occasional sentences and paragraphs when feeling breaks through almost in spite of the writer's intentions.[18] For this reason Burn's extended and detailed discussion of his relationship with his parents and step-parents, and to a lesser extent with his siblings, adolescent girl-friends, and his wives and children, is of particular interest. He began with a general intention to "furnish a faithful narrative of the whole chain of events which have acted upon me through life up to the present time . . ." (p. 39) but his decision to place so much emphasis on the influence of his various parents flowed more directly from an acceptance of a Wordsworthian view of the psychological significance of childhood.[19] For Burn, the child was very much the father of the autobiographer, and consequently he made a sustained and sensitive attempt to come to terms with the interaction between his relationship with his various parents and what he terms "my under-developed sensibility". It is in this context that one of the great strengths of the autobiography, its concentration on the connection between his evolving personality and all outward "impressions", a key term here, becomes most apparent.

The dominant character in the early years is not his natural father, whom he has yet to meet and for whom he develops an unreasoning dislike, nor his mother, who remains a palely drawn figure despite Burn's evident sympathy for her, but his step-father, William McNamee, who is one of the great achievements of the book. His personality and its profound impact on the growing boy are drawn with a fine combination of insight, affection, and literary skill. The set-piece descriptions of the man's appearance and character and of some of the more dramatic incidents in the father–son relationship are vividly realized, and he managed to combine a clear estimation of his father's glaring faults with both a genuine sympathy for the harshness of McNamee's own life, which he saw as a palliative, if not a justification, for his sins, and a heartfelt appreciation of the positive contribution he had made to his step-son's upbringing, concluding that: "I owe him an eternal debt of gratitude for having left an indelible impression of the noblest aspiration of

---

[18] A few of the autobiographers, notably Bamford (op. cit., p. 174), Clare (op. cit., pp. 16–17, 44–6) and John Bezer in his "Autobiography of One of the Chartist Rebels of 1848", reprinted in David Vincent (ed.) *Testaments of Radicalism* (London, 1977), dwell upon adolescent affairs of the heart, and most give some account of their childhood, but few come close to Burn in range and depth of feeling.

[19] For a discussion of the impact of the "romantic" view of childhood in English thought and literature see Peter Coveney, *The Image of Childhood* (Penguin, 1967), pp. 52–83 and *passim*. The absence of the concept of "original sin" from Burn's account is a further example of the secularization of his outlook discussed above.

11

his mind upon my own" (p. 55). But in the end McNamee was part of the general failure of his parents to provide Burn with the physical and above all emotional security which he saw as essential to the development of a complete adult.

The constant theme of Burn's childhood is one of abandonment and betrayal. Before he is even conscious of himself, he has been deserted by his natural father and deprived of a significant portion of the basic information about his identity, not least the date of his birth, which he never seems certain about. In many respects his step-father could have been an adequate substitute; there clearly develops a strong bond between the two of them, but the inherent instability of both the man and the life he led finally undermined whatever was achieved. As the economic strategy of the family dictated, Burn was separated first from his mother to go begging with his step-father, then taken off by his mother on a journey to London, then having survived several attempts to purchase him from the family, he was casually hired out to a passing farmer, and then equally casually extracted from the family of his step-father, whom he never sees again, and dropped into that of his natural father, whom he has never seen before, where he is made to feel the stranger that he is. Even when he is able to keep in physical contact with his parents, the emotional relationship is never stable. McNamee's temperament was such that, Burn wrote, "I have known him kick and caress me in almost the same breath" (p. 61) and Burn always had to compete for his affection with his own children: before the final separation he notes that, "any little hold I formerly had upon McNamee's good graces seemed to be waning" (p. 60). His mother refused to sell him on several occasions, but then hires him out and abandons him in Ireland, and on his return Burn is uncertain about his reception and such spasmodic contact as he maintains is finally broken by her remarriage, when, once more, he is made "a stranger in what should have been a home to me" (p. 106).

To a point, the chronic insecurity of Burn's childhood was a product of a pattern of circumstances which individually were not that uncommon in the period and the section of society in which he lived. The high level of mortality in these decades meant that the chances of a child losing a parent or one or more siblings before reaching maturity were high.[20] Few of the autobiographers, themselves the survivors of levels of child mortality which in some of the expanding towns, including Glasgow, where Burn later tried to raise his own family, reached fifty per cent, escaped the death of at least one

---

[20] Anderson has calculated that in Preston 47 per cent of children died before their fifth birthday and only three out of five of those alive at 25 reached the age of 50 and only two out of five that of 60. The situation in Glasgow will, if anything, have been worse than this. Michael Anderson, *Family Structure in Nineteenth Century Lancashire* (Cambridge, 1974), p. 34. For the incidence of orphanage, see P. Laslett, "Parental Deprivation in the Past in England" in his *Family Life and Illicit Love in Earlier Generations* (Cambridge, 1977). He calculates that at least one child in five lost one or both parents in the period 1599–1811 (p. 166).

close relation in childhood; and a considerable number experienced the loss of a parent.[21] Further, the practice of leaving children in order that the father or parents might travel in search of work was common at all levels of working class life. Burn himself, having achieved the status of a skilled artisan, later leaves his own wife and young child to go on the tramp.[22] Had McNamee possessed the wit and wherewithal to apprentice his step-son at the normal age of about fourteen, he would have been removed from his family to that of a master at much the same time as his enforced separation in Ireland. It was Burn's misfortune to suffer from a combination of all these circumstances in their most acute form, and if the elements of typicality in his experience enable the historian to understand a little more about the situation of working class children in general in this period, they did little to alleviate his own sense of injury.

The crisis of identity which had been set in motion by his desertion by his natural father at the time of his birth reaches a climax when he is reunited with and in his turn deserts his natural father in Ireland. It is at this point that he symbolically removes two syllables from his name, and "thus . . . wandered forth into the wide world a fugitive from kindred and from home" (p. 78). There is a touch of melodrama about this section of the account, but the description of the deep sense of emotional deprivation which precedes it is both moving and convincing. His father is overdue on a fishing trip, and as he analyses his hopes while he waited together with other friends and relations for the return of the missing fishermen, he realizes just how divorced he has become from normal human contact: "my condition of mind was a solitary exception to that of every being in that anxious crowd. The circumstance was just one of those which was well calculated to bring charity to the part of duty, but all my best feelings were covered as it were by a mountain of selfishness. Until the boat reached the beach in safety, my hope was against every other hope, and when the hope of the people was realized, mine was blasted" (p. 75). His inability to prevent the sundering of all effective emotional relationships has left him in a state of complete isolation. He summarizes his position in one key sentence, ". . . the world had no care for me, yet I had a world of feeling within me which was continually acting and

[21] Bereavement in childhood was such a commonplace occurrence that many of the auto-biographers passed over the event with a minimum of comment. See for instance the anonymous "Working Man's" laconic summary of his family history: "There was a wonderful large family of us—eleven was born, but we died down to six." (Anon., *The Autobiography of a Working Man*, London, 1862, p. 1).

[22] For the practice of "tramping" see below. Although the working class lived predominantly in nuclear families, it seems to have been an accepted convention that in times of crisis, such as the death of one or both parents or the temporary absence of the head of the house-hold for economic reasons, the remainder of the household would merge temporarily with that of a close relative. In such circumstances the autobiographers Christopher Thomson, William Adams, Robert Butler and William Lovett were left with grandparents and Ebenezer Elliott, Samuel Bamford and William Brown with other relatives, and none of them expressed any surprise at the temporary boarding out and subsequent reunification with their parents. For family structure see Michael Anderson, op. cit., pp. 43–56.

13

re-acting upon itself" (p. 73). In the eyes of the child, parents were the world, their failure was the world's failure, his divorce from them was a divorce from society as a whole. The more his feelings became trapped within himself, the more his uncertainty about his own identity increased. Only by establishing emotional contact could he know that he existed and that he had an identity. There is a point, at the end of the section on youth and childhood while he is wandering in London, far away from his vague geographical "home" of the North Tyne Valley, when he feels as if he has become almost totally invisible: "I was fairly lost in a wilderness of human beings; I was a mere atom in a huge mountain of humanity! and as it were an unclaimed particle of animation—a thing that belonged to nobody. In fact I looked upon myself as one of the outside links in the chain of civilized society. If I could have become a part of the monument somebody would have looked at me and have set their wits to find out my use" (p. 116).

The whole of Burn's account rests on an implied assertion of the importance of a stable family life in the development of a child's personality, and as an analysis of the consequences of a range of family failings which separately and in a less intense form were experienced by a large number of working class children in this period, the narrative is of great interest to the historian. In Burn's eyes his family experience is related at a number of levels to his wider social and economic situation at this time. In a practical sense, one aspect of his parents' inadequate care of him was their failure to educate him or to find him an apprenticeship at the usual age. When he does eventually try to get himself apprenticed on his own initiative, he is held back by lack of anyone to stand security for him, a role normally fulfilled by an apprentice's parents. There is also a more general connection. A constant theme in his family life was, as we have seen, his failure to control his relationships with his family and from this initial failure flowed his overall inability to secure his place in his world. The general point is made in the final summary of his family life: "I think if ever a poor wretch was the football of crooked circumstances such was my fate. I had been blessed with three fathers and two mothers, and I was then as comfortably situated as if I never had either one or the other, excepting that I was a living monument to the folly of both father and mother" (p. 106). His family experience in part causes, and in part symbolizes, his overall sense of powerlessness in the period before his apprenticeship. It fails to provide him with a home and an occupation, and in the years following his final separation from his family, he is continually at the mercy of broader economic forces in his society. Without property, without a trade, without personal connections, he is, as he writes, "kicked about the world" (p. 108), or, "like a vessel at sea without a rudder" (p. 109), or again, "the slave of circumstances" (p. 121)—the imagery is interchangeable with that used to describe his situation in his family. Here his private family history merges with that of the economic and social conditions of his period. In the industrializing society, generations of young men were leaving the land, voluntarily or otherwise, and drifting into the towns, rootless and powerless. Burn's plight was more dramatic, his movement greater, his isolation more profound, but the basic causes were the same. Most migrants to the towns were, like Burn, in their late teens or early twenties, single or only just married;[23] having left known communities and supportive families, they had abandoned a fixed if repressive place in the world, and now found themselves in strange communities in which their capacity to withstand the forces of the market economy was pathetically small. Recent research has suggested that some family connections survived such a transition, and that most migrants were not quite as alone as Burn.[24] However, if their connections were marginally more substantial, few would possess the enterprise and persistence to seek out and eventually attain the obvious solution for a man in Burn's position, an apprenticeship to a skilled trade which would enable him at last to become visible, "whereby I would be looked upon", as he writes, "as an honest member of society" (p. 105) and which would give him some control over his circumstances. Thus he goes forward to his apprenticeship to a journeyman hatter in Hexham hoping to reunite himself with his world, and in so doing bring together the two conflicting themes in the first half of the autobiography, his general affirmation of the order, morality and progress of his society and his deep personal sense of alienation and failure.

III

An autobiographer, like any historian, is always faced with the dual task of analysing events both as they happen and as they seem in retrospect. Reconciling the appearance of an event as it is taking place with its meaning when the outcome is visible is often very difficult, but Burn has few problems as he comes to the subject of his apprenticeship. Writing with all the experience of his fifty-odd years at the end of the autobiography, he saw it as "the grand turning point in my existence; to me it was the half-way house between the desert of my youth and the sunny lands of my manhood" (p. 200). Whilst from the perspective of the nineteen-year-old it feels as if he is "now . . . upon the eve of entering upon the real voyage of life with something like a man at the wheel" (p. 123). The voyage takes him, as an apprentice, from Hexham to Otley via a tramp to Dublin, and having served out his time he goes on the tramp once more, walking up to Edinburgh and Glasgow, and then south to Sherborne and London before returning, at the end of 1830, to Glasgow where he remains for twenty years, with brief interludes in Greenock and Paisley. Although his final departure from Glasgow is not a turning point of the same significance as the beginning of his apprenticeship, there is a unity in the period before 1850, with the remaining five years covered by the autobiography standing as a confused but in the end apparently triumphant coda. His experiences between 1822

[23] See Anderson, op. cit., pp. 39–40.
[24] Anderson, op. cit., *passim*; Peter Laslett, ed., *Household and Family in Past Time* (Cambridge, 1972), chs. 4–7.

15

and 1850 may be divided into two broad areas—his occupational and domestic affairs, and his life as an activist, first as a trade unionist and radical politician in the 1830s, and then as a leading Oddfellow up to 1847.

Burn's optimism as he began work with Mr. Rutherford in Hexham rested on solid foundations. For a working man of this period a move from the situation of a casual labourer to that of a skilled artisan would in any circumstances appear to hold out the prospect of a major advance in income, security and social status. Hatting was a moderately well paid trade, with wages ranging from about 25s. a week in the provinces to as much as three or four guineas for "finishers", the elite of the trade, in London. The hatters had one of the oldest traditions of trade unionism, and their organized strength had enabled them to ignore the repeal of the Statute of Artificers in 1814 which removed legal protection from the institution of apprenticeship. Entry to the trade was still strictly regulated, and consequently the journeymen retained considerable bargaining power over levels of wages and conditions of employment.[25] The new sense of security encouraged Burn to branch out in other directions. McNamee had taught him to read when he was a child, but in his early twenties he was still unable to write and had no opportunity to get hold of any serious literature. Then late in 1826 a friend gave him an old edition of Chevalier Ramsay's *Life of Cyrus* which "opened up to my inquiring mind a rich field of useful knowledge" (p. 130).

"Useful knowledge" was a key concept in the vocabulary of the self-improving working man at this time. It stood for serious literature as against the frivolous or even degrading material to be found in chap books and sensational novels. It stood for works which would break down the narrow boundaries of the mind of the uneducated working man and allow him to range over time, across continents, and, as Burn rather rhetorically puts it, "to hold communion with those master-minds who had scattered the beautiful flowers of their intelligence in the garden of humanity" (p. 130).[26] It stood also for knowledge which would allow him to understand the causes of things, not only how the natural world worked, but how the social, economic and political structures functioned and were changed. If useful knowledge was Chevalier Ramsay, it was also the historical works that he

[25] See R. Lloyd, *Lloyd's Treatise on Hats* (2nd ed., London, 1819), pp. 31–5, *Report from the Select Committee on Artisans and Machinery* (1824), PP. 1824, V, 73–99, 150–4; S. and B. Webb, *The History of Trade Unionism* (London, 1911), pp. 38, 46–7, 75, 80; P. M. Giles, "The Felt-Hatting Industry, c. 1500–1850, with particular reference to Lancashire and Cheshire", *Transactions of the Lancashire and Cheshire Antiquarian Society*, vol. LXIX, 1959, pp. 104–32.

[26] He returned to this theme at greater length in Letter XII which is largely concerned with the value of education and literature. Like all the self-educators Burn was fascinated by the sheer accessibility of knowledge. In almost every area of experience his horizon was limited by the circumstances of his birth and occupation but in the field of knowledge, despite the immense practical difficulty of obtaining literature, he was free to travel wherever and with whom he wished. "Books give us," he wrote, "the experience of thoughtful men, who lay their knowledge before us like so many free-will offerings, and enrich us by the possession of that which taketh nothing from the donor." (p. 196).

later borrowed from Mr. Walker's circulating library in Otley, and the political information he obtained from the newspapers. In purely material terms, however, such knowledge was almost always useless. Book knowledge and occupational skill were still separate categories of information; Burn learnt his trade by practice and imitation, not by reading.[27] Neither he nor the great majority of working men had any reason to hope that reading books would make them wealthier; indeed, given the high cost of literature, the reverse would more often be the case. The pursuit of useful knowledge and the seven years' toil of an apprenticeship were of little direct relevance to each other, but both were a means by which a working man might hope to begin to exercise some control over his circumstances—knowledge of the realities of his situation was the first step towards power for a working man and equally membership of the skilled trades, which had a virtual monopoly of effective trade unionism in this period, was the most certain means of keeping at bay the forces of the market economy—and both were a means for Burn of achieving respectability. As an artisan he would no longer be looked down upon as a vagrant, but would have the status of a respectable working man, and in Otley his pursuit of knowledge enabled him to improve his manners and his conversation and meet on equal terms "a number of respectable tradesmen of the town." (p. 132).

He was now also free to begin to reconstruct his family life. Within twelve months of his arrival in Hexham he met and fell in love with a young servant girl called Kitty who lived in the same street. Their courtship was prolonged at least in part because his late apprenticeship meant that he was earning in his early twenties a wage normally thought appropriate for a boy of fifteen, but three years later they were married.[28] After the detailed treatment of his relationship with his parents and the long account he gives of an intense but distant passion he developed for another Hexham girl in his adolescence, the portrayal of the girl he marries is disappointing. The language is conventional and generalized. All we learn is that her parents were "honest and industrious people", and that, "as to herself, never a more single-hearted, amiable, and virtuous woman, adorned the home of a working man" (p. 126). Otherwise we are left with the undoubted fact that on his side at least, the marriage is founded on romantic passion: "I was ten thousand fathoms deep in the indescribable regions of love," he confesses, "and I had some vague idea that matrimony would be the legitimate cure." (p. 129). Despite early financial

[27] For the training of the new industrial workforce, see Sidney Pollard, *The Genesis of Modern Management* (London, 1965), pp. 174–81. The middle-class enthusiasts for working-class adult education, led by Henry Brougham and the Society for the Diffusion of Useful Knowledge, hoped that book knowledge would increase the skills and inventiveness of the workforce, but an artisan of this period required little more than a basic literacy and numeracy.

[28] The reviewer in *Tait's Edinburgh Magazine* viewed the marriage with disapproval: "Like other improvident vagabonds he married during his apprenticeship, and brought the responsibilities of a family upon him before he was able to appreciate them, much less meet them creditably." (Vol. XXII, November 1855, p. 701).

difficulties, the marriage was a success, and on 31 December 1828 his eldest son Thomas was born. At last he had a family upon which he could rely, and perhaps symbolically we finally discover to whom all the experiences contained in the autobiography are addressed. He now had an outlet for his feelings.

It was not long, however, before the foundations of his expectations began to crumble. His first master became bankrupt, he quarrelled with the son of his second, and reluctantly decided that he had to leave "the home I had so long sighed for" (p. 130). After a journey to Dublin he served out his time in Otley, only to discover that being a qualified hatter meant that he travelled even further and changed jobs even more frequently than he had as a vagrant. Within twelve months he had virtually circumnavigated Britain, finding and losing jobs in Edinburgh, Glasgow, Sherborne in Dorset (after a "tramp" of 1,400 miles) and London, before returning to Glasgow and at last obtaining what appeared to be permanent work. After four years he had accumulated sufficient confidence and capital to set up on his own account, but following a move to new premises in 1836 his business began to fail, and he left the trade to run a public house for those of his brethren still in employment. The initial success of the "Hatter's Arms" proved illusory and after two years he moved to Greenock where he opened and was speedily forced to close a spirits cellar. He went back to his trade, working briefly for a manufacturer in Paisley, before returning to Glasgow to set up his own business once more. The venture proved to be under-capitalized and had to be abandoned, he took on another public house, moved to a second, and when that failed found himself "left without a shilling to commence the world in some new line." (p. 171). It was 1848, eighteen years after his long awaited entry into the trade, and he was now in his mid-forties. In the meantime the stability of his family had also been seriously undermined. In 1837 his beloved Kitty died in a typhus epidemic, and despite Burn's careful nursing the youngest of his five children, an eight-month-old boy, soon followed her. Then his step-brother Robert, to whom he had been very attached, returned from the West Indies, took to drink and like McNamee before him, died of alcoholism. "These successive shocks," he recorded, "rapidly altered my position, and cast a gloom over my hope for the time being." (p. 148). In 1838, however, he remarried and began to rebuild his family life.

The challenge for Burn as he composes his account is to explain why his apprenticeship had so signally failed to enable him to exercise some control over his economic circumstances. His overall conclusion is clear enough: "I left Glasgow, a ruined man . . ." (p. 200), but how did this happen? Where lay the responsibility? What is interesting here is that whereas the historian can, at almost every point, find explanations in the economic history of the period, in the character and problems of the hatting trade, and in the general position of an unemployed artisan in Glasgow in the 1830s and 40s, Burn is almost wholly preoccupied with his personal responsibility. It can be argued

18

that the mobility and instability that he experienced were almost inevitable. Hatting was a seasonal trade, most journeymen would expect occasional periods of unemployment and the hatters had developed one of the most elaborate systems of tramping to facilitate mobility of labour within the trade.[29] It was also a common practice for journeymen to serve their apprenticeship with small masters in the provinces and move into the larger industrial centres on completion of their articles.[30] Furthermore, Burn was heading for a period of major crisis in the British economy, culminating in the worst slump of the century between 1837 and 1842, and the impact of the cyclical depression was compounded by the fact that the section of the trade which he had entered, felt-hat making, was about to be overtaken by a new style for silk hats. By about 1840 the skills which he had so painfully acquired were virtually useless.[31] Again, his move into the licensed trade, which, in view of his oft-stated and quite understandable hostility to drink, seems quite extraordinary, can be explained. Unemployment forced him to look outside hatting, and the prospects for a jobless artisan in Glasgow at this time were bleak. The New Poor Law did not reach Scotland until 1845, and although Glasgow had by now adopted a rating system, it was incapable of coping with the scale of cyclical poverty.[32] Running a public house was one of the few means by which a working man with very little capital and no outlet for such skills as he possessed could provide himself with a temporary living. Estimates of the proportion of licensed to unlicensed houses in Glasgow in the 1830s reached as high as one in ten,[33] and it was clear that in many instances they were not alternative professions, but merely a form of outdoor relief financed by marginally more prosperous working class families. It was that or begging again.

[29] The hatters are known to have used the system as far back as 1708, and the emblem of the trade showed different versions of a hatter on tramp, sometimes being welcomed at a turn-house with money and a pot of beer, while a motto declared, "We assist each other in time of need". They adopted the "blank" system, whereby a man in good standing was given a "blank" or certificate which he would present at houses of call. (Lloyd, op. cit., p. 32; Giles, op. cit., p. 120; E. J. Hobsbawm, "The Tramping Artisan", in *Labouring Men* (London, 1968), pp. 34–63).

[30] Under the rules of the trade it was forbidden for a master to have more than two apprentices at any one time. Consequently, rather than train their own apprentices, the larger firms in the industrial centres tended to recruit journeymen who had served their apprenticeship in the country.

[31] Burn discusses the replacement of felt-hats (made out of horse hair and beaver) by silk hats on p. 144 and on p. 441 of the 1882 edition. His account is confirmed by J. R. McCulloch in his *Statistical Account of the British Empire* (2nd ed., London, 1839), vol. 1, p. 729, where he notes that "of late years the manufacture (of felt hats) has rapidly declined".

[32] For an account of the state of the poor in Glasgow during the period in which Burn was running the "Hatter's Arms", see *Observations upon the Poorest Class of Operatives in Glasgow in 1837* (Glasgow, 1838).

[33] See *Report from the Select Committee of Inquiry into Drunkenness* (1834), PP. 1834, VIII, Q 1601; *Report from the Select Committee on Combinations of Workmen* (1838), PP. 1837–38, VIII, Q 1986; James Cleland, *Enumeration of the Inhabitants of the City of Glasgow and County of Lanark for the Government Census of MDCCCXXXI* (2nd ed., Glasgow, 1832), pp. 112–13.

Burn is aware of some of the forces working against him. Following his final failure as a hatter he provides a quite accurate account of the decline of the felt-hat industry. However, his comments as he introduces this section of his life, his explanations of various misfortunes along the way and in particular his concluding discussion of his career in Glasgow, make it clear that he attaches most of the blame to himself. In one sense he approves of his commercial shortcomings: his failure at tavern-keeping he ascribes to his respectability and antipathy to the whole culture of drink. But the overall tone is self-critical. The retrospective passage as he is on the point of leaving Glasgow for the last time summarizes his attitude: "I never had any trouble in analysing my own mind, and could therefore put my hand on my weak points, but strange as it may appear, I have ever allowed *pride* and *confidence* to retain the whip hand of my judgement. With all my numerous imperfections I know I am not without many of those feelings and virtues which lend a charm to our nature." (p. 172). His feelings had found a satisfactory outlet in his family, despite the disaster of his first wife's death, and they had also enabled him to feel a real sense of community with other working men. Yet they were not enough, his want of middle class "business habits", of "cunning", of "confidence" and of "calculation",[34] overthrows almost all that has been achieved. Instead of looking to the more general economic forces bearing down on his class, and his own section of it in particular, he turns the blame back on his supposed defects of character. This induces not only a general fatalism, but a real division within himself; he cannot usefully connect his feelings to his external circumstances. Thus the isolation and lack of a sense of a place in his world is still with him, and he is coming to feel that his lot, "is somewhat like that of the 'Wandering Jew—doomed to wander on through continual changes'." (p. 149).

Burn had first become interested in politics towards the end of his apprenticeship when he began to read the newspapers and join in the discussions in the bar-parlour of the New Inn at Otley. Almost as soon as he had established a permanent base in Glasgow, he became actively involved in the intensifying struggle for political and economic power. His membership of the hatters' union took him in one direction into the Glasgow Trades Committee and thence to the committee of the Glasgow Reform Association, and in another to the national delegate meetings of hatters held in Manchester in 1833 and Liverpool in 1834. He was at the centre of the confused pattern of radical politics in Glasgow in the years following the passage of the 1832 Reform Bill, and then moved into the Chartist movement during his brief sojourn in Greenock. He finally abandoned politics after the 1839 Chartist Convention had called for a "National Holiday" or general strike, and turned to the Oddfellows, playing a leading role in the establishment of the movement in south-west Scotland, writing what is still the definitive history of the organization's early years in that area, and rising rapidly

[34] See pp. 145, 150, 196.

through the local and national hierarchy until he was elected to the Board of Directors at the Annual Conference in Bristol in 1846. At the end of a year of office he retired from public life, and three years later left Glasgow altogether.

The first conclusion to be drawn from the account of these activities is that Burn was clearly a man of great energy and considerable powers of leadership. His rise in radical politics, where he became a member of the central committee of the reform association within a year of his arrival in Glasgow; in the hatters' union where he was the delegate for all the hatters in Glasgow and vice-chairman of the national general meeting a mere three years after completing his apprenticeship; and in the Oddfellows, where he was one of the few working men to penetrate the upper echelons of the organization's bureaucracy, was in each case remarkably swift. By the time he left Glasgow the anonymous beggar boy had established a name for himself which, in the case of the hatters and Oddfellows, extended far beyond the boundaries of the city.

However, as elsewhere in the autobiography, the real interest of the account lies not so much in the events, though it should be noted that the work remains one of the major sources of information on the history of all three areas of activity in Glasgow in this period, but in the way in which Burn interprets his participation in them. Here the most significant feature of his treatment is that in each case the record of commitment and leadership is framed with comments intended to undermine the meaning of his participation and, by extension, the status of the movements themselves. The entry into union affairs and politics is prefaced by general remarks about the extent to which, in the years following 1830, "my passions dragged me headlong through the by-ways of folly" (p. 138). He describes himself as "politically mad" (p. 139) as he becomes involved in the Reform Bill crisis, and on his final departure from politics in Greenock he writes that "I had run the gauntlet of political folly, and while in that town I had got completely cured of my *monomania*" (p. 157). His work with the Oddfellows is treated in much the same fashion. Burn's view that his judgement was at fault throughout his career is apparently justified by the fact that he was involved in much infighting during the mid-1830s, and that after eight years of often intense activity he discovered that the radical movement was committed to a policy to which he was fundamentally opposed. Yet it can be argued that the conflicts in which he was involved stemmed not from his personal waywardness but from more general tensions within working class radicalism and that between 1831 and 1839 the movement underwent a major transformation which could very well have left a man such as Burn feeling wholly out of sympathy with it. From an historian's point of view his most salient character trait during this period is not instability but, to the contrary, immobility, a failure to fully respond to the rapidly changing climate of politics in the period following 1832.

Burn's political consciousness had developed before the passage of the first Reform Bill. The formative influences were the radical journalists of the post-Napoleonic war period, men like Wooler of the *Black Dwarf* and William Cobbett. By the time he settled in Glasgow at the end of 1830, he had acquired an outlook which was in many respects typical of the radical working class movement which he soon joined. It was an outlook founded on some sense of class identity. The language of both Burn's account and of the radical newspapers of the period, particularly the *Herald to the Trades Advocate*, to which he refers, was a language of class which assumed the existence of two separate communities, each with its own range of interests and aspirations. Unlike most of the working class radicalism in England, the movement in Glasgow grew out of the trade unions, with a loose grouping of skilled and semi-skilled trades, which had previously come together at the time of Peterloo, reforming and developing a political programme which was moderate in its ends and flexible in its means.[35] As with Cobbett, and as with Burn, the main enemy was not the representatives of industrial capitalism, but aristocratic corruption. The great hero of the *Herald* was the Benthamite radical leader Joseph Hume, it was the Trades Committee which took the initiative, early in 1831, in the attempt to form a coalition with the middle-class Glasgow Reform Association, and his post-reform participation in parliamentary elections fitted the general pattern. He was on the side of the majority in his dispute with Dr. John Taylor in 1837 which resulted in Taylor's temporary political eclipse, and his hostility to the call by the 1839 Chartist Convention for a National Holiday was shared by most of the Scottish Chartists. There was a strong "moral force" wing in Scotland, and when the proposal was put to the Scottish Chartists by Taylor it received support only from three areas.[36]

The intensity and finality of Burn's reaction, however, went far beyond the general feeling of disenchantment which followed the 1839 Convention. In part his response seems a product of the fact that though he retained throughout the thirties a genuine disrespect for the major political parties and continuing sense of his own class identity, he was not capable of developing his pre-1832 outlook into a full commitment to a class conflict which placed at its centre the economic division of interest between the classes. Faced with a call for a general strike he found that he no longer had a place in the political movement. Yet Burn's lack of ideological mobility was far from unique and it does not explain why he sees himself not as a member of a dissenting wing of the movement, as, for instance, another disillusioned Chartist, William Lovett, was to do in his autobiography, nor even as a representative of an outdated generation, but as an isolated individual, pursuing a lonely path to a position of total opposition to the politics of his

[35] For the details of Glasgow radicalism in this period, see the notes to pp. 139–47.
[36] Namely Forfar, Kirriemuir and Dundee. (See Alexander Wilson, *The Chartist Movement in Scotland*, Manchester, 1970, pp. 70–8).

own community. The prevailing image throughout the account of his political life is that of irrationality bordering on insanity. Dismissing himself at the outset as "politically mad", he goes on to blame the 1839 crisis on "the mad conduct of a few leaders" (p. 150), and of the leadership in general he concludes: "All I can say is, if these men were honest they must have been mad, and if not mad, no conduct could have been more infamous" (p. 151). His long-standing preoccupation with his inability to use his reason to control his circumstances had merged with the middle class analysis of the nature of the Chartist movement which was becoming orthodox history at the time at which he was writing. That analysis attempted to divorce the leadership from the mass membership, dismissing the latter as politically immature and the former as corrupt and, crucially, insane. The convenient fact that the movement's most prominent leader, Feargus O'Connor, had had to be committed to a lunatic asylum in 1853, greatly strengthened an attack which, by assailing the rationality of leadership, sought to undermine the significance of the programme and ideology of the movement as a whole.[37] Such an explanation exercised a fatal attraction for a man like Burn. What had been an authentic description of his situation, where, for instance, he writes, "Before I went to the trade my life had been like a feather on the stream, and I was continually whirled along from one eddy to another" (p. 137), now becomes an evasion: "Here, then, I got into the gulf stream of political activity, and was carried onward with amazing velocity" (p. 139). The label of irrationality allowed him to escape the responsibility of providing a coherent analysis of his career and the movements to which he belonged. In this manner the feeling of separation which had grown as the politics of the late '30s had begun to move away from him, was compounded by the adoption of a framework of analysis which had at its centre a dismissal of all that he had ever fought for.

Burn's treatment of his career as an Oddfellow remains something of a mystery. His motives for espousing the cause are quite comprehensible. They are formally set out in the lecture on Oddfellowship which appeared in 1840. The movement would generate an a-political, moral revolution in the situation of the working class, it would provide working men and their families with a sense of respectability, with financial security, and perhaps most important for a man like Burn, with a feeling of community; "If I should wander to the farthest part of England", he wrote, "or take my flight across the wide Atlantic I should still feel at home".[38] In a personal sense his hopes were largely realized. He received considerable material and moral support from the movement at a time of crisis for his family, and was proud of "the

---

[37] For the middle-class treatment of Chartism, see J. Saville, "R. G. Gammage and the Chartist Movement", introduction to 1969 reprint of R. G. Gammage, *The History of the Chartist Movement* (1894); David Vincent, op. cit., pp. 4–6.

[38] *Lecture on the Moral, Social and Friendly Character of Odd-Fellowship of The Manchester Unity* (Glasgow, 1840), p. 8.

substantial proof of friendly regard I received from a large body of my fellow-men" (p. 155). His career in the organization was remarkably success- ful, and after playing host to the General Annual Moveable Conference in 1845, he reached the summit of the bureaucracy in 1846, when he was elected to the Board of Directors. Once elected it was normal for a director to serve for several years and Burn might have looked forward to holding the rotating office of Grand Master of the entire Order, but after twelve months he withdrew from the organization altogether, leaving us with a single dis- missive sentence in lieu of an explanation: "I am almost sick of relating my own folly; but the record of my strange life would not be complete if I withheld it" (p. 161). Despite his avowed intention, the record here is far from complete. Unlike his political career we are given no reason for his apparent disenchantment with the movement, and it is possible that his departure was precipitated by financial rather than ideological factors. The Board of Directors was drawn largely from the professional classes, despite the working class character of the movement as a whole, because few working men could find the time and money which the unpaid membership of the Board demanded.[39] Burn succeeds the narrative of his life as an Oddfellow with an account of the gradual failure of his public house and it may be that he simply could no longer afford to remain a member of the Board. Perhaps his silence was due to pride, or perhaps it was just too easy to sweep the failure of his Oddfellowship career into the established explanation for the failure of his life as a politician.

IV

By 1848, the "real voyage of life with something like a man at the wheel, had run aground. Despite occasional periods of prosperity as a hatter and publican, and considerable achievements as a politician, trade unionist and Oddfellow, he had been unable to secure a place for himself and evidently had become increasingly uncertain about the cause of his continued in- security. For most of the remainder of his life covered by the autobiography his problems repeated themselves in an ever more acute form. He worked in a temporary and undisclosed capacity for an old friend who was an engraver and lithographer, but that business was failing and he took a post as travelling representative for a firm launching a system of book-keeping for use in schools. In March 1850, he moved with his family from Glasgow to York to set up a base for his operations, but after two months on the road he discovered that "my undertaking was a dead failure". He moved on to Leeds, and then Liverpool, where he laboured for a couple of months as a warehouseman and held a temporary post selling off the stock of a hatter's, and thence to Manchester to work for nine months as a book deliverer. Redundancy forced him to change jobs once more, and for a year he served as a member of a firm compiling commercial directories, first in Manchester,

[39] See P. H. J. H. Gosden, *The Friendly Societies in England 1815-1875* (Manchester, 1961) pp. 71-93.

then in Guildford and then in Hull. Between January and May 1853, he journeyed throughout Scotland and the Midlands collecting subscribers for a commercial magazine. Thus after twenty years of relative geographical stability in Glasgow he was back to his old life of constant travelling, and unlike his days as a beggar boy when the North Tyne valley seemed to exert some centripetal force in his wanderings, he now seemed completely detached from any particular area or community. His renewed and more intense rootlessness is mirrored in the quality of his passing observations on events and places. The series of "views" of various towns he has visited which occupy the first ten pages of Letter X reflect Burn's interest in literature and his fascination with the "march of improvement", but are otherwise devoid of any feelings of personal involvement and response. The description of the "transformation" of Newcastle upon Tyne could have been written by the town's mayor, there is no sense of the impact such changes would have on the experience of a particular working man. Some of the tension has gone out of his writing here. He has become not so much a traveller as a tourist in his own society.

He was still unable to escape the cycle of tenuous prosperity and destitution. The same phrases and sentences re-occur as he describes his financial affairs: in 1848 he is "left without a shilling to commence the world in some new line" (p. 171), and after a succession of jobs, during which time, "I was . . . carried headlong into a stream of unbending circumstances, and like a chip of wood amid the boisterous waves of a stormy sea, I was dashed hither and thither without any controlling power of my own" (p. 173), he finds himself, three years later, "once more steeped to the lips in poverty, while my prospect for the future was full of gloom" (p. 180). As his family increased, so the troughs deepened. There is a moving passage describing the plight of his family as they lodged in a bug-infested house in Liverpool in 1850. His wife falls ill following the birth of their fourth child and for eight weeks Burn has to leave work to nurse his wife and child and manage the household, and is gradually forced to sell off their possessions to keep the family from starving (p. 177–9). However, in May 1853, he reaches what appears to be the concluding turning point. He at last obtains a respectable and permanent post, and as the journey of his life reaches its destination he sets out to cast his final interpretation of the meaning of his long and chequered career.

Although it is possible to deduce a number of general motives for writing the autobiography, the immediate circumstances of its composition remain unclear. The book's publisher, William Tweedie, was the main publisher of temperance literature, and later became a personal friend of Burn, but we do not know who made the first approach or whether Tweedie had any influence over the content of the work. There is also the larger problem

[10] Tweedie published at about this time a second important working man's autobiography, that of Robert Lowery, in the columns of his *Weekly Record of the Temperance Movement* (12 April 1856 to 30 May 1857).

of how a man with no formal education of any sort, who was still unable to write his own name in his early twenties, came to have the confidence and capacity to compose what is a highly literate and in some ways literary piece of work. As with so many other working men in this period his literary confidence was founded in his participation in various forms of organized working class activity. He will have gained some experience in self-expression and written communication when he took part in the nightly debates during the Reform Bill crisis and became involved in the management of large-scale demonstrations. His work as a delegate of the hatters' union will have given him further experience in this field, but it was as an Oddfellow that Burn first emerged as a published writer. The movement provided him with a training, a forum, subject matter and finally a market. Following the founding of a lodge in his public house in 1838, he became involved in proselytizing the cause in and around Glasgow, speaking first to small gatherings and then giving public lectures. In 1840, a local firm published one of these in the form of a twenty-eight page pamphlet. It was a fluent and somewhat rhetorical piece and appeared to be a straight transcription of the original lecture. It was a comparatively short step now to his first full-scale work, an 180-page book entitled *An Historical Sketch of the Independent Order of Oddfellows*.[41] This was a heterogeneous work, combining history— some highly speculative, some factual accounts of his own activities— a description of the movement's practices and objectives, and the un-doctored minutes of the 1845 Glasgow G.A.M.C. It contained much that was useful and some that was eloquent and was well received by the move-ment.[42] The beggar boy, who was still only a not too successful publican, could consider himself an author. With the experience and confidence he had gained with the Oddfellows he could now branch out in other directions. His next publication was a strange work entitled *The Language of the Walls* which he wrote sometime during the early 1850s.[43] He summarized the book as an endeavour "to describe the chicanery and dishonest practices of the age as they really exist".[44] Some of the targets were the familiar ones of intemperance and election malpractice, but it contained a detailed attack on various forms of food adulteration and a genuinely perceptive and pro-phetic onslaught on the subject of the book's title, brand-name advertising, then in its infancy, which he rightly saw as the new "circulating library for

---

[41] Published in 1845 by the Manchester firm of Abel Heywood.

[42] The work was reviewed in the *Oddfellows Magazine* for April 1846, pp. 65–7. "Mr. Burn's work," the reviewer commented, "is one which must have entailed upon the author a great amount of labour and inquiry, and we have great pleasure in bearing testimony to the skill and judgement with which he has arranged the materials at his command." (p. 65). It was described as one of the two best books so far published on the movement.

[43] According to the list of his publications in the 1882 edition, the work was published in 1853 by "Patterson, London", but the only edition I have discovered, *The Language of the Walls: and a Voice from the Shop Window or The Mirror of Commercial Roguery by one who thinks aloud* was published in 1855 by "Abel Heywood of Manchester, Sold by William Tweedie of London".

[44] Ibid., p. V.

the million".[45] By 1854, therefore, Burn possessed all the necessary literary qualifications to attempt the task of transmitting a tradition of oral reminiscence which he had learnt as a child as he travelled with McNamee, and which had been strengthened by his familiarity with, and pride in, the lyrical ballads of the Borders, into a formal autobiography.

His experience and confidence do not, however, fully explain the quality of the writing. In many respects the book is a monument to the achievements of a self-educated working man. McNamee had taught Burn his letters, but he had taught himself how to read in the fullest sense of the word, how to seek out, persist with and find meaning in full-length books, a more alien and difficult task than it may appear to those of us who have had the benefit of a lengthy formal education. The range and substance of his subsequent learning is reflected not only in the scope of his literary references,[46] which include besides his great love Burns,[47] and of course the Bible, Shakespeare, Pope, Defoe, Gray, Goldsmith, Cowper, Wordsworth, Byron, Tannahill, Swift, Dickens, Homer and a smattering of classical tags, Cervantes, Voltaire, Alison and Cobbett, but also in the sophisticated use of language throughout the autobiography. His commonest device for catching and retaining the attention of his readers is the ironical use of the diction of polite literature to counterpoint the extremely impolite events and circumstances of the world in which he lived. Here, for instance, he is describing one of McNamee's drunken bouts which plunges the family back into destitution: ". . . he owed himself a treat for his past good conduct, and of all men in the world he was the last to allow such a debt owing to himself to go unpaid. With the high resolve of liquidating this obligation, he called a meeting of his creditors, and so relieved his mind of further anxiety about the matter. After three days and nights, the ass, his panniers, and myself, were all that remained of our worldly effects." (p. 44). The effect is constantly stimulating, often elegant and witty, and fulfils a more serious role in that it reinforces Burn's overall intention of challenging complacent assumptions about the extent of the gulf between respectable and non-respectable ways of life. The educated reader is led into the narrative by concepts and language which he would normally employ to describe his own activities and then brought up sharply by the realization of what this language is now referring to. There is also an element of display in the self-conscious juxtaposition of middle class language and Border and Clydeside dialect and thieves' slang. Burn is proud of his hard earned ability to stand with a foot in either culture, though at times, as for instance at the beginning of Letter X, the writing gets out of hand and appears mannered and artificial. This very facility, moreover, perpetuates rather than resolves the problem of determining his natural place in society.

[45] Ibid., p. 3.
[46] The frequent minor errors in Burn's literary quotations suggest that he was genuinely quoting from memory and not from the results of specific literary research.
[47] He became chairman of the Burns Society in Edinburgh in 1859 while he was working there for Mr. Hill (1882 ed., p. 246).

The twin journeys of the autobiography, that of Burn's life, and that of its interpretation which was itself written on a journey, from Aberdeen to London, over the course of twelve months, reach what appears to be a successful conclusion in the final paragraph. The beggar boy has at last risen to a position of respectability: "The ground that I walked over as a beggar, I have also traversed in the character of a gentleman, and upon more occasions than one, at the houses where I once sought alms I have been saluted with the respect due to rank far above my own. For the last two years, I have held a situation of considerable responsibility, during that time I have come in contact with many of the first-class commercial men in the United Kingdom" (p. 201). Equally his family life, the source of so much anguish in his childhood and youth, is now a scene of tranquillity: "My home is the abode of happiness, and my own, and the lives of my family gently glide down the stream of existence in peace and contentment". It was a conclusion which the reviewers of the autobiography were happy to accept at its face value.

With the exception of a contemptuous dismissal by the *Athenaeum*,[48] the book was favourably received by the daily and periodical press, their reviews both reflecting and encouraging considerable public interest.[49] Although we have no figure of total sales, demand was sufficient to sustain two further "editions" (in fact reprints) in 1856, and a "Cheap Edition" in 1859, which sold at half the original price of 3s. In 1882 Hodder and Stoughton brought out a genuinely new edition which was revised and extended to cover Burn's life in the intervening period. The reviewers saw the book as a gratifying example of self-improvement. The depth of Burn's original social condition and what the *Spectator* called the "hard literal reality" of the writing gave a refreshing scale and drama to the climb, and the comments on the progress of society together with the condemnation of radical politics, particularly Chartism, were gratefully received. He was linked with Dickens, in part because of the colour of his life and his apparent good humour in the face of his frequent reversals of fortune, which led *The Times* to liken him to Micawber, and in part perhaps because Burn's long account of commercial insecurity echoed a preoccupation of Dickens and of a middle class readership whose new-found prosperity was felt to be constantly threatened by the

---

[48] See No. 1471, 5 January 1856. "This title-page looks like a desperate attempt to 'get up' an interest in the life of the 'beggar boy'. The 'autobiography' has all the cant of imposture, being mixed up with a dreary mass of platitudes on temperance, politics and literature. The incidents are not very remarkable, but had the materials been adapted for a narrative, they would have been swamped by the author's prolixity. In style, the book hovers between a newspaper paragraph and a penny lecture. If it be a genuine autobiography, the writer had done well to describe the life and to reserve his opinions. The writer has had, apparently, some converse with men and things; but he has not learnt the art of writing."

[49] See, *Spectator*, no. 1426, 27 October 1855, p. 1118; *Morning Chronicle*, Friday, 14 December 1855, p. 3; *Tait's Edinburgh Magazine*, vol. XXII, November 1855, pp. 700–1; *Times*, Thursday, 27 December 1855, p. 4; *Nonconformist* and *Londonderry Standard*—undated reviews printed on covers of 1859 "cheap edition".

sort of disasters which Burn had experienced and, crucially, survived.[50] The didactic character of the autobiography seemed to place it in the mainstream of the Victorian literature of success. Smiles himself could not improve on comments such as, "one thing [is] certain, that well-directed energy, backed by habits of industry and common prudence, will always make way for itself in spite of the cold conventionalism of the world" (p. 189).[51] Burn's own success was not in doubt. He had finally achieved "respectability", a word which occurs in every single review which is more than a précis.

Yet if we read the autobiography a little more carefully, it is clear that Burn himself had considerable doubts as to the nature and the permanence of his achievement. In the first instance he twice states in the final letter that he cannot be sure that his present prosperity may not be as insubstantial as all the other "turning points" of his life. "For aught I know", he writes, "the future may be to me a dark passage of misery without the buoyant energy of youth or manhood to spur me into the last battle of life" (p. 199). His uncertainty was quite justified. In the autobiography he coyly refused to give any details of his ultimate occupation and employer. He was in fact working as a debt collector for the Rev. William Hill, the ex-proprietor of the *Northern Star*, the leading Chartist newspaper.[52] His respectability, in other words, was sustained by the financial instability of the respectable class. Doubts about the solvency of his employer led him to take a post collecting subscriptions for the *Ladies Journal* in Dublin. The venture was not a success, and by Christmas, he was back in London and broke, a mere two years after the completion of the autobiography. He had 1s. 6d. with which to begin again. He rejoined Hill and went to Edinburgh to manage an office, but by 1860, his employer had joined the ranks of his clients. He was kept on by Hill's successor and then in 1861, left to set up a similar business of his own. Predictably it failed almost immediately and he was "stranded again on the lee shore of poverty" (1882 ed., p. 245). William Tweedie gave him some employment out of charity, he worked briefly again for the resilient Hill who was now trying to compile a "Handbook of London", and then a son-in-law who had emigrated to the United States sent him an invitation and £3 towards the fare. Although he was now in his early 60s, the travelling man needed no second bidding and the family took passage immediately. Once arrived at Newark, New Jersey, Burn could not live off his relations and the wheel came full circle as he found intermittent employment as a hatter. On his return to England in 1865, he went back to Northumberland to work first as a hatter in Newcastle and then as a journalist on the *Hexham Courant*. In almost every respect he was back where he started, forty years earlier, but

---

[50] At the same time that the autobiography was published Dickens was bringing out the first numbers of *Little Dorrit*, the first half of which is set in Marshalsea debtors' prison.

[51] For Smiles and the literature of success, see J. F. C. Harrison, "The Victorian Gospel of Success", *Victorian Studies*, vol. 1, December 1957.

[52] For Hill's earlier career, see E. Glasgow, "The establishment of the *Northern Star* newspaper" *History*, XXXIX, 1954; M. Hovell, *The Chartist Movement* (Manchester, 1925), p. 311.

his journeying was not yet finished. He moved down to London where a barrister named Thomas Baker, who was introduced to Burn through William Tweedie, found him a place as a clerk and messenger in the Salmon Fisheries Office in Westminster.

By now he had written three more books: *Commercial Enterprise and Social Progress*, published in 1858, an elaboration of the material and themes contained in the passages in his autobiography on the changes in urban, social and economic life during the first half of the century; *Three Years among the Working Classes of the United States, during the War*, published in 1865, an account which exploited public interest aroused by the Civil War and cast a somewhat jaundiced eye over what Burn considered to be an unduly materialist and aggressive society; and *A Glimpse at the Social Condition of the Working Classes of the United Kingdom during the early part of the present century*, published in about 1868, a work which despite its title was a contribution to the current debate over trade unions and the law, and took the form of a defence of the basic rights of trade unions coupled with an attack on the more extreme forms of their activity. There was one further work to come before the final edition of his autobiography: in 1871 he brought out *The Educational Places of Amusement in London*, described in the preface as "a trustworthy guide to all the really innocent and instructive places of amusement in London", which may have been based on the work he undertook for Hill ten years earlier. Although the 1882 edition lists his publications, he is curiously silent about their composition and reception. That the works were a product of his own initiative and journalistic talent for relating his material to topical events is suggested by the fact that each was published by a different firm, but apart from a passing mention of an offer of £20 made by Routledge for *Three Years*,[53] there is no reference to his income from his writings and we are left to assume that as he was unable to give up full-time work until he was eighty the direct rewards cannot have been large. However, there were indirect benefits. Mr. Baker not only found him employment but also, in 1869, secured him a grant of £30 from the Royal Literary Fund. He received a further grant for an unspecified amount about ten years later. Another patron, Lt.-Colonel Manby, arranged a job as a clerk at Crystal Palace and then, in 1871, obtained him his final post, symbolically, with a railway company, the Great Eastern, for whom he worked as inspector of stores, first at Ipswich and then at Brandon. In 1881, following the death of his second wife, he at last retired and went to live with a married daughter in Hammersmith.

With his occupational life now at an end, Burn made one final review of his life. He made numerous small changes to the content and the style of the first edition of the autobiography and attached an account of the succeeding twenty-five years, concluding with a more general historical review of the

[53] See 1882 edition, p. 309. The work was eventually published by Smith, Elder and Co., perhaps because they made him a better offer.

social changes he had witnessed during his lifetime. In almost every respect his revision weakened the original work. The epistolary structure was clumsily excised, presumably because Thomas had died in 1870, and his surviving children were now too old to need his advice. He seemed almost frightened by his old vigorous self and went through the text making extensive but trivial stylistic amendments which greatly dissipated the energy of the writing.[54] Some of the additional detail is of interest, but it is counterbalanced by a thorough bowdlerization of the narrative. All references to sex and the bodily functions were dropped or smudged over,[55] evidence that either Burn had become more prudish as he had advanced in years or that he or his publishers perceived a change in the standards of the society for which he was writing. The chapters on his life after 1855 amounted to little more than a recitation of events. The writing rarely matched the intensity of the first edition and with the inclusion of the long historical section the work became extremely unwieldy. How little his further experiences had solved the problems with which he had been faced, or had yielded fresh insights, is revealed by the fact that the conclusion of the 1855 version is simply transferred to the end of the final narrative and made to do service for the additional quarter century as well. The little new material reinforced his preoccupation with movement and respectability; in the end he was happy with the defensive assertion that "in the history of a life like mine, which is full of quickly recurring ups and downs, . . . I never lost caste" (1882 ed., p. 447).

If Burn's journey had reached a temporary stopping point rather than its final terminus in 1855, the first edition of the autobiography, which was unchanged in the two editions of 1856 and the cheap edition of 1859, remained in every respect far superior to the final version of 1882. Indeed it can be argued that the 1855 edition, which is reprinted here, is the most consistently interesting of all the nineteenth century working men's autobiographies. Several other works, particularly those of Bamford, Bezer, Brierley, Cooper, Frost, Gutteridge, Shaw, Somerville and Thomson, could at times match Burn for the quality of his prose and the variety of the events and social practices which he experienced and described, but he stands alone in the intensity of his attempt to understand all that he had seen and done. It was with some justification that he claimed on the penultimate page that "You have now before you an honest history of my life up to the present

---

[54] For instance, "A man who either writes his own life or has it written for him may be said to be dragged from the crowd of his fellows and placed naked upon an elevation . . .' (1855 ed., p. 39) becomes, "The man who either writes his own life, or has it written for him, may be said to be withdrawn from the crowd of his fellows, and placed to a certain extent naked upon an elevation . . ." (1882 ed., p. 1).

[55] The description of Rooney's character "tending to three points in the compass of human actions, namely fighting, whoring and roguery" (p. 98) is deleted, as are the passages describing the orgy at the home of the gentleman of colour, Peters (pp. 94–5), and the attempt by the wife of Burn's master to seduce him (p. 120). His step-brother Robert now finds an officer not in bed with his wife but merely insulting her (p. 148). References to passing water and urine are dropped from pp. 81, 113 and 124.

31

time" (p. 201). The history is "honest" in the sense that it is consistently concerned with the relationship between Burn's inner self and his situation in the outside world. In this respect his honesty makes the autobiography a far more complex piece of work than his middle-class reviewers imagined but equally it is a major factor in undermining its final achievement. For Burn's search to find his place in his world after he has been cast loose by the domestic and economic disasters of his childhood has not succeeded and this failure is reflected and perhaps intensified in the confusion of his interpretation of his adult life. As we have seen, many of the forces which prevented him from finding his true identity as a worker or as an activist were a product of the general situation of the working men of his location and time. There was little he could have done about the structural changes in the hatting industry and few working men possessed the political flexibility and skill to ride the working-class movements of the 1830s without losing their balance at some point. Yet rather than fully identifying himself with the working class, he appropriated a set of values and assumptions with which to define his goals and measure his failure which conflicted with the realities of his situation. He judged his career as an activist through the spectacles of the middle-class outlook on working-class activity and thus alienated himself from the movements to which he had contributed so much. Equally he attributed his repeated economic failure to his lack of the middle-class virtues of prudence and business acumen. Throughout this period the notion of respectability was fraught with ambiguity, embodying at once a deep sense of working-class pride and an abdication of working-class values in the face of middle-class contempt and perhaps Burn's most representative quality lies in his exemplification of the dilemmas inherent in that idea. Although Burn could not properly harness its power for his own journey he saw the middle class as the motor of history and it was for this reason that the reviewers were content to accept the apparently happy ending, but it was also for this reason that we find many unresolved problems beneath the surface. His central task as he began his apprenticeship was to establish a firm connection between his inner self and the outside world but such hope as he had of doing so in the face of the pressures bearing down on him was thrown away by his adoption of an explanation which suggested that his most spontaneous feelings were responsible for his failures. Consequently, he wrote at one point when discussing the career of a fellow Glaswegian, "His difficulty in life was precisely that of my own, he had a talent for everything but business! and carried on his shoulders a world of experience, which was the same to him as a miser's gold, being neither of use to himself or anybody else" (p. 175). His belief in the middle-class view of the world further explains how he was unable to resolve the tensions, which are found in the first half of the book, between his general view of progress and his personal sense of failure. His relationship to the middle class was one of aspiration and admiration. He never felt sure of membership, even in his most prosperous periods, and in practice his commitment served only to intensify his self-reproach. The persistent contradiction between his interpretative values and his actual situation explains the painful but in his own terms honest confession as he summarizes his multiple failure in Glasgow: "I may, therefore, say that my character through the best part of my life has been a living lie, and at the end of fifty years, I am even more disappointed in myself than I have been in all the world beside." (p. 172). He had found no home, not even in himself.

Background Reading

Related working men's autobiographies include: Samuel Bamford, *Early Days* (London, 1849); Thomas Cooper, *The Life of Thomas Cooper, written by himself* (London, 1872); William Green, *The Life and Adventures of a Cheap Jack by One of the Fraternity*, edited by Charles Hindley (London, 1876); William Lovett, *The Life and Struggles of William Lovett* (London, 1876); Alexander Somerville, *The Autobiography of a Working Man* (London, 1848); Peter Taylor, *Autobiography* (Paisley, 1903); William Thom, *Rhymes and Recollections of a Handloom Weaver* (London, 1844); John Younger, *Autobiography* (Kelso, 1881). For other relevant memoirs, see: Henry Cockburn, *The Journal of Henry Cockburn*, 2 vols. (Edinburgh, 1874); Peter Mackenzie, *Old Reminiscences of Glasgow and the West of Scotland*, 2 vols. (Glasgow, 1890); George Robertson, *Rural Recollections* (Irvine, 1829); Martha Somerville (ed.), *Personal Recollections from early life to old age of Mary Somerville* (London, 1873); Thomas Somerville, *My Own Life and Times 1741–1814* (Edinburgh, 1861). There are no standard works on the main areas of Burn's career, but useful material is contained in: Michael Brock, *The Great Reform Act* (London, 1973); P. H. J. H. Gosden, *The Friendly Societies in England 1815–1875* (Manchester, 1961); Thomas Johnston, *The History of the Working Classes in Scotland* (4th ed., Glasgow, 1946); John K. M'Dowall, *The People's History of Glasgow* (Glasgow, 1899); A. Allan MacLaren, ed., *Social Class in Scotland: Past and Present* (Edinburgh, 1976). W. H. Marwick, *A Short History of Labour in Scotland* (Edinburgh, 1967); L. J. Saunders, *Scottish Democracy 1815–1840* (Edinburgh, 1950); T. C. Smout, *A History of the Scottish People* (London, 1969); G. M. Trevelyan, *The Middle Marches* (Newcastle, 1934); J. T. Ward, *Chartism* (London, 1973); Alexander Wilson, *The Chartist Movement in Scotland* (Manchester, 1970). See also three unpublished Ph.D. theses: Bernard Sharratt, *Autobiography and Class Consciousness: An Attempt to Characterize Nineteenth Century Working Class Autobiography in the Light of the Writer's Class* (Cambridge, 1974); Robert A. Cage, *The Scottish Poor Law 1745–1845* (Glasgow, 1974); Fiona Montgomery, *Glasgow Radicalism 1830–48* (Glasgow, 1974).

THE

AUTOBIOGRAPHY

OF

A BEGGAR BOY;

IN WHICH WILL BE FOUND RELATED THE NUMEROUS TRIALS,
HARD STRUGGLES, AND VICISSITUDES OF A STRANGELY
CHEQUERED LIFE ; WITH GLIMPSES OF SOCIAL
AND POLITICAL HISTORY OVER A PERIOD
OF FIFTY YEARS.

———

LONDON:
WILLIAM TWEEDIE, 337, STRAND.
———
1855.

TO

CHARLES DICKENS, ESQ.

Sir,

      I beg to offer you this little tribute of my admiration for the services you have rendered in the cause of Humanity, in scattering the beautiful and fragrant wild flowers of your thoughts and feelings in the paths of humble life. In common with the majority of your numerous readers, I have not only been amused but highly instructed by the perusal of your works. I think you will agree with me, that the highest compliment which can be paid to an Author is being told that he has identified himself with the best feelings of his reader; and this you have never failed to do with me. The manner in which you have arranged your numerous groupings,—the happy distribution of your lights and shadows, and, above all, your amusing treatment of the foibles of humanity, have given you a place in my esteem by which you have made me your debtor; I hope, therefore, that you will accept this expression of my regard as a small instalment of what I owe you. In conclusion, I trust you will be long spared to delight and instruct your countrymen with the bright emanations of your fertile imagination.

I am, Sir,

Yours very sincerely,

THE AUTHOR.[1]

Chancery Lane, London,
    August, 1855.

---

[1] The second edition of the autobiography, published early in 1856, is dedicated not to Dickens, but to the Queen, in the hope that "your Majesty may have an opportunity of learning the struggles and difficulties which beset the lives of many of your Majesty's subjects, but more particularly that class, who lives, as it were on the outskirts of civilisation." A note is attached from a Colonel Phipps, announcing the Queen's acceptance of the book. The third and fourth editions carry no dedication, and the revised 1882 edition is dedicated to "Thomas Baker Esq. of the Inner Temple", who had met Burn through his publisher William Tweedie and had helped Burn find employment in his late sixties.

Preface

THE AUTHOR has been induced to publish this little volume, from a consideration that a perusal of the numerous trials and hard struggles of his life, may have a tendency to stimulate young men to an endeavour to overcome the obstacles and difficulties which may surround their early positions in the world. This brief history of an eventful and highly chequered career, he thinks, cannot fail to impress upon the youthful reader a lesson of useful import. Men in their daily intercourse have frequent opportunities to study each other's history, but as they cannot keep up the connection in the regular order of events, their narratives necessarily become disjointed. There is also another consideration of still greater importance to the proper understanding of a man's character, which is a knowledge of his motives! Could we but see the hidden springs which prompt men to action, we should often be less liable to judge harshly of each other's conduct, and, instead of censuring, find it our duty to praise!

The first division of the book will introduce the Author in the character of a wandering vagrant. It will be seen, that when he was cast upon his own resources, he was placed in circumstances of extreme danger, being exposed to the two-fold temptations of poverty and bad company. It may be said that he overcame the difficulties of his truly critical position by the energy and determination of his character.

The second division will show the reader the misdirected energies of an uneducated man, whose ambition was fettered by the want of early training. In this part of the work the Author has endeavoured to open up the whole volume of his mind, and thereby expose its most secret springs. It will thus be seen that many of his commercial failures have arisen from a pure want of caution, and like many a well-meaning man who has split upon the same rock, instead of looking for the sources of his numerous mishaps in his own want of judgment, he has frequently attributed them to causes which never existed!

The third epoch of the Author's life may be said to have been ruled by a series of conflicting circumstances, over which he appeared to have had little or no control; however, the reader will not fail to observe that the same laudable determination of character which saved him from moral shipwreck in early life, still enabled him to weather the storms of adversity in more advanced years. On the whole, the narrative will be found to be a series of natural incidents arising out of their various causes, and the Author has made no attempt either to heighten their colour, or enhance their importance. Much of the reflective matter in this volume will be appreciated, or otherwise, according to the pre-conceived opinions of those into whose hands it may fall, the Author has only to add, that his notions of men and things, whether right or wrong, have been produced by much rubbing with the world, and in the *meantime*, they are the honest expressions of his mind.

THE AUTHOR.

Letter I

Aberdeen, September 20th, 1854.

MY DEAR THOMAS,[2]—I have often thought of giving you some account of my early history. I have now made up my mind to do so, in the hope that my numerous trials and difficulties, and the experience of my chequered life, may be of service to you in guiding your steps in the path of duty. As a general rule, I take it for granted that the life of a mere working man can be of very little interest to the public. I am sensible that there are exceptions to this rule; when a man has worked his way from the obscurity of humble life by the force of genius—such, for instance, as some of the early painters and poets: the lives of such men become public property, and we learn by their noble example to persevere if we would conquer. Biography forms the most pleasing part of history. It sets before us the character of such men as may have become eminent for their virtues or notorious for their vices, and it withdraws the veil from their motives to action. By it, too, we learn the motives which led them to aspire to deeds of glory, or the delusions which carried them into the snares of vice. In reading the life of a man, if honestly written, we are placed in a favourable position, whereby we are able not only to observe all his actions, but we can also see the whole machinery of his mind, the workings of his various passions, and the strength of the regulating power of his judgment. A man who either writes his own life or has it written for him may be said to be dragged from the crowd of his fellows and placed naked upon an elevation, so that all may witness his noble qualities as worthy of imitation, or his defects which are calculated to impress upon us the weakness of human nature.

In reading the lives of many of our statesmen, one would almost imagine that life was an idle dream and virtue an empty sound. In many instances, men of this class have looked down upon the people as a distinct and separate creation from themselves, worthy of their notice only when they could make use of them for their own sordid interest or petty ambition. For my part, I think it would be well for society, if the lives of all such men were comfortably consigned to oblivion. In giving you a history of my life, I will endeavour to furnish a faithful narrative of the whole chain of events which have acted upon me through life up to the present time, keeping in the back-ground only

[2] Thomas was his eldest son, born at Otley on 31 December 1828. He died of a kidney disease on 3 March 1870.

those things which are trivial or otherwise unworthy of notice. It is true that I have never achieved any act worthy of public notice: the relation between my name and fame has been as distantly remote from each other as the poles. But, as a recompense for the want of bold adventure, deeds of daring, and noble enterprise, you will find much that is worthy of reflection, and, in some cases, my conduct may be found not unworthy of imitation. Like a large number of my own class, I was born in poverty, nursed in sorrow, and reared in difficulties, hardships, and privations. It is only such as have passed through the various substrata of civilized society who can justly appreciate the feelings and sufferings of the thousands who continually live as it were by chance. When we know the numerous petty shifts and dishonest subterfuges which characterize the conduct of a large portion of those members of society whose position places them out of the reach of want, we cannot feel surprised at the dishonest practices of that miserable class of beings who hang upon the outskirts of civilization. The man who can dine is very differently situated to the poor wretch who, after he has had one meal of victuals, has no idea where or when he may be blessed with another! Those members of society who are blessed with a regular supply of food and raiment may be said to be antipodes to the accidental feeders, and their modes of thinking are, in every sense of the word, as opposite as are their ways of living!

You have only known me since I was what may be termed a free man; or, in other words, since I became independent by the application of my energies to honest industry. To attain this position was with me a work of years of toil and ardent hope. The great majority of young men who are put to trades are generally prepared in some measure, ere they are sent to masters, to pass their probation for the duties of life. You will learn, as you proceed, that my case, upon entering into the busy arena of the world, was very different.

Where or how I came into the world I have no very definite idea. The first place I found myself in was a garret in the main street of Dumfries.[3] The date of this extraordinary occurrence I have lately learned was somewhere about the year 1806.[4] Among the first great events of my life, I remember the circumstance of having been held up in my mother's arms to witness an execution; the person's name was Maitland Smith, who suffered death for

[3] In the 1882 edition Burn gives a more detailed description of the garret: it had "sloping roof for side walls, and it had the recommendation, in a natural history point of view, of literally swarming with rodents, known more commonly by the name of rats. I can well remember my mother having to keep a switch by her side when we were taking our food; otherwise I believe they would have had the lion's share of it." (p. 2). For descriptions of the town and the surrounding area by contemporary travellers see, Thomas Newte, *Prospects and Observations on a Tour in England and Scotland* (London, 1791), p. 49; Henry Skrine, *Three Successive Tours in the North of England and Great Part of Scotland* (London, 1795), pp. 35–6; Dorothy Wordsworth, *Recollections of a Tour made in Scotland A.D. 1803* (3rd ed., Edinburgh, 1894), p. 7.

[4] Burn never seems to have been certain when he was born. The calculation here, and the reference on p. 72 to his being "somewhere about twelve years of age" late in 1815 suggests he was working from a birthdate of 1802–3, but in the final 1882 edition he appears to have settled for 1800, and accordingly this date of 1806 is put back to 1804.

the murder of a cattle dealer, in Dumfries, in 1806.[5] From this effort of memory, I conclude that I must have been from three to four years of age at that time. My mother then was earning her living by carding hatters' wool, which I believe to have been a very laborious occupation. Poor woman! she had been unfortunate in placing her affections upon my father, who had deceived her, and left her with myself in her arms as a recompense for her lost honour and slighted affections.[6] Shortly after this event she must have left the North of Ireland, and migrated to Dumfries; how long she remained there I have no recollection. The next event which clings to my memory was my mother's marriage with a discharged soldier, whose health and constitution had been sacrificed before the altar of patriotism and glory in the Peninsular war. This gentleman's name was William McNamee. What sort of a figure he made in the war I know not, but I am aware he was no ordinary person in the estimation of all who had the honour of seeing him. In height he was upwards of six feet, and as perpendicular as the gable-end of a house; his bones were so poorly protected with anything in the shape of muscle, that he looked like the frame of a man being set up. The first time I saw him, and ever after, he wore buckskin smalls (a part of the uniform of the foot guards); his limbs were so slender that he put one in mind of Death's shanks in Burns's inimitable *Death and Doctor Hornbook*.[7] Whether it was the fashion to wear the hair long at that period I cannot say, but Mac wore his hanging down upon his shoulders; the colour was that of a dark chestnut, and it hung in graceful natural curls. When a young man he must have been very good-looking; his face was still prepossessing, and his bearing characterized by a commanding military air. The marriage was celebrated in a common lodging-house in Gretna Green. I believe the ceremony was performed by a knight of the hammer. How long the marriage festivities were kept up I cannot say; but this I know, that after this event the world became to me a scene of continual vicissitudes and hardships. It is true, I had a reversionary interest in it; and how I turned this patrimony to account will be seen in the sequel. My new-found father and good mentor was a man who possessed a goodly share of common sense; he had seen a good deal of service while in the army, having been in several general engagements, and was with the Duke of York in his memorable Dutch campaign. His scholastic attainments, I believe,

[5] The murder in fact took place on 16 April 1807, when Maitland Smith, a ruined spirits dealer from Dumfries, robbed and shot a cattle dealer named Alexander Williamson. He was executed outside the new gaol in Dumfries (see William McDowall, *History of the Burgh of Dumfries*, Dumfries, 1906, pp. 687–8).

[6] The Irish working class population in general observed a much stricter code of sexual morality than their Scottish counterparts, which would have accentuated the disaster of the desertion of Burn's mother. Her subsequent apparently successful marriage to McNamee conformed much more closely to the behaviour of the migrant Irish population. See T. C. Smout, "Aspects of Sexual Behaviour in Nineteenth Century Scotland" in A. Allan MacLaren, *Social Class in Scotland* (Edinburgh, 1976).

[7] "They were as thin, as sharp an' sma' As cheeks o' branks" [a kind of wooden curb for horses] (l. 41).

were limited to reading and writing imperfectly. He was a member of the Church of Rome, and a rigid observer of all its forms. Poor man! he had one failing, but this one was followed by a thousand others; if he once tasted intoxicating liquors he had no power to close the safety-valve until he either became prostrated, or his finances were exhausted. When he was in his sober moments, Mac was as honest a man as the sun could shine upon, and strange to say, when under the influence of drink he was quite the reverse. The most dangerous of his drunken foibles was an everlasting propensity for polemical discussion, accompanied by an obstinacy of character like that of Goldsmith's village schoolmaster—

"For e'een though vanquished, he could argue still."[8]

This superabundance of religious zeal often caused him to receive treatment, anything but in keeping with the charity of the Gospel. Like the majority of his countrymen, (the name will indicate that he was an Irishman,) the mind of my step-father was largely surcharged with strong feelings of religious prejudice. It will be remembered that people professing Catholicism in those days were marked with the hateful *brand* of the national stigma. They were therefore continually labouring under a painful sense of their unmerited wrongs. The members of the Church of Rome, though British subjects, and contributing to the national wealth, and submitting to all the conditions of society, were debarred nearly all the rights and privileges of common citizens. They were not only continually subject to the gross and brutal attacks of the ignorant, but their wrongs were frequently used as stepping-stones to state preferment by the rich and powerful. It was thus that the deadly embers of religious animosity were kept alive, and one class of society was continually made the foot-ball of the other. I have no doubt but my step-father's mind must have been soured by the overbearing conduct of his comrades while in the army, who took occasion to prove their sense of religion by a system of heartless persecution, which was at that time sure to find favour with their superiors. Of course this was no justification of his foolish conduct: I merely mention it as matter of palliation. Men who are goaded by the unjust treatment of their fellows, seldom regulate their conduct by the principles of reason: unmerited wrongs are sure to produce a spirit of revenge; and in my opinion he would be more than man, or less than man, who could passively submit to such degradation. From the above traits in my step-father's character, it will be seen what manner of man he was; it may, therefore, be readily imagined that a mind so formed would necessarily exercise no small influence over the building up of my own.

McNamee had never learned any trade, having gone to serve his country when he was little more than a boy. After his constitution had been fairly shattered, he very imprudently took his discharge upon request, by which means his long service of twenty-eight years was unrequited. When my

[8] From Goldsmith's *The Deserted Village*, 1.212. The quotation is both accurate and apposite in that the schoolmaster's arguments are with the parson.

mother put herself under the protection of this gallant defender of his country, he was making an honourable living by appealing to the charitably disposed members of society.[9] I believe she had been earning her own living, as a travelling merchant, by retailing to her patrons such small wares as she could carry in a basket.

Shortly after the marriage, it was arranged that my mother should continue her business, and that my father should take me along with him, in order to increase the commiseration of the benevolent public in his behalf. As I was said to be the oldest of three, and rather a prepossessing looking little fellow, I was considered a pretty good subject to stimulate the kindly feelings of all good Christians. My existence up to this eventful period may be said to have been in the dream-land which lies beyond the confines of memory. It is true I recollect some little land-marks, which left their impress upon my plastic memory; but their importance is of so infantile a character, that I deem them worthy of undisturbed repose. My capacity for thinking was at this time beginning to expand, and my mind began to chronicle passing events. In the course of a few years after this, I had passed through a life full of hardships and romantic adventures. Within the space of two years I had been the inmate of every jail in the south of Scotland.[10] My poor father's love of drink, and his religious dogmatism, continually embroiled him in scrapes, and, being his squire, of course I always came in for a share of his rewards. I have still a vague remembrance of nearly being made food for a colony of rats in the tolbooth of Moffat. I remember, too, having been fed upon brose,[11] with brose as a condiment during fourteen days, in Greenlaw gaol.[12] I am not without some pleasing reminiscences of the *gude toun* of

[9] Begging in Scotland was far from honourable, and unlikely to provide an adequate living. Under the Scottish poor law the poor had no legal right to relief and were encouraged to rely on private charity. If that failed they could apply to the Kirk Sessions where the Elders would scrutinize the moral character of the applicant, and McNamee, as an alcoholic and a Catholic, would be viewed with little favour. Successful applicants could expect little, the average relief given in this period was a mere 1s. 5d. per week. The total number of mendicants receiving some official support amounted to 44,000—about 2½ per cent of the population compared with a figure of around 9 per cent in England. *Third Report from the Select Committee on the Poor Laws (1818) Appendix: Report of the Committee of the General Assembly*, PP. 1818, vol. V, pp. 24–36; Sir James Sinclair, *Analysis of the Statistical Account of Scotland* (Edinburgh, 1825), pp. 141–222; Alexander Dunlop, *A Treatise on the Law of Scotland Relating to the Poor* (Edinburgh, 1825), pp. 40–89.

[10] Besides suffering the penalties for fighting and stealing, McNamee and his son were also put at risk by their begging. The English Act of Settlement did not apply in Scotland, but to become eligible for relief a beggar had to be resident in a parish for three years. Travelling beggars could be arrested as vagabonds and were liable under a Proclamation of 1692 to a month's imprisonment for a first offence and branding on the face for the second, although this latter penalty was no longer carried out. Burn's Irish connection was a further problem. All travelling Irish were generally regarded as vagabonds, irrespective of their actual status, and not until 1824 was it finally established that it was illegal to refuse relief merely because the applicant was Irish. Dunlop, op. cit., pp. 90–3; Sir G. Nicholls, *History of the Scotch Poor Law* (London, 1856); James E. Handley, *The Irish in Scotland 1798–1845* (Cork, 1943), pp. 157–203.

[11] A kind of porridge made by pouring water or broth on meal.

[12] Changed to Duns jail (7 miles away) in the 1882 edition.

Hawick, having been boarded and lodged in the tolbooth there for the space of seven days.[13] This circumstance arose out of the following little incident. My father had been on the *fly* in that town for nine or ten days, and when his money was all done he sallied forth into the country upon a begging expedition. The first place we landed at was a farm-house, a little way out of the town: I remember this house well; and while I was in Hawick a short time ago, I had the curiosity to visit the locality, in order to see if the house was still standing. It is not like the ruined cottage, where none shall dwell; after forty-seven years, I hailed its thatched roof and dingy walls, little altered since my first visit. My father had only been in the house a short time before he had fairly enlisted the sympathy of the farmer by "fighting all his battles o'er again." After the subject of the wars had been sufficiently exhausted, my good angel wound up with a religious disquisition: on the whole, the good farmer seemed much satisfied with the abilities of the old soldier, and rewarded him accordingly. When my father was passing out of the lobby, or rather the passage which separated the dwelling-house from the byre, his evil genius led him to steal a hair rope, or tether, which temptingly hung against the wall; the farmer, following us out at the same time, caught him in the act. Poor McNamee's boasted religion, like Paddy the Piper's music, flew up to the moon. The consequence of this escapade was, the honour of the board and lodging I have noticed above. It will be seen that my early training must have been pretty well attended to.

About nine months after this event we were located in a small village of the name of *Hightee*, in the neighbourhood of Lochmaben, in Dumfrieshire, and had considerably bettered our condition, in consequence of my father having abstained from drink during the course of some four or five months. We were dealing in hardware, and had so far climbed the hill of prosperity, that we were enabled to keep an *ass!* It would have been well if it had been the first in the family! ! In consequence of being out of an assortment of goods, three of us were sent off to Dumfries to obtain the required stock; I mean my father, myself, and the ass! Burns has truly said, "that the best laid schemes o' men and mice gang aft a gee." So it was with poor Mac: he owed himself a treat for his past good conduct, and of all the men in the world he was the last to allow such a debt owing to himself to go unpaid. With the high resolve of liquidating this obligation, he called a meeting of his creditors, and so relieved his mind of further anxiety about the matter. After three days and nights, the ass, his panniers, and myself, were all that remained of our worldly effects. There is a climax to all worldly things; so, like the immortal

---

[13] Henry Graham described the prison accommodation of the period as follows: "The receptacle for prisoners in a village was a 'thieves' hole', a little hut with damp earthen floor with hardly a glimmer of light from the tiny damp opening, through which the snow drifted and the wind swhirled in mad career through the room, and out again, under and above the ill-fitting doors . . . A small country town for its residence for prisoners had a vile thatched room, perhaps fourteen feet long, dark, filthy and fireless, and in winter perishingly cold . . ." (*Social Life of Scotland in the Eighteenth Century*, London, 1901 ed., pp. 503–4).

Tam O'Shanter, the time had arrived when we required to "*tak* the gate"; like him, too, we set out upon our journey when bordering upon the midnight hour.[14] Our way lay through Locker-Moss, this was a barren moor, without anything in the shape of a regular road. When crossing this moor, I was set upon the back of the ass, and, being fairly worn out with sleep and fatigue, I tumbled off Neddy's back somewhere about the middle of the moor; and, as the night was very dark, the ass and his companion journeyed on; being sound asleep, I lay, quite comfortable, until daylight, when my father, after a good deal of trouble in finding me, picked me up, and flogged me well for parting company without leave.

About the time I am writing of, this village Hightee, or *Hytee*,[15] must have been a regular *rendezvous* for wandering vagabonds. I remember one very ludicrous scene, which was like to have ended in tragedy. Among the swarms of beggars, tinkers, and *gipsies*, there was a woman who had been in the neighbourhood for a considerable time. This lady was short of the sense of hearing, or at least she made it convenient to be so. She had successfully levied black mail upon certain of the fair sex, under the pretence of telling them what good things the Fates had in store for them. It had come to pass that the oracles of this Sybil were not always in keeping with the truth. Upon the occasion in question, a large number of the villagers of both genders carried the poor deaf and dumb lady to a pond of water which embellished the village green, and, after having bound her body with a horse halter, by way of trying the hydropathic cure, they dragged her body and soul back and forward through the water. Her complaint seemed hopelessly incurable; but, as the good lady was determined not to go to heaven by water, she at last allowed the water to do for her what it undoes in many others, and, when the villagers found that they had rendered the woman such a service as that of restoring her hearing, and, what was of more importance in a female point of view, the use of her tongue, they consigned her to the care of the Procurator Fiscal. I have often seen her after that as deaf and dumb as any fortune-teller could wish to be.

People who look down from the comfortable eminence of social life, will necessarily imagine that all class distinctions will cease to exist among the wandering *nomads*, who live upon the charity of the well-disposed. In this they are very much mistaken. In whatever walk of life men are placed, talent will always take the lead. Among beggars, there is an aristocracy as exclusive as any that prevails among the higher orders of society. The difference between a common beggar, who earns his daily bread by cadging for *scran*,[16]

[14] The opening lines of the poem run as follows: "When chapman billies leave the street,/ And drouthy neibors neibors meet,/ As market-days are wearing late,/ An' folk begin to tak the gate;/ While we sit bousing at the nappy,/ An' getting fou and unco happy,/ We think na on the lang Scots miles,/ The mosses, waters, slaps, and styles,/ That lie between us and our hame/".

[15] i.e. Hightae, a village eight miles east of Dumfries.

[16] Remains of food.

and the genteel high-flyer, is as marked as the distinction between a peasant and a peer. The man who can successfully pass himself off as the innocent victim of an awful calamity, can afford to live in a very superior style to the common every-day beggar, who receives alms as a matter of course. The one can generally afford to live like a lord, while the life of the other is a dull round of drudgery. Vagrants are not wanting in ambition; and the genius of one successful member is sure to stimulate the energy of some of his compeers. I have known men made up for the charity market in a hundred different ways; I have even seen some adepts in the profession who were able to personate half a dozen characters, and successively impose upon the feelings of the benevolent in each. While we were in the neighbourhood of Hytee, there were three men, and the same number of females, who were all first-class professionals: these fellows could make themselves up in an astonishing variety of ways, and they continued to go over the same ground with un-diminished success in fresh guises. One day, one of these fellows was ruined by fire, and the next he lost his all by shipwreck; then again he was the victim of a foul conspiracy, by which he was robbed out of his patrimony. No man can be a successful actor unless he can identify himself in the mind of the audience as the real Simon Pure; it must, therefore, be admitted that the *artistes* I have alluded to above were no mean ornaments to their honourable profession.

Amongst the wanderers in these days, there were a great number in Scotland who carried the meal *poke*.[17] Many of the farmers' wives kept what was then called an *aumous*[18] dish; this was a small turned wooden dish, and was filled according to the deserts of the claimants or the feeling of the donor. Those who did not keep one of these vessels, were in the habit of measuring the amount of their alms by a single handful of meal, or by a double handful, which was styled a *goupen fou'*. Some people gave alms in oatmeal, and others in barley-meal. The oatmeal was always preferred by the applicants, inas-much as they could always find a ready market for it, and at better price than could be obtained for the barley. I know not whether it arises from the march of intellect and the progress of scientific knowledge, but I find there is one class of beggars who used to excite the sympathies of the good people on the north side of the Border, who appear to have gone down into the greedy gulf of oblivion. I allude to the handbarrow beggars. These human counter-irritants for acting upon the best feelings of our nature, were at one time a source of infinite trouble to the people in the wild sequestered parts of the country. The manner in which these dilapidated and crumpled-up fragments of the *genus homo* were transported from one locality to another, imposed no small tax upon the time and kindly feelings of all who were honoured with a visit. These creatures were either seated upon their barrows, or reclined upon soft couches, and when one of them was set down at a

17 Small bag.
18 Alms.

farmer's door, it required two able-bodied people to remove the living lumber to the next house. This was frequently no easy task, as the meal pokes were often as heavy as their owners. Now it often happened when one of these animals was planted at the door of a farm-house, especially in the summer season, when there would only be a single female at home, the he, or she, and the barrow would have to remain until the servants came to their victuals. In many instances, these living loads had to be carried several miles before they could be deposited at the door of another farm-house.[19] I knew one case where a lady of this class was made to find the use of her limbs, by those who had charge of removing her taking it into their heads to souse her into a comfortable cold bath in the river Esk, which they had occasion to ford. Her ladyship, instead of "taking up her bed and walking," arose from her bed and ran! ! ! After her bath she was no more seen in the beautiful valley of the Esk.

Up to the period I am writing of, which would be somewhere about the year 1809, I had twice narrowly escaped drowning. While my step-father continued sober, he treated me with all possible kindness, and not unfrequently evinced as much real affection for me as if I had been his own child; but unfortunately when he was in drink, and, of course, got into trouble, I was continually made his *scape goat*, and all his sins were sure to be visited upon my devoted head. About six months after the Dumfries expedition, my father had been drinking for some days in New Galloway, a small place in the wilds of Kirkcudbrightshire. After he could remain no longer in this town, he sallied forth late in the evening of a cold October day, and he knew not whither. In the course of a short time we had arrived upon a wild and desolate moor, the face of the sky was covered as with a pall, and the rain fell in torrents. I can never forget how he dragged me along the dreary waste he knew not whither. His tall, gaunt figure, was frequently brought into fearful relief by the flashes of lightning which followed the fitful claps of thunder, and he looked like the genius of the storm, with a young victim in his hand ready for a peace offering. During that awful night we floundered through its dreary hours, and had so frequently measured our lengths amid the bogs and swamps of the moor, that we actually became a part of it. By daylight we found ourselves in the neighbourhood of a lonely shepherd's cottage. The inmates of this house kindly received us; we were both completely exhausted, and I believe if we had not met this relief at the time we did we should have both perished. As it was I could not be removed for eight days in consequence of having been seized with a fever.

During the whole of this time my mother had been very industrious; but the great misfortune with her was, she had no sooner accumulated a little property than her thoughtless husband squandered it in dissipation. Poor

---

[19] For similar accounts of the handbarrow beggars see Martha Somerville (ed.), *Personal Recollections from early life to old age of Mary Somerville* (London, 1873), p. 13; H. G. Graham, *The Social Life of Scotland in the Eighteenth Century* (London, 1901), p. 235.

47

fellow! there never was a man in the world with a better set of good intentions; but as a set-off to these unfinished virtues, he possessed a stock of evil ones which were like Pharaoh's lean kine—they continually devoured the good ones. Being a creature of impulse, his whole life was a continual round of sinning and repenting; and I firmly believe that he was as honest in his resolves of amendment as he was industrious in crushing his good intentions. In consequence of his frequent rounds of dissipation he was subject to fits of *delirium tremens*. At that time I had no idea of the cause of this fearful malady, and as a consequence was often nearly frightened out of my life. The first circumstance of this kind occurred at a place called Wark; this is a small village upon North Tyne, twelve miles from Hexham, in Northumberland. My father had been drinking in this place for some days; whether he was obliged to leave the place surreptitiously, or did so upon his own account, I cannot say; but this I do know, that I shall never forget the occasion as long as I live. We left Wark between ten and eleven o'clock at night, in the middle of winter; he had made up his mind to go to Hexham, but instead of taking the direct road by Chollorford, he forded the Tyne, and took the road by Barrisford, which was at least three miles further round. How he got safely through the river I cannot imagine, but it must have been attended with no small danger; all I now remember is that we were both as wet as water could make us.

We had not proceeded on our journey more than half-a-mile after having forded the river, when my father brought up in the middle of the road. Up to this time, he had been talking to himself a great deal of incoherent and disjointed stuff. This was an ordinary occurrence with poor Mac, when under the influence of the *jolly god*. The moment we came to a dead stand, he pointed his hand to the devil, who was standing on the middle of the highway, at the comfortable distance of about five yards in advance of us. We stood still for a few minutes, during which time my father seemed resolving the matter over in his mind, as to whether he should retrace his steps or go on. At last, he crossed himself, and we moved forward. The devil, in the most friendly and accommodating manner, did the same. In order to satisfy himself of Satan's identity, my father made an attempt to pass him; but, however fast we walked, we were not able to lessen the distance a single inch, or, however slow we paced the ground, our relative positions remained unchanged. My poor little heart fluttered like a new-caught bird in a cage, and I was in a state of the most indescribable fear. I did not see the devil, but imagined we were in the company of thousands. My father was a person who, under ordinary circumstances, possessed a large amount of moral courage; but he must have been more than mortal who could encounter the devil single-handed, and that devil a *blue* one. For some time, the perspiration exuded from every pore of his skin, and every now and again he crossed himself, cursed, or mumbled a prayer! All this time he grasped my trembling hand with convulsive energy, and I clung to him for my very life, and did not dare to turn my eyes either to the right or the left. Although the night was extremely cold and my clothes were saturated with water, the powerful emotion of fear must have sent my blood galloping through my system: otherwise I must have perished. Our journey home was one of continual mental suffering. Every bush and tree, and every gust of wind, were to me as many devils, and, during the whole time, my father continued talking to himself and blackguarding his satanic majesty, who still acted as our pilot. When we arrived at Hexham Bridge, our unsocial companion silently took his leave of us, after having travelled over fifteen miles of a bleak and solitary road. It would be impossible for me to described my own sufferings during that dreadful night. My father continued to see and to hold converse with the devil for some days after, and it was more than a month before he recovered from the effects of his debauch and nocturnal journey with the Master of the Blues!

Upon another occasion, some time after this, my father had been drinking in Lauder, a small town in the south of Scotland. We left this place in consequence of the active character of some of his amiable propensities. When we left Lauder, my mentor was in a state of beastly intoxication. We took the Edinburgh road—I should think by chance. This road passes through a wild and desolate moorland country. How far we had travelled I cannot say, but during the night we lay down upon the moor, by the wayside. We had not been there long, when a continual succession of stage-coaches began to pass and re-pass us. The whole of these vehicles were laden with passengers. Some of the passengers were ugly demons of every possible shape and form, some were merry imps, and others mischievous rascals. They all seemed to know poor Mac. Some of them invited him to take his place as an outside or inside passenger; others grinned at him with horribly distorted faces. Some were for hanging him: others preferred the amusement of drowning; some suggested roasting, while others demanded a show of hands for boiling him. For hours these infernal coaches kept rattling past us, and my poor father kept my horrors alive by directing my attention to what the devils were saying. It is true I did not see any of them; but I heard my father attending to their remarks, and when he saw them, it was quite enough for me—I could feel more than sufficient without ocular demonstration. I really believe, that, up to the date of our encampment upon the *Lammer Muir*, the road had never been honoured with anything in the shape of a coach higher in character and condition than a rude country cart.[20]

I remember another occasion, when these blue fellows held him in their hellish thrall for six days and nights. This was while we were being storm-staid in a lonely ferry-house in the island of Skye. I think he suffered more

[20] Burn referred to Tam o' Shanter in his account of crossing Locker Moss and he may have had the poem in mind in these two incidents. Tam, like McNamee, is assailed by the Devil and other supernatural horrors on his drunken ride home. Given the general background of wild country and hard drinking, both Burn and Burns will have been connecting with a widely shared experience.

upon this occasion than either of the former. He was surrounded by legions of devils, who tormented him in every imaginable way. During the whole of this time, I was in a continual state of terror, and, what made my condition one of continual and unmitigated agony, I had none to console me. We had left my mother in the Low Country, and the people of the ferry-house were as ignorant of the English language as if it never had existed. If you can imagine an innocent being chained to a dissipated devil and dragged through the slime, and mire, and scenes of horror which lie in the path of the drunkard, you may form some little opinion of my position when my father unchained his lawless desires.

If I were inclined to moralise upon the sin of intemperance, and make known my own experience during my journey of life, O! what scenes of horror, misery, wretchedness, and crime, I could hold up to the scorn and pity of all rational men. I am firmly convinced that the foul and brutal Demon of Intemperance has done more in defacing the image of God among the sons of men than all our other vices put together. It may be truly said, that to this "monster we owe all our sin and woe." How humiliating it is to see a man come down from the high and god-like dignity of his reason, and leave his moral nature behind him, that he may revel in madness! Every instinct and feeling of humanity goes by the board, and we behold the noblest work of the Almighty scathed and blighted—the pitiful wreck, of what ought to be the temple of wisdom, alone remains. This frightful insanity severs every tie of kindred, love, duty, and affection. The home of the drunkard becomes a scene of desolation, and his friends have occasion to mourn him a thousand times more than if he were dead. The sin of intemperance is a fearful vice in man, but in the female it is an hundredfold more hideous. O! what sight is there in Nature so truly sickening, as to see the mother of a family brutalized with drink? With her there is no redeeming quality left; she becomes a maudling maniac. Shame, which guards the outposts of female virtue, flies from its duty; the common decencies of life are cast to the winds, and she becomes a thing of filth and loathsomeness. Every duty she owes as a wife, a mother, and a member of society, are all swallowed up in her beastiality. She has no love, but for the damning cup; no affection, but for the foul craving of her fiery stomach. Her home becomes the abode of misery, her family are orphans, and if her husband be a sober man, she has covered him, body and soul, with a pall of living thorns. In her madness she blindly staggers on until she tumbles into a premature grave. This is no overdrawn picture; such scenes are being witnessed every day—and every hour.

I have frequently thought, when I have seen the people of this country, with the instincts of self-preservation, prepare to defend themselves against an attack of cholera, or some other pestilence, (and with what anxiety they endeavoured to ward off the dreadful malady,) that had they taken the same pains to stay the ravages of intemperance, which is a thousand times more fearful in its consequences than any plague, or indeed than all the combined scourges that have ever afflicted humanity, they would then have been doing a duty to themselves, their country, and posterity. I know there has been much pity expended upon the victims of this dreadful scourge; and we have periodical displays of excited feelings, and the ventings of honest indignation; yet fire-water sweeps on in deadly torrents through the fair fields of humanity, and carries thousands annually into the gulf of eternity. That we may see the deformity of this monster in a clearer manner, let us imagine three hundred thousand drunkards, male and female, all congregated together in one locality, so that their united actions could be observed. I ask, would not their madness make the very angels weep, and humble the thinking witnesses of the revel to the dust? Depend upon it, the £50,000,000 the people of this country spend annually upon intoxicating drinks, and narcotics, is quite sufficient to manufacture this number, large as it may appear. The statistical returns of our huge criminal department prove that 150,000 human beings annually pass through our gaols. From my own experience, I would say that the great majority of these have been initiated in crime by passing through the cursed portals of the gin-palace. If we could only watch the melancholy but transient career of these 300,000 self-devoted victims, and see them reeling over the precipice of eternity with fearful rapidity, how should we shudder with all the pity, fear, and horror of our natures! The historian and the moralist may paint the revolting horrors and direful calamities of war; but I am satisfied that the blood-stained sword of Mars never produced so much human suffering as alcohol has done.

I may be excused this digression,—the subject is one on which I feel deeply; moreover, I thought it necessary to call your attention to its manifold evils, in order that you may avoid the numerous temptations which lead to destruction. Drunkenness is one of those vices into which men fall by degrees. In its first stages it is surrounded with many pleasing and apparently innocent pleasures. The social cup frequently seems as it were the key to men's best feelings; and thus we are led on to taste its various joys, and indulge in the fascinating pleasures of kindred congeniality, until we are ensnared, and ultimately lost!

When we come to reflect upon the awful penalties this vice imposes upon its victims, we cannot but feel surprised at the self-immolation of so many thousands of human beings. With the drunkard, the infatuation is as blind and reckless, as the retribution is sure, and few are able, after entering the gulf-stream of dissipation, to check their headlong career until they are totally wrecked.

I have said that my step-father's health had suffered much while he was in the army. All the time that I knew him he laboured under a severe asthma, and was subject to continual attacks of coughing; and his breathing was often so laboured, that one would imagine his machinery was fairly worn out. I often think, when I reflect upon the matter, that, considering the brutal manner in which he used himself, if he had taken even ordinary care, he might have prolonged his life much beyond the date of his death. In the latter part of 1810, McNamee took it into his head to visit London, to see if he could obtain sufficient recommendation to pass the Board at Chelsea, in order to become an out-pensioner. By this time my mother had increased the muster-roll of our family by two, a boy and a girl, we therefore numbered the round half dozen.[21] A journey to London in those days was no trivial matter; however, as wandering was our destiny, it mattered little where we roamed. After we crossed the Border, my father made application for a pass in Carlisle, which was readily granted by the magistrate, when he learned the object of our journey.[22] This pass enabled us to get relief in the various towns and villages through which we had occasion to travel. As this turned out a profitable speculation, we embraced nearly all the towns over the half of the kingdom on the way up. This journey initiated us into the genteel mysteries of vagrant life in England; and when my father could afford to keep himself sober, we could save money, and live like fighting cocks into the bargain. I can well remember the marked difference in the etiquette of the English and Scottish beggars; at that time, the manners and habits of these strollers were as different as it is well possible to conceive. The English beggars were then characterized by an independent, free, and easy style; of course the distinctions of class were rigidly maintained on both sides of the Border, but in all cases the Scotch were far behind the *genteel civilisation* of their southern neighbours. The manners of these people, I imagine, are formed and regulated much in the same way as those of gentlemen's servants.

I have found that nearly every class of people in the kingdom have a moral code of their own, and every body of men has its own standard of perfection. Your professional pickpocket looks down with contempt upon a knight of the *scranbag*, and the *highflyer* turns up his genteel proboscis at the common cadger. A lady who may have shared the bed, board, and affections of an aristocratic letter-writer, would feel herself as much humbled in allying herself with a plebeian *charity irritator*, as my Lord Noodle's some time affection receiver would have in espousing one of his lordship's ploughmen. From what I have witnessed in my early life, of the manners, habits and feelings of the wandering tribes of humanity in Great Britain, I am the better able to reflect upon their modes, and compare them with those whose position is higher up in the social scale. Honesty may be said to be the basis of human virtue. This consciousness of what is right is liable in the minds of

[21] The fourth child was a son, the eldest of McNamee's children by Burn's mother.
[22] During the eighteenth century a system grew up of providing paupers with certificates of character which would enable them to demand free passage and sustenance from parishes en route to an agreed destination where the pauper had reason to expect relief. Discharged soldiers and sailors were especially provided for under an act of 39 Eliz. C 17, re-enacted in 1803. By 1821 it was claimed that at least 60,000 were perpetually circulating up and down the country at the public expense. (S. & B. Webb, *English Poor Law History*, Pt. 1, London, 1927, pp. 387–91).

certain people to an amazing amount of latitude. In some people, the perception of this principle becomes "small by degrees, and beautifully less." In comparing men's actions and motives, I have found that the difference is very frequently only in the degree, for instance, I have seen a beggar barter his wife for a pot of ale, and I have known a nobleman who got clear of his better half for 40s. damages. I remember when in York, along with my father and mother, we were lodging in a house where there were about fifty travellers, male and female, congregated; among this heterogeneous group of all ages, conditions, and nationalities, there was one jovial young fellow who found himself inconvenienced by the possession of a very good looking young woman—I should think her age was not more than nineteen. This pair of turtle-doves had been moistening their clays pretty freely for three or four days. At the expiration of this time, the gay Lothario, either sated with love or full of generosity, kindly transferred his lovely nymph to the keeping of another gentleman, and gave him half-a-gallon of beer into the bargain. I have no doubt such a transaction as this would be highly offensive to the feelings of people trained in the genteel walks of life; yet it is no uncommon thing for the young fast sailors among our aristocracy to act in the same manner—with this difference in their favour, namely, that they have had the despoiling of their victims and covering their families with shame and ignominy before they cast them off.

After a good many vicissitudes and two incarcerations, we arrived in London, and took up our abode in that sylvan retreat where the motley inhabitants spoke all tongues, from Kerry to Constantinople—Church-lane in St. Giles. "Sad thy tale, thou idle page!" The ruthless hand of progress has swept this place of a *million* memories, and many a thousand dark deeds from the map of the world! If I remember correctly, we paid nine-pence a-night for one bed in a large barrack of a building, the proprietor of which kept a provision-shop. This fellow was both as ugly and as dirty as if he had been bespoke so. The very atmosphere of London, or else its *gin*, very soon produced an exhilarating effect upon the nervous system of my father. In the course of a few days, his libations had reduced us to the most miserable state of destitution, and, to add to our hapless condition, we were left among strangers, many of whom were brutalized into heartless grinning savages by drunkenness. My father's discharge was backed with an excellent character. The commanding officer under whom he had last served was then Governor of the Tower.[23] As soon as he got himself into full marching order, by being free from the influence of drink, he presented himself before Colonel Cook and was very well received. The colonel promised to use his influence in my father's behalf, and, in the mean time, made him a present of two pounds; as I was with him at the interview, I was introduced as his own son. The colonel also made me a very handsome present, and requested that my father

[23] Burn downgrades Colonel Cook to "an officer of the tower", "Probably keeper of the Regalia" in the 1882 edition.

should introduce my mother upon his next visit. For some time after this all went "merrily as a marriage bell." The colonel was an old bachelor, that is, if my memory does not fail me—he took a very strong liking to my little person, and was very anxious that my mother should *invoice* me over to him, in order that he might train me up in his own way. What obliquity of feeling or false sentiment made her cling to me, by which means my fate was to continue to be chained to the car of evil destiny—I know not. As a proof that the colonel had no idea of how we were living—he purchased me a splendid suit of clothes, made in a sort of a half military form, with an immense number of gilded bell buttons. Poor old man! he little thought he was dressing me like a puppet for the charity market!

After we had been about a month in London, my father obtained an interview with the Duke of York. I cannot say whether he promised to interest himself in my father's favour, or not; however he made him a present, and, on leaving us at the Horse Guards, he patted me on the head, and inquired my age. Passing the Board proved an utter failure, which I believe was entirely owing to the everlasting drinking propensity of my father. When all other resources failed for raising money, he used to make charity sign-posts of himself and the other two boys, along with me. Human sympathy is a strange thing—it binds men of all ages, countries, and conditions, in the god-like bonds of universal love. To those who have not got occasion to think upon the subject, it would be a matter of surprise to learn the amount of real charity which exists in London. If my father had taken care of the money he had given him during his begging campaign in London, I am satisfied that he could have gone into some business, by which means he would have been enabled to have rubbed the vagrant rust off his character, and become a respectable member of society. The hungry devil in his stomach seemed ever ready to swallow up every good resolve the poor man could make.

I need not say that my mother's life was one of continual misery. When left to herself, she was a woman that could always make a living, both for herself and family, but unfortunately, the proceeds of her industry went to swell the river of our calamity. London soon became too small for my reckless father. During the time we were in town, he had wantonly, and repeatedly, abused the kindness and generosity of the Governor of the Tower. During some of his escapades there, I had the honour of three nights' confinement with him in the old guardhouse; of course he was put there to keep him from a worse place. During these small events, which went to make up the history of my father's life, my own years were increasing, and impressions were being made upon my undeveloped sensibility, which stamped themselves upon my memory, or passed like shadows.

I was a thing without a mind, and might be said to have neither body nor soul of my own—that plastic part of my nature, which was to become my only patrimony, was being moulded under the most degrading influences and corrupt examples. It is true, and strangely so, whether McNamee was drunk or sober, he never forgot to pray, morning and evening: and it was an amiable trait in his character that, whether in prosperity or adversity, he never let any of us forget the duty we owed to God, and our dependence upon his Divine will. I owe him an eternal debt of gratitude for having left an indelible impression of the noblest aspiration of his mind upon my own. This redeeming living reality of his existence haunts me in my happiest waking dreams, and causes me to revere his memory with a holy affection. I often think that there is a soft and holy influence steals over our souls when our memories calls up the living forms of those who taught us to lift our eyes to Heaven, and say, "Our Father who art in Heaven!" I know that other influences have wound themselves round my existence, and that I had received impressions of men and things which were well calculated to cramp the energies, and strengthen the bonds of my mental slavery. These peculiar circumstances were inseparable from my condition, and it required no small effort, in after life, to cast off the silent working influences of such an education. The difference in physical organization between a fool and a philosopher is often very small, if my step-father's duplicate bumps of caution had been a little more developed, he certainly would have been a very excellent character. The want of this single element was the cause of all the other faculties of his mind living together in a state of continued disorder. This insubordination among the servants of his system, set his judgment at naught, so, poor fellow, he had to march through the Coventry of life with a pack of real ragamuffins.

In my next letter I will notice a few of the changes which have been effected in the progress of events in Modern Babylon since my first visit, after which I will resume my journey.

Letter II

MY DEAR THOMAS,—Forty-five summers and as many winters have cast their broad lights and deep shadows over the face of the earth, and millions of human beings have performed their parts upon the stage of life, and made their exits, leaving room for others to run the same routine, since my first sojourn in London. The irresistible logic of time is change. To-day only is! Yesterday has passed into the greedy gulf of eternity, and the future is rapidly hurrying to the same goal. While time whirls past with surprising velocity, and man pushes forward on the highway to the outer boundary of both time and space, the endless chain of cause and effect continually keep unfolding new combinations in the magic kaleidescope of nature. Amid the universal transformations of things in the moral and physical world, my own condition has been like a dissolving view, and I have been so tossed in the rough blanket of fate, that my identity, if at any time a reality, must have been one which few could venture to swear to.

In looking back from my present position, I have only a very faint recollection of London in 1810. Still, there are many circumstances and places which yet live fresh in my memory. The character of the locality in which we resided, and the many strange scenes there, will ever retain their hold upon my recollection. The St. Giles of my youth with its stirring memories, huge sufferings, savage life, and innumerable crimes,—is now a respectable locality of comfortable-looking houses and civilized inhabitants; while the dark deeds of the past are only to be found pictured in works of fiction or recorded in the exciting narratives of the Newgate Calendar. Change has, therefore, swept over this once living hive of heterogeneous humanity, like a mighty wave, and washed away all traces of its very existence. St. Giles is not the only place in Modern Babylon that has been sacrified to the levelling *genius* of progress. St. Catherine's was another of these dark spots in the wilderness of London, where vice and crime flourished in tropical luxuriance. I have often been taken through Swan-alley, which was then looked upon as being one of the most consummate sinks of iniquity in London, and I have frequently feasted my juvenile eyes upon the savage male and female patrons of the *Black Boy and Tankard*, where the first gentleman of the age was wont to enjoy himself in the refined society of coal-heavers and other amphibious denizens of that *ultima thule* of civilization. One of the principal differences between these two saintly localities was to be found in their respective *vernaculars;* in the one you had the blackguard slang of landsmen of all nations, mixed up with the technicalities of prigs and professional beggars; while in the other, you had the benefit of the jargon of salt junk and the *Fo'-castle,* refined with coal-dust and the elegant vocabulary of Billingsgate. This modern Gomorrah has been changed into pools of water—St. Katherine's Docks and a range of huge warehouses now cover the site of the whole locality—in these days Tower-hill was honoured with the title of Rag-fair, and the traffic of dilapidated garments, impressed with the fashions of a preceding age, was divided between the Jews of the stock of Jacob and those of St. Patrick.

I well remember that the Tower Moat then lay stagnant and green, sending up its sweet *effluvia* as a sanitary offering to the surrounding district; at that time the roar of the lions, the tinsel, red faces, and party-coloured dresses of his Majesty's showmen in the Tower were well calculated to fill a young mind with awe, wonder, and admiration—I observe that there are still extant a few of these *rara avis,* formerly known by the cognomen of "beef-eaters"—poor fellows, they look as if they were ruined by the luxuriant rankness of their pasture, and the onerous smallness of their labour. I can also remember the tidal industry of the water-wheel at the north-west end of London Bridge. The present London Bridge is like a young colony, it has not seen sufficient human misery to have a history. Waterloo and Southwark Bridges were then snugly sleeping in their quarries about Aberdeen and Falmouth. The two blacksmiths in the front of St. Dunstan's, in Fleet-street, hammered the passing hours with equal industry, to the amusement of little boys. The British Museum and the National Gallery have since then become monuments of our national progress. The new Palace in St. James's Park, and the Parliament Houses, indicate our growing prosperity, and, as far as the Parliament House is concerned, our peculiar bad taste in architecture. Several men who were then climbing the slippery hill of Fame, have long since gone to the home of silence, but I observe that their names, and their country's gratitude, have in several instances been perpetuated in marble and bronze. Many of the old-fashioned narrow streets, with their dingy and dropsical looking houses, have been displaced by spacious thoroughfares and magnificent places of business. The addition of nearly a million of human beings has been the means of sending a large portion of the town many miles into the country for the benefit of its health; the consequence is, that the London of 1855 is fully one-third larger than the old rickety London of 1810.[24]

During the last forty-five years, centralization has been the means of entirely changing the old order of things. The numerous modern facilities for travelling must have greatly contributed to swell London into its present

[24] The population of Greater London had in fact doubled over this period—from 1,327,000 in 1811 to 2,685,000 in 1851.

gigantic proportions. The continual multitudinous ingress and egress of strangers must have been the means of producing a gradual change in the social condition of the people, as well as contributing to the general prosperity of the town. In the early part of the present century travelling was a thing of rare occurrence among the great body of the people. I have known scores of respectable country people who were never fifty miles from home in their lives; among the same class of people in the present day, it would be difficult to find men who had not visited the principal towns in the kingdom, either upon business or pleasure. Within the last twenty years the rail has set the whole world in motion; from this state of human locomotion, it must be evident that a large portion of the London people must be continually employed in ministering to the wants of their country cousins. Amongst the numerous changes which have been effected by the innovating march of progress, I find that the *Cockney* phraseology of my young days has lost much of its primitive simplicity, a married lady is now no longer a *vife*, and the *osses* eds have generally become embellished with Hs, a *wessel* now *veighs* anchor after the W has relieved the V from the dog watch; but it must be remembered that times were then *werry ard*, and *weal*, *vine*, and *winigar* not *werry* comatable, still the good people swilled their *arf* and *arf*, whether *ot* or cold. The natives of London have also been divested of much of their one-sided views of men and things, and the consequence is, that they have left much of their old-fashioned prejudices behind. When I was a boy, a north countryman was sure to be branded with the title of a Scotchman, which then implied half savage, half knave; and all Scotchmen were supposed to have been fed upon *brose, braxy,*[25] and *oatmeal*. Our growing commercial relations, and the consequent fusion of the people, have done much to effect a revolution for the better in these matters, and if we are not more religious, we are at least more charitable, which is certainly a move in the right direction.

I cannot say what understanding was come to between my father and mother before leaving London; it is certain, however, that some arrangement was made, which I believe was in no friendly spirit, in consequence of my father's continual dissipation. My mother took the whole of the children into her charge, and made application at the Mansion House for a pass to Hexham, in Northumberland, as a soldier's widow, which she had no difficulty in obtaining; with this pass we visited nearly all the towns and villages on the east coast of England between London and Newcastle-upon-Tyne. As my mother preferred taking the journey at her ease, and her own time, she frequently had the benefit of the cash that the overseers would have had to pay for sending us forward in a conveyance, and at the same time she had the advantage of the intermediate relieving officers, who were often glad to get clear of us at the expense of a shilling or two. During the time we were in

[25] Salted mutton from sheep that had died from natural causes, particularly from the disease of braxy, a common intestinal complaint brought on by lack of fresh food in winter.

Scarborough, a little hunchbacked gentleman, who was a sweep by profession, had taken a notion to add one to his family, by appropriating my
small person; I dare say he imagined that if I had been made to order, I
could not have been more suitable for his honourable profession, so he had
me kidnapped while I was playing on the beach one evening. I was in his
sooty honour's custody during three days and nights—while I was with him
he used me like a prince. How my mother hunted me out I cannot say; but
I am aware that the little fellow offered her a hundred pounds down for me,
and, if she would relinquish all future claim on me, he offered to make me
his heir.[26] It is said that there is a tide in the affairs of men, which if taken,
&c.; if there be anything of such a nature in the affairs of boys, my affectionate mother always stood between me and the flood which leads on to
fortune. Be that as it may, it appears that I was neither destined to be the
pet of Colonel Cook, nor the heir of this lonely being who seemed to require
a receiver for his over-flowing affections! ![27]

Our vagrant journey thus far must have been very profitable, and I
believe my father's to have been equally so. I do not remember what plan he
adopted, but I believe he operated upon the charitably disposed with his
discharge, and the certificates he had obtained to enable him to pass the
Board while in London; however, a re-union between him and my mother
took place while we were in Yorkshire. After they had compared notes, and
agreed upon their plan of future arrangements, we proceeded to Newcastle-
upon-Tyne. The begging trade, with its gross deceptions, to say nothing of
its dangers, I believe was somewhat repugnant to the feelings of my parents;
whether they left the business from conscientious scruples, or from a feeling

[26] cf. an attempt by a sweep to purchase the young Thomas Cooper (b. 1805) who was
travelling with his widowed mother in the countryside near Gainsborough: "We were not
half way towards Lea, when we were met by Gammidge, a master chimney-sweeper, and
his two apprentices bending under huge soot bags. He began to try to entice my mother
into an agreement for me to be his apprentice, and took out two golden guineas from his
purse and offered them to her. She looked anxiously at them, but shook her head, and
looked at me with the tears in her eyes; and I clung tremblingly to her apron, and cried,
"Oh mammy, mammy! do not let the grimy man take me away!" "No my dear bairn,
he shall not", she answered; and away we went—leaving the chimney-sweep in a rage,
swearing after my mother that she was a fool, and he was sure to have me sooner or later,
for that she could not escape bringing herself and me to the workhouse." Thomas Cooper,
The Life of Thomas Cooper, written by himself (London, 1872), pp. 9–10. The 2 guineas
offered for Cooper is a more likely figure than the huge sum of £100 Burn claims was
offered for his services.

[27] In the 1882 edition Burn adds to this passage an account of another attempt to purchase
him on the same journey. They are staying in the house of a Jew in Scarborough: "This
old man took a very decided liking for me; he frequently got me to walk with him; and
upon more occasions than one he showed me some of his valuables, which consisted of
jewellry, among which were two gold watches, one of which was ornamented with
diamonds; and he told me if I would remain with him the whole of what I had seen should
be my own. He had several consultations with my mother, in which he used all the
persuasion he was master of to induce her to turn her eldest son over to his keeping, in
which he pledged himself to be more than a father to me but his pleading was to no
avail." (1882 ed., p. 35).

59

of independence, I really do not know, but after our arrival in Newcastle, we became transformed into respectable travelling merchants, or what were then regularly termed "pedlars." Our stock in trade was composed of a medley of hardware and small ware goods. For a considerable time we made Hexham our chief *rendezvous*, and travelled, as it were, in a circle; in the course of a short time we cultivated a very general acquaintance, and we also obtained no small share of confidence and respect. While we travelled in the rural districts our expenses were very small; the inns we put up at were the farm-houses, where our quarters were free, and we invariably had our victuals into the bargain.

Before our journey to London, I had been the constant companion of my father, whether he was drunk or sober, like Sancho Panza, I was sure to be at his heels, and if the Don was honoured by being tossed in a blanket, I was sure, like Paddy the piper, to come in for my share. My brother Robert was now grown to be a fine active boy, but at the same time a very headstrong one. Affections are things, I believe, people have very little power over; be that as it may, any little hold I formerly had upon McNamee's good graces seemed to be waning, and a transfer to be gradually taking place. This change was daily being facilitated, by Robert and myself always being in each other's way. In consequence of this unfortunate change of things the house became divided against itself; the childish quarrels of my brother and myself were magnified into matters of importance; every offence was deemed an act of malice; and I was always made the scape-goat for both his sins and my own. My mother, therefore, took me under the wings of her kindly protection, and every quarrel between the young ones was sure to cause a rupture between the old ones.

Some little time after we left Newcastle my brother and I happened to quarrel about some trifling matter. I had bled his nose, whether by accident or otherwise I do not now remember, but he had sufficient tact to make the most of it in representing the matter to his father, as he knew I should be well punished; the consequence of this little escapade was likely to be rather a serious affair, inasmuch as I escaped with my life almost by a miracle. My father was in the habit of carrying a pocket knife, with a long Spanish blade, as a life-preserver: in his passion he stabbed at me with this weapon three times in succession; how the blade missed finding its way into my body, considering the power with which it was wielded, I cannot imagine, but the only injury I received was a slight cut on my side little more than skin deep. The first stroke cut the side of my jacket open, and the second severed the waistband of my trowsers, while the third cut open the brim of my little felt hat; any one of these blows, if rightly directed, would have spoiled my music, and precluded this biographic sketch.

It was only a short time after this, while we were at home in Hexham, I had been plagerising time, and making use of it for my own special amusement, by bathing in the river Tyne. I had been absent without leave from seven o'clock in the morning until five o'clock in the afternoon; I remember I was sporting in the water like a young dolphin, when I beheld the gaunt form of my dear father, with a smile of satisfactory vengeance curling about his mouth, coming towards me with giant strides; like a lamb in the presence of a wolf my little soul felt all the alarm of the coming danger. As he neared me, I observed that he had a new cut switch in his right hand, which he endeavoured to conceal behind his back, I lost no time in making for the river bank as speedily as possible; I knew if I could only clear the water before he came upon me, I could soon enlarge the distance between us on the land, in consequence of his short-windedness. Notwithstanding my good intentions, however, before I got fairly landed, I had half a dozen welts between my head and my hips, each as thick as an ordinary finger, and as lively in the colour as a ripe cherry. Before I could reach home I had to run fully three-quarters of a mile, and to make my journey pleasantly exciting, one-half of the distance was through the leading street in the town. It was somewhat amusing to the natives to see me scampering naked along the public street, like a young American Indian, with my back scalped instead of my head, and my merciless tormentor following behind with my toggery under his arm. I imagined that when I should gain the citadel of home, I would escape all further punishment, but this was an idea I did not realize; inasmuch as I received satisfaction in full. I will leave you to judge whether my punishment was anything like proportioned to the offence, when I inform you that I could not suffer my clothing to be put on for nine days, and during the greater part of this time was confined to my bed. These little things would not be worth notice, only in as far as the severe treatment to which I was subject might have a certain influence over my own conduct in after-life. I know that my step-father never used me with cruelty without regretting it afterwards; in the whole course of my life, I never knew any man who was more a creature of impulse: I have known him to kick and caress me in almost the same breath. One hour he would be all sunshine, and the next, his whole being would be swelling with rage; this storm would very likely be caused by some trivial circumstance; and if he was depressed by small things, he was equally liable to be comfortably excited by mere childish matters. McNamee sober, and McNamee under the influence of drink, was like Philip, he was not the same man; but it happened very unfortunately for me, that whether he was drunk, or sober, I had no appeal from his authority, and the punishment he awarded me when under the maddening influence of drink, could not be repealed when he was sober. Although I was continually subject to capricious severity, and unmerited suffering; still, my life was nor without its sunshine; every storm is succeeded by a calm, and the smaller our power of reflection the more transient our sufferings.

During the time we were engaged in travelling, my duty was to carry the rags, horse hair, and other articles which we received in barter for our merchandise; when our bags were made up of these materials, I have often laboured under my burthen until my heart was like to break, yet with the buoyancy of youth when the day's labour was ended, I have enjoyed myself in the very fulness of soul; if in the summer season, by wandering by some *wimpling* burn, or through the woods and dells, where nature revelled in her own wild beauty. I can now, after the lapse of forty years, call to remembrance many of the occasional haunts of my boyish days. I knew every farm-house from Hexham to Kielder Castle, at the head of North Tyne, and from Redesmouth to the Carter Bar.[28] While travelling our rounds, we had certain farm-houses we honoured by taking up our lodgings in, where there were children of my own age, and I was as much at home with them as if I had been one of the family, and of course entered freely into all their juvenile sports, and pastimes. When I was a beggar-boy, I received as much real kindness, and found myself as much on terms of equality with the sons and daughters of respectable farmers' children, as if I had been one of themselves. Amid all my sorrows and sufferings, I cannot look back upon my wanderings in Northumberland without feelings and emotions of real pleasure; and I can never forget the hospitality, and in some instances, the more than parental kindness, I experienced from the unsophisticated natives. I have eaten many a *whang*[29] of barley-bannock, buttered with the *gude wife's thumb*, and I have been frequently consoled with the application of the homely adage, "That *nae* body could tell what a rugged *cout* (colt), or a ragged *callant wad* come to."

Up to 1812, we travelled over nearly the whole of England, Wales, and Scotland, sometimes in the capacity of beggars, and at others as itinerating dealers, and in consequence of my father's unsteady habits, continually exposed to everchanging vicissitudes. While we were in Northumberland, there was only one thing to prevent my father from saving as much money as would in a short time, have enabled him to open a shop; but after we had obtained a comfortable standing, and a good stock of merchandise, he opened the greedy trough of his stomach and swallowed all; and after the wreck of our fortune, we removed over the Border to the Scotch side. During the next two years we continued to travel in the valleys in the south of Scotland, but our circuit was chiefly confined to Eskdale, Liddesdale, and Tiviotdale; and when we required to renew our little stock of goods, we had to go either to Dumfries, or Carlisle. After our removal from Northumberland, my father once more put the rein upon his intemperance, and we were again upon the high way to prosperity.

During the severe winter of 1813 and 1814, we were located at a little

[28] Burn came to regard Redesdale and the North Tyne valley as his "home" during his childhood and youth. Though he rarely stayed in any one building for any length of time, he always returned to the general area when he had been away in other parts of the country. The best evocation of the area is to be found in G. M. Trevelyan's essay *The Middle Marches* (Newcastle, 1934). Redesdale and especially the North Tyne Valley had long been notably lawless regions although by the time Burn began to travel through them the restraining influences of the Presbyterian Church and improved communications had begun to exercise a sobering effect on the population.

[29] A large slice.

town in the south of Scotland of the name of Langholm. Although travelling was both a dangerous and difficult business during that memorable stormy winter, yet we were able to turn our industry to good account; hare skins were then in great demand, and it was generally admitted that the skins produced in these vales were the best in the kingdom. At that time the article had obtained its maximum price; the skin trade was then regulated by the *Backend* Fair, which was held annually in Dumfries, and at that time full skins were bringing thirty-six shillings per dozen. In consequence of the severity of the winter, the poor hares had little chance of escaping with their lives, and it was no unusual thing for a farmer to have two or three dozen skins hung up in his chimney corner. The trade-manner of casting skins was by arranging them into whole, half, quarter, and pelts, of course, the country people had little knowledge of these technicalities of the trade, and the dealers were sure to have the advantage. During the course of this winter, my father and mother made a good deal of money, but in doing so they encountered no small amount of hardship.

Upon one occasion I was out with my mother in the wilds of Eskdale above Langholm; we had a very narrow escape from being swallowed up in a snow-wreath; and if it had not been for the timely assistance of a shepherd we should have both perished. I remember seeing several cottages completely blocked up with snow, the inmates having to cut their way out in the morning. In some of the more sequestrated parts of the country the people were nearly perished for want of fuel. I knew one lonely house where the inmates had to burn no inconsiderable part of their furniture in order to keep themselves alive from the cold. Upon another occasion, I was out with my father upon the moors between Langholm and Newcastleton, then known by the name of Copshaw-holm. In this district the houses are few and far between; during a snow-storm we had lost ourselves on the trackless waste; we laboured in vain, for hours, to find our way to some house; at last we got into a sort of a dell where there was an old sheep-fold, and by this time the night having come on, we were obliged to content ourselves with the shelter the lee side of the fold afforded us. My father had on a soldier's great coat, and he folded me under this cover and hugged me as close to him as possible during the long, dreary, and cold hours of that dreadful night. When morning arrived, we found little to console us: around, on every side, lay a dreary and monotonous waste of snow, and my poor father seemed quite lost as to what direction to take. We were both nearly foundered. He, at last, made an essay to find our way to some friendly dwelling, and as Providence would have it, we had not gone above a hundred yards from our cheerless quarters, when we heard the barking of a shepherd's dog. Poor Mac looked upon the dog as an angel of rescue: after he had shouted two or three times, he was answered by the shepherd himself, and we were not a little delighted to ascertain, when we found our bearings, that we were not more than a quarter of a mile from a farm-house, the only one within two miles: we were kindly received by the farmer and his family, and, although we had suffered severely, kind treatment soon revived us. We were storm-staid in this place for three days, during the whole of which, we were most hospitably entertained; but during which time my mother suffered intense mental agony, having fully made up her mind that we had perished in the storm.

By this time she had given birth to five children, two of whom had died while we were travelling in England—the remains of one pretty little girl lie in the quiet and sequestered church-yard of Staindrop, in the county of Durham; and the other, a boy, found a resting-place in Gainsborough in Lincolnshire. The time is now drawing nigh, when my own condition in life is about being materially changed; but, before taking leave of this part of my history, I cannot help making a few reflections upon the state of society on the Borders in the early part of the present century. I can still look back through the dim vista of forty years to the happy days I spent among the primitive, but kind and hospitable natives. The inhabitants of the numerous sequestrated vallies on both sides of the Borders were then really an unsophisticated class of people. Every house on the Border at that time was a welcome home for the wayfarer—the beggar was treated kindly and bountifully supplied with food—he had his bed for the night comfortably made up in the barn or the byre; and in many farm-houses bed-clothing was specially kept for this class of wanderers. The *pedlar*, or travelling dealer, was treated somewhat differently: he was lodged in the house, and generally took his meals with the family, and found himself as much at home as if he had been at his own fireside.[30] In these times the farmers were content to dispose of their produce at the market towns which were most easily come at, and they occasionally sold their stock to factors, who paid them periodical visits from the large towns: this was the manner in which the sheep farmers disposed of nearly the whole of their wool. In the Lowlands, travelling merchants purchased the butter and cheese in the same way; others bought up the poultry and eggs; and the butchers of Newcastle and Carlisle were wont to scour the country for calves and such cattle as they could not obtain at the regular markets.

Travelling, among the country people in these secluded districts, was then a thing of rare occurrence, and they knew little of what was passing in the busy world, except what they obtained from hearsay. The times were then equally as exciting as they are now. The French war was then carrying desolation over a large portion of Europe, and there were few of the people

[30] George Robertson remembered how such tradesmen were entertained in the main living quarters of the isolated farmhouses, the kitchen: "It continued to be the great rendezvous of the passing travellers, and of the various country-tradesmen employed by the family. It might be called the news-room of the establishment." Again, beggars remained outside the house: "But no visitors were so frequent as the common beggars. Hardly a single day passed without some of them making their peculiar *chap* at the door; nor a single week, without some of them getting a night's lodging in the barn." (George Robertson, *Rural Recollections*, Irvine, 1829, pp. 108, 109).

even in these lonely, and sequestered vallies who had not occasion to mourn some dear relative who had fallen in the service of his country. If these people had not heard the martial sound of the bugle, or the roar of the murdering cannon, many a loved one was missed from the family circle, and the homely, but social board, and many a tender loving heart was left with an empty void which might never be filled.[31] There were few newspapers in these days, and it was a thing of rare occurrence for any of them to find their way into these regions. The various classes of people who made their living by travelling among these wilds were then the real news-mongers, and of course, were always welcome guests at the *ingle* of the farmer, or the cottar.[32] When my father kept himself sober, no man in his position ever found a more hearty welcome, or could receive kindlier treatment from the country people, upon whom he was in the habit of calling. The fact was, his information was generally looked upon as good change for their hospitality. His knowledge of the seat of war, and the operations of the contending parties, with the general intelligence he brought to bear upon his subjects, caused him to be looked up to as no mean authority. He was equally *au fait* upon religious subjects; his mind was well-stored with historical gleanings, and in polemical debate he rarely found his match. When he was sober he was cool in argument, and patient as a listener. I am aware that much of his knowledge was of a very superficial character, yet the manner in which he used it made him frequently pass as an oracle. Oft has he

"Talked o'er his deeds of sorrow done,"

and if he did not

"Shoulder his crutch and show how fields were won;"[33]

---

[31] The British regiments which took part in the Napoleonic Wars recruited heavily from the Scottish lowlands. The extent of popular interest was reflected in the number of memoirs of ordinary soldiers and sailors which were published after the war. Memoirs of Scottish servicemen include: Anon., *Recollections of an eventful life chiefly passed in the army. By a soldier* (2nd ed., Glasgow, 1825); Robert Butler, *Narrative in the Life and Travels of Serjeant B. Written by himself* (Edinburgh, 1823); Anon., *Vicissitudes in the Life of a Scottish Soldier. Written by Himself* (London, 1827); "G.B.", *Narrative of a Private Soldier. Written by Himself* (Glasgow, 1829); Anon., *Life on Board a Man-of-War, by a British Seaman* (Glasgow, 1829); W. H. Fitchett (ed.), *Wellington's Men, Some Soldier Autobiographies* (London, 1900). The other source of information for the families was letters written by their sons. Alexander Somerville, a native of the lowlands and a soldier of the following generation, considered that the relatively high incidence of literacy among Scottish recruits, compared with those from England, meant that far more was known about the exploits of Scottish soldiers than about those of soldiers from other parts of Britain. Alexander Somerville, *The Autobiography of a Working Man* (London, 1848), p. 188.

[32] Referring to the same area through which the family was wandering, James Russell wrote, "The news of the day were slow of finding their way into remote valleys like ours. Beggars and pedlars were the great newsmongers". ("Reminiscences of Yarrow" in J. G. Fyfe (ed.), *Scottish Diaries and Memoirs 1746–1843*, Stirling, 1942, p. 553). See also Martha Somerville, op. cit., p. 13; Thomas Somerville, *My Own Life and Times 1741–1814* (Edinburgh, 1861), p. 351; Marjorie Plant, *The Domestic Life of Scotland in the Eighteenth Century* (Edinburgh, 1952), p. 245; T. C. Smout, *A History of the Scottish People 1560–1830* (London, 1969), p. 303.

[33] See Goldsmith, *The Deserted Village*, lines 157–8.

65

many a time he has held the farm circle in breathless suspense, while delineating the havoc of the battle, or the dreadful carnage of the siege, the clash of arms, and the horrors of the sacked town.

In the course of my vagrant wanderings on the Borders, I had learned much of its legendary lore, and romantic history. Often while we occupied the chimney nook of a moorland farm-house in a winter's *nicht*, the daring deeds of some border reiver, would be related in the broad vernacular of the district, or tales of ghosts, witches, and fairies, would go round until bed-time. Many a time my hair has been made to stand erect at the recital of some tale of blood and murder; and often has my young imagination been filled with wonder at the fairy legend of a by-gone age. At that time the people on the Borders were proverbial for their superstitious notions.[34] I have known scores of people whose illness was caused by supernatural means. Such complaints as were not common, or where the causes could not be probed by the limited understandings of the natives, were sure to be produced by evil eyes. Children were then said to be cured of the hooping-cough by being passed nine times under the belly and over the back of an ass, or being dipped nine times in a south running stream.[35] In these times, the poor innocent cattle were frequently made to suffer for the sins of their owners. Some people were proof against the power of the evil one in their own persons; when such was the case, their live stock were sure to suffer. I remember we were once lodging at a moorland farm-house between Moss Paul and Hawick, where we were to stay over Sunday; on the Saturday one of the cattle belonging to the farmer had been bewitched, and the poor animal went mad—it was in such a rabid state that it was found necessary to kill it. The farmer was quite aware to whom he owed this act of devilry. The old lady who had used her spell lived in the neighbourhood—but the best of the matter is yet to come. On the Sunday we had a part of the identical cow served to us along with broth for dinner. I don't know whether my father and mother were too saucy to partake of this fare, or that they were afraid of the sanitary consequences; however, be that as it may, we made our dinner of the pota-

[34] Thomas Somerville remembered that, "numerous vestiges of that wild superstitious credulity, which had been nurtured amidst the darkness of the middle ages, still survived in Scotland" (op. cit., pp. 365–6). The hold of superstitions over daily life had been losing ground for half a century before Burn's childhood, but much clearly remained. See H. G. Graham, op. cit., p. 215; L. J. Saunders, *Scottish Democracy 1815–1840* (Edinburgh, 1950), p. 54. Burn returned to the topic in the appendix to the 1882 edition, adding further detail about a variety of supernatural beliefs (see pp. 475–7).

[35] M. C. Balfour in *Examples of Printed Folk-Lore concerning Northumberland* (London, 1904), p. 49, quotes four more contemporary "cures" for whooping cough: "Children have been brought for some distance to the lime kiln at Hawkwell, a quarter of a mile south of this place, and carried backwards and forwards through the smoke"; "A child [is taken] under the belly of an ass and between its forelegs. A piebald pony is also very efficacious"; "Another plan is putting a trout's head into the mouth of the child affected, and, as their sages say, 'let the trout breathe into the child's mouth' "; "another receipt is to make porridge over a stream running from north and south." The micro-organism which causes whooping cough, coccobacillus, was not discovered until 1906.

66

toes, and the beef and broth were destroyed. The most noted places for witches and fairies that I remember, and where they lingered longest in the face of civilization, were *Cannoby* and *Buecastle;* the latter place, is a wild moorland district in the most northerly part of Cumberland, and I believe has been famed from time immemorial for the *honesty* of its cattle dealers, and the superstition of its rude Saxon natives. At the time I am writing of, there was not a glen, a homestead, a mountain-stream, or a valley, but had its ghost story, or some attendant genius in the shape of a good or evil-disposed fairy. In these days it was quite a common thing for one of the *wee* folk to assist in doing the necessary work of a farm-house; and in order that they might perform their labour without interruption, it was always done when the inmates were in the arms of *Morpheus.* One of the common methods in which the witches were in the habit of exercising their infernal art was by casting their *glamour*[36] over the *kirn*[37] of the farmers' wives to whom they owed any little debt of revenge. When the spell rested upon the milk, all the churning in the world would not produce butter.[38] This species of credulity very frequently led to serious consequences. I have known several instances where females who were suspected of being witches, were all but sacrificed to the godly fury of innocent believers, the fact was, that to be sceptical upon this subject was tantamount among the country people to disbelieving the Bible. The Witch of Endor, and the command that a witch should not be suffered to live, were looked upon as unquestionable authority upon the subject, and there were few at that time who had the hardihood to call these divine truths in question.

I never knew any body who had a better appetite for a belief in supernatural agencies than my mother; under the most trivial circumstances of bodily ailment or ill-fortune, she was sure to have recourse to charms. My brother, who died in Gainsborough, was a weak and puny child from his birth, and from the nature of his ailment was unable to assimilate his food. My poor mother was as firmly convinced that the child was bewitched as she was of her own existence, and she used several exorcisms to break the spell—among several valuable charms she had the heart of some domestic animal stuck full of pins, and roasted before a fire,[39] and at the same time she used a variety of incantations; how the operation failed in producing the desired effect I am not aware. I dare say you will imagine that this subject is not worthy of a moment's consideration. I grant you that it would not, were it not that the manners and habits of the great body of the people, fifty years ago, form a striking contrast to those of the present day, and I have no doubt but the change will be equally as great fifty years hence, when the present age is contrasted with the future.

[36] Enchantment.
[37] Churn.
[38] The spell could be lifted by putting a crooked sixpence into the churn (Balfour, op. cit., p. 54).
[39] This was a common device for warding off evil spirits (Balfour, op. cit., pp. 52–3).

Having received a considerable part of my education in such a romantic school, it would be strange indeed if I could have escaped without being subject to the impressions consequent upon such a course of training. Since I have attained to manhood, I can assure you it has frequently required all the little philosophy I possessed to keep the invisible agents of the other world from regulating my affairs, and directing my conduct to suit their caprice or convenience, and many a sturdy battle my reason has had with my fears upon their account. I think, on the whole, I have been able to overcome the numerous busy tormentors of my youth, and whenever my fears became alarmed, judgment is sure to come to the rescue; however I must confess that the battle is sometimes little better than a drawn one.[40] I am not sufficiently master of psychology to understand how the lingering impressions of super-natural agencies should continue to alarm us after the reasoning faculties of the mind have passed judgment upon them, and found them mere creatures of the imagination, unless it be that Mr. Imagination, who acts the part of a vigilant sentinel, by being always upon guard, and easily alarmed, should be necessary to keep Mr. Reason in healthy employment, by lending fear the use of his aid and counsel in all cases of real or imaginary danger. I believe there are very few men who are not less or more liable to be acted upon by supernatural fears, and yet they are conscious that such feelings are mere dreams. When ghosts, fairies, and witches cease to live in the belief of a people, the character of such a people must lose much of its poetry. The age of superstition is one of ideality, in which imagination takes the lead of reason. The mind of a nation is in a continual state of transition, and the farther it flys off from the superstitious element, the more utilitarian and the more sceptical it becomes. A few centuries ago criminals were tried by ordeal; in the early part of the last, respectable females were roasted for witchcraft, and the age of ghosts is only just passed away. It must not be supposed, however, that because we cannot believe in these things, that imagination has ceased to hold its empire over us. The loss we have sustained has been of late partially compensated for in other supernatural and electrical agencies. We have now our table turning, spirit rapping, and mesmeric *clairvoyance*. It is said by sensible people that the devil is the agent in these things, but if people are pleased to have the aid of the devil in ministering to their amuse-ments, I really don't see why any one should find fault; for my own part, I think that his majesty might be much worse employed.

---

[40] See also a similar confession by William Lovett, who grew up at the same time in the Cornish village of Newlyn: ". . . the numerous stories regarding those nocturnal visitants, told to me in infancy, reiterated in boyhood, and authenticated and confirmed by one neighbour after another, who had witnessed, they said, their existence in a variety of forms, riveted the belief in them so firmly in my brain, that it was many years after I came to London before I became a sceptic in ghosts." *Life and Struggles of William Lovett* (1st ed., 1876; 1967 ed., p. 9).

Letter III

My dear Thomas.—The first two chapters in the history of my life can be of very little interest either to you or any body else. Their principal value will be found in their connection with after events. Every man's life is made up of a chain of causes, some of which produce direct or immediate effects, others would seem to act upon us in the remote periods of our existence, and exercise an influence over our very destinies. I am not a fatalist—at least, I think not—yet I have often found myself led and acted upon by feelings and influences which I could not account for by any little philosophy I possessed. This short-sightedness may arise occasionally from attributing certain acts and circumstances in our lives to proximate rather than to distant causes, or *vice versa*. As you proceed with this narrative, you will observe that my life has been one of epochs, or, more properly speaking, I have been carried forward by a succession of trade-winds without any directing power of my own. I may mention a circumstance here, which, though trivial in itself, will prove that we frequently labour under feelings and hold ideas we cannot account for upon any rational principle—at least, that such has been my case. From my earliest recollection, I was impressed with a feeling of the most unmitigated hatred against my own father: when, how, or where such a feeling took hold of my mind, I have not the most distant idea. I had never seen him, rarely ever heard his name mentioned, and never heard him described. I therefore knew not what sort of a man he was, and yet I hated him with a downright honest hatred. It is said, that "Coming events cast their shadows before."[41] Whether this be the case or not, you will learn by the sequel whether I did not receive treatment to confirm this mysterious feeling in his regard.

In the month of May, 1815, while we were travelling in the valley of North Tyne, between Falsestone and Kielder Castle,[42] our family being all together at the time, we were resting, about the middle of the day, by the side of the river, my brother Robert and myself were amusing ourselves in the water,— when a young man came up, on horseback, and introduced himself to my father without any ceremony, by requesting to know if he would allow his

---

[41] From Thomas Campbell's *Locheil's Warning*.
[42] Changed to Thorneyburn (3 miles to the East of Falstone rather than 6 miles to the West) in the 1882 edition.

auldest callant to *gang* wi' him to herd *nowt* for *twa* or three months. A short palaver was held between my father and mother; I was recalled from my aqueous sports and was requested to dress, not for dinner, but for a journey. I had a second shirt folded up in a piece of paper, was told my mission, helped on to the horse, behind the young man, and away we went. Our destination was a shepherd's cottage near the head of Warksburn: the distance from where we set out might be somewhere about twelve miles as the crow flies. The name of my new home was *Cauldrife*, and no name could possibly have been more appropriate. The house stood upon a wild moor, completely isolated from the civilized world. I had my instructions that night, next morning was called up at four o'clock, and while I took my breakfast my new mistress packed my dinner up ready for me to *gang* to the hill. My dinner consisted of barley bannocks, a *whang* of skimmed milk cheese, facetiously denominated *Peg Walker*, from the peculiar cohesive character of its particles. This, with a tin flask of milk, was a sample of my *stereotyped* dinners. After breakfast I went off to the hill, which was distant about a mile and a half; my charge was a large herd of oxen, which were sent up to graze from the low country in the summer months, and were returned at the end of the season, in order to be fed for the winter market at Morpeth. I went on pretty well in my new avocation, until the novelty of the thing was past. After I began to reflect upon my position, my lonely and dull monotonous employment was like to break my heart. I rarely ever saw a human being from one week's end to another, except the inmates of the cottage when I went home in the *gloaming*, which was generally about nine o'clock at night during the time I was there.[43]

I endured this monotonous life for three months, and during the whole time I never either saw or heard of my father and mother. While I was in this place my mind was continually filled with all sorts of uncomfortable reflections, and as the term of my servitude drew near, I had made up my mind that I was cast adrift upon the world, and my childish prospects were, as you may imagine, anything but cheering. During my sojourn in Cauldrife, I witnessed a little incident of rather a peculiar nature: one night I was lying awake in my bed, there being other two beds in the same room, one of these was directly opposite mine, and contained two men who were *mowing* for the season. About two o'clock on the morning of the night in question, both these men simultaneously arose in their bed, and sat upright, and carried on a regular conversation for nearly half an hour concerning the French war, which was about being brought to a close, during the whole of the time the men remained asleep. After they had thoroughly discussed the question, they both lay down as if by mutual consent. What was very singular, neither of the men knew anything of the matter when questioned about it in the morning.

[43] In the 1882 edition he adds that "While at Cauldrife I had a faithful friend constantly at hand, my collie dog, who shared my meals and lightened my duties" (p. 66).

At the expiration of my time I bade adieu to Cauldrife and travelled over to Bellingham, which was about nine miles distant; as good fortune would have it, I found my father and mother, and my clothing being in a sad state of dilapidation, my father took me down to Newcastle and rigged me out with second-hand toggery, upon which he spent the whole proceeds of my three months' servitude, which amounted to fifteen shillings. If I could have torn the veil from the future, it would have humbled my innocent pride, these same garments covered me when I was frequently steeped to the very soul in grief. It is often well for us that "enough for the day is the evil thereof."

My father had by this time continued a faithful disciple to the cause of temperance for two years, and the consequence of which was, that my mother and he had accumulated a considerable amount of property, and instead of carrying their packs, as they were wont to do, they had wisely enlisted the services of a pair of asses, so that they had really become respectable pedlars.

My father, as I observed before, had left home when he was very young, he had left several brothers and sisters behind him, and had never heard anything of them during all the years he had been away. Finding that he was in comparatively comfortable circumstances, he made up his mind to visit the land of his birth. Whether he had any idea of remaining in Ireland or not I never learned; however, everything was prepared for the journey, and in due course we arrived in *ould* Ireland without any incident worthy of notice. As we journeyed to the residence of my step-father's relations, we required to pass through Killaleagh,[44] in the county of Down, while in this place my mother learned that my own father was married and living there. Here then I am on the eve of another change in the wheel of my capricious fortune. My mother had an interview with my father, after which I was duly consigned to his care. I cannot describe my feelings at this sudden and unlooked for change. My step-father, with all his faults, on the whole had been a kind and not unfrequently an affectionate father to me; on the other hand, my own father was an utter stranger, and I went to him with my mind surcharged with a living hatred of his very name. I have observed that he was married—he had a family of three children, the oldest of which was a boy about five years of age, and the two younger were girls. I therefore lost my own mother and a step-father, with three brothers as dear to me as if we had all owed our being to one father. In place of these I found a step-mother, by whom I must naturally be looked upon as an unwelcome intruder. My new-found brother and sisters were strangers to me, and from the peculiar circumstances of our left-handed relationship, and the unlooked-for nature of my introduction, it was very likely we should remain strangers to each other, at least in feeling. If you will imagine to yourself a number of people obliged to live upon short allowance of food, and forced to receive an additional member without a corresponding addition of victuals, you will be able to

[44] i.e., Killyleagh, a small fishing port 14 miles south-east of Belfast.

71

form a pretty correct idea of my reception in the ungenial home of my father. My step-mother was certainly placed in a very unpleasant position, before my unlooked-for appearance she was not aware that any other duplicate of her dear husband existed except her own loved boy. After I was introduced, the poor woman did not know how to treat me, and I knew she never could love, if even she could bring her mind to tolerate me.

From the peculiar sensation my presence created, I could observe that my father found himself in no very comfortable position; I was there as a living memento of his perfidy, and while under his roof, I was a standing reproach to him for the faithlessness of his conduct. My new mother was a very quiet, easy, thriftless sort of a person; when she was ill-natured, or in a passion, she told the object of either the one or the other—the nature of her feelings through the medium of her eyes instead of her tongue. My father was a peaceable, industrious, sober, and well-meaning person, he had nothing marked in his character, if I except a strong hatred of popery. At this time, he was in humble circumstances, and his young family required all his industry for their support. His trade was that of a corduroy weaver, at that time employment was scarce, and the work was very badly paid for. I should then be somewhere about twelve years of age, but I was both small in make, and low in stature; however, as a set off to these natural deficiencies, I was both sharp and active. It was not likely that I was going to be allowed to eat the bread of idleness, so I was set to the business of winding bobbins for my father.[45] As there was no accommodation for me to sleep at home, I was sent to lie with my uncle John, who had then only returned from the army, where he had seen some service—he was lodging with my paternal grandfather, whose dwelling was next door to my father's. The old man rented a small plot of ground, by the cultivation of which he contrived to earn a scanty living. I think his age was then seventy-six, he had, when younger, been a very strong man. The proceeds of his early industry had been swallowed up in rearing a large family, who were then all married except one girl who was living with them, and my uncle John. The first out-door employment I had, was in gathering potatoes for my father when he went out to dig by the day, which he was in the habit of doing in the season. While this business lasted I fared pretty well, as we got our victuals from the farmers where we were employed.

When my father settled down to his loom again, I was honoured with a new employment; in addition to winding the bobbins, I was made caterer for fuel for the establishment. Sometimes I was sent to the moss for turf, this place was fully three miles from Killaleagh, what turf I got I brought home in a bag, you may form a very good notion of the quantity of this material I could carry such a distance at my age. When I did not go to the moss, I was

[45] For more detailed descriptions of the life of a bobbin-winder, see Samuel Bamford's *Early Days* (London, 1849), p. 101, and Benjamin Brierley's *Home Memories and Reflections of a Life* (Manchester, 1886), pp. 18–19.

sent into the fields and woods to gather sticks and furze. By this time the winter had set in, and I was neither inconvenienced with shoes nor stockings. In consequence of my professional rambles through woods and fields, my clothes were reduced to rags; indeed, no young urchin could possibly have a better suit for ventilation, and what was more, I had a numerous *live stock* on my body with the addition of the itch to keep me warm. If cleanliness be a virtue, my guardians seemed to have very little respect for it, and as to any care they had over me, that appeared to give them even less concern. It is really surprising what an influence dirt exercises over the mind, and how soon a person is likely to lose all feeling of self-respect when proper care is not taken with the person. The avenues to morality require the frequent application of soap and water, otherwise the noblest faculties of our nature soon become clogged and inactive. Poverty in rags is a thing that is seldom allied to romance; had I been transferred from the nursery of some rich man's family, the circumstances of my suffering condition would have been well calculated to create sympathy in my regard; as it was, the world had no care for me; yet I had a world of feeling within me which was continually acting and re-acting upon itself. I knew I had no one to look up to; I therefore kept my sufferings, and my thoughts as much to myself as possible. Often when I was wandering in the fields gathering firewood, I have poured out my pent-up feelings in a flood of tears. Young as I was, I could see that my future in life must depend upon my own exertions. I had one idea that was continually before me, and haunted me in my night visions and waking thoughts, which was to fly from my miserable bondage, but how that was to be effected, I knew not, still I felt a melancholy pleasure in tossing the thought in my mind.

During the winter my feet were hacked into innumerable fissures from which the blood was continually starting, when I washed them at night before going to bed (which was as seldom as possible), my sufferings were intense, added to this, my heels were as elongated as any black man's, with the action of the frost, which caused me either continual pain or an itching, which was nearly as bad to bear. Notwithstanding my hard lot, neither my father nor mother ever noticed me, unless to do their bidding; the fact was, I was a complete stranger in my father's house, and continually treated with marked coldness and neglect. Had it not been for my grandfather and grandmother, and my uncle and aunt, who always treated me with uniform kindness, I should have frequently suffered from hunger. My uncle was at that time rather a rakish young fellow, he occasionally broke the dull monotony of my existence, by taking me with him to some of the rustic dancing parties he was in the habit of attending. The only Irish wake I ever had the pleasure of seeing was in his company. I believe the Irish character is no where to be seen to better advantage, than at a wake or a fair, for in both cases, the whisky brings it into bold relief. The peculiarly excitable nature of the Irish temperament, seems to know no medium, the transition from fun to fighting, is often instantaneous. At that time it was no uncommon thing to see men

73

shaking hands one minute, and industriously breaking each others heads the next.

During my sojourn in Killaleagh, I had frequent opportunities of witnessing those outbursts of feeling which arise from party spirit. This infatuation has been a national curse to Ireland; the idea of men killing each other for the love of God, has something in it so extremely repugnant to common sense, that did we not know the weakness of human nature when labouring under strong prejudice, we could not believe in such a state of things among people who were even half civilised. I am aware that Ireland has suffered much from English misgovernment arising from an illiberal and short-sighted policy. Until lately, our rulers have uniformly endeavoured to keep alive a spirit of antagonism among the people; in this conduct they have evinced a very small philosophy, and a still smaller christianity. But however much the English have been to blame, the Irish people have ever been their own greatest enemies; there are few countries blessed with so many natural advantages; and I am certain that no civilised people could have done less to develop its numerous resources. Instead of extending the commerce of their country, cultivating the soil, and adding to their social comforts, their time and energies have been wasted in party feuds, and savage forays upon each other. From this state of things, the Irish character had become a problem to the rest of the civilised world, and neither statesmen nor philosophers could find a key to its solution. There is another trait in the Irish character which has ever been a drag upon her prosperity; I mean the want of national independence. Her people, instead of depending upon their own energies, courage and industry, have vainly looked forward to their country being redeemed by acts of Parliament. O'Connell had frequently edified his countrymen by quoting Byron's saying,

"He who would be free himself must strike the blow;"[46]

but had he impressed upon them the truth, that a nation that would be great must be united and industrious, it would have been more applicable to their condition. In my opinion "the love of savage justice" which has always characterized the Irish people, would long since have died a natural death, had it not been for the religious feuds which so long continued to divide the nation against itself. I am glad to think that a happier morn has dawned upon the nation, and that she is now beginning to cast off the chains of her mental slavery; and that the time will soon come when she will not be last in the great race of civilisation.

In the early part of the spring of 1816, my father went out to the herring fishing, with a party of men who, along with himself, were joint proprietors of a boat and net. The party had been at sea all night, and early in the morning it came on to blow a gale; the weather continued so stormy that

[46] A popular misquotation. The line from *Childe Harold's Pilgrimage*, actually runs, "Hereditary bondsmen! know ye not / Who would be free themselves must strike the blow?'

great apprehensions were felt for their safety. The friends and relations of the boat's crew were in dreadful alarm, and by break of day the beach was covered with a crowd of the townspeople, anxiously looking out to sea. During the whole of my life I cannot say that I ever felt a feeling of revenge; on the contrary, such a state of mind seems foreign to my nature. What I am going to state may seem both unnatural and unholy; yet, upon that occasion the only fear I had was, that my father should *not* be drowned. The chance of escape from bondage such an event would give me was the all-pervading feeling of my soul. If the half of the world must have been wrecked along with him, the feeling would have been the same. The dreadful consequences to the families of the men who formed the boat's crew never entered into my mind; my only thought was to be free. During the fearful suspense and the vacillating hopes and fears of those interested in the safe return of the party, my condition of mind was a solitary exception to that of every being in that anxious crowd. The circumstance was just one of those which was well calculated to bring charity to the post of duty, but all my best feelings were covered as it were by a mountain of selfishness. Until the boat reached the beach in safety, my hope was against every other hope, and when the hope of the people was realized, mine was blasted. Up to that time my feelings had never suffered with such intensity, if they had been steeped in the devil's molten furnace they could not have been more hellish. His safe return kept me in chains, and restored my anxious step-mother her husband!

I have often thought if my father had treated me with even a small amount of kindness, he might have been able to subdue my hatred. My young heart yearned for something to love, but that feeling required to be drawn out by a kindred one. I knew my step-mother could not love me—it was not in the nature of things for her to do so; my father had deceived her in hiding my existence, it was therefore no wonder that she treated me with so much coldness and disdain. My father's harshness and want of duty to me may have been greatly regulated by the opinion she would form of his conduct to me, and the favourable contrast she might be able to draw of his fatherly treatment of her own children.

During the whole time I was with him, he never once called me by name, his uniform manner of addressing me was, by the withering and degrading title of "sir!" Had he but known how truly I hated him, and his unmannerly term, he might have acted more in accordance with the character of a father. The affections of young people cannot be outraged with impunity, it is true they may be trampled upon, but duty never can supply the place of affection and gratitude. I have reason to think that my father has often reflected in the bitterness of his heart on his cruel conduct to me.

Had he done his duty to me as a father, I might have been able to repay him when he most required the dutiful attentions of a son. If he had sent me to school, which he could have done, and assisted me to go into the world with only an ordinary education, he would have saved me from being the foot-ball of fortune, and leading the life of a wandering vagrant for years. He was frequently in the habit of taunting me with the old soldier, as he was pleased to call my step-father; had he known how immeasurably he fell in my estimation in the comparison, he would have been more cautious in his observations. He had learned that McNamee was a Catholic; this of course with him was an unpardonable sin, and he frequently told me with much bitterness of feeling, that if he thought there was a particle of Popery in my body he would cut it out! Poor man! from what I could observe, his hatred of Catholicism, like that of many of his countrymen, constituted nearly all the religion he possessed. The progenitors of my family were originally an importation from Scotland, and being Cameronians, the deep hatreds and strong prejudices of that sect seemed to cling to them through their generations.

I often think it strange, when I reflect upon the matter, that, during the whole time I was in Ireland, I had never cultivated a boyish acquaintance nor had a single playmate, if I except a little girl, the daughter of one of my father's neighbours—I was drawn to her by pure kindness. We never met but she had a smile and a kind word of greeting for me; she was first drawn to me by pity, and then she loved me. This dear little creature was like a good angel to me, and I loved her with the fondness of a brother. We often met when going errands, and upon such occasions we were never at a loss for conversation. I frequently told her of my travels and the strange sights I had seen, until her little innocent mind was filled with wonder. Even now, after the lapse of so many years, I can picture her little dumpy form, red face with the dimple in her chin, and the sweet pleasing smile playing about her small mouth, as if we had only parted yesterday. I remember, upon one occasion, while we were upon some message together, I was reciting some of the tales of my travels to her, when she interrupted me by inquiring, What sort of a town England was? Since then I have had similar questions asked by older heads than hers. A short time ago I was in Aberdeen, where I lodged with a very kind and amiable old lady. One evening I was making inquiry of her as to the position of *Nairn* and its distance from Aberdeen, at the same time wishing I had a map of Scotland to refer to. She observed that she could *sune gie* me *ane*. The dear old lady was as good as her word, for she presently supplied me with a map, or lithographed plan of the seat of war in the Crimea! I laughed at her good-natured simplicity, and observed that her geography was confined to the latitude of the tea-pot. " 'Deed," quoth she, "ye may say *dat*, for in my young days there was *nae sic'* new fangled things *thoucht o' !*"

The winter of 1816 had passed away, and spring with its glorious train of vernal clothing, sunshine, and flowers, had once more decorated the face of nature. But in the face of returning gladness to the earth, my spirits were steeped in sadness, and summer and winter were all the same to me. When I have been in the fields gathering my daily load of firewood, I have often envied the joyous lark, as he poured forth his full flood of song, his glorious freedom. A being in my situation could have very little sympathy with external nature: my sores made me savage, and my isolated condition turned all my thoughts upon myself. Since then, I have often thought that the man must be callous indeed who can listen to the joyful strain of these sweet warblers, as they hail the early morn, without feeling in his soul emotions of heaven-born pleasure. That is a beautiful poetic fancy of Tannahill's, where he describes the "Laverock *fanning* the *snaw*-white clouds."[47] I have often thought that the delightful warblings of this *prima donna* of the feathery choir was well calculated to draw men's souls from earth to heaven: many a time I have felt their music act like a soothing charm upon my troubled mind. I sometimes think when men's souls are not in harmony with the love and sympathy of nature, that they cannot feel the true enjoyment of life. There is many a honest John Bell to whom a daisy is just a daisy, and nothing more than a daisy: this, however, is the bliss of ignorance. In bringing this reflection to a close, I am obliged to admit that there is one condition necessary to those enjoyments which spring from a proper appreciation of the beauties of nature. I confess it is a vulgar one, but not the less necessary—I mean an *orderly stomach*.

In the middle of April, 1816, my father took me with him to assist some neighbouring farmer in making his turf. It seems to be a regular practice in that part of the country for the neighbours to assist each other in getting in their winter's fuel; this operation always takes place in the early part of the season, in order that the turf may be thoroughly dried through the course of summer. Two little circumstances occurred to me upon this occasion, which would not be worth notice but for the after consequences of one of them. The one was having enjoyed a good dinner, and the other having my right foot severely wounded on the instep, by the tramp of a horse. I have already observed, that my feet were in a very bad condition in consequence of being always exposed to the weather, my new wound was therefore, a very unacceptable addition to my catalogue of sorrows.

As the season advanced, my yearnings for liberty increased, and my resolves began to assume something like a tangible form. One day in the early part of May, I was sent to the moss for a bag of turf; this was after I had done winding bobbins for the day; the wound on my foot was extremely painful, and what made it more so, I had no commiseration shown me, and no one seemed to care whether I felt pain or pleasure, so long as I could perform my tasks. I had got to the moss, had filled my bag and got my load resting on the highway; this was the direct road from Killaleagh to Belfast. After standing reflecting with the mouth of the bag in my hand for a few minutes, my final resolve was made; I tumbled the turf out on the road, put the bag under my arm, and turned my face towards Belfast, and my back to a friendless home. I had no such feeling as Jacob experienced when he left his

[47] See below, p. 195.

father's house; my mind was made up that whatever might be my lot in life, no consideration should induce me to return. From the moment I made up my mind, I threw myself boldly upon the world, and for ever broke asunder every tie that connected me to the name I bore. I had neither staff, nor scrip, nor money in my pocket. I commenced the world with the old turf-bag. It was my only patrimony. In order that I might sever the only remaining link that bound me to my family, I tore two syllables from my name;[48] and thus I wandered forth into the wide world a fugitive from kindred and from home. I had no fear but one, and that was of being followed, and taken back. I travelled sixteen Irish miles that afternoon. The excited state of my feelings kept down the pain I otherwise must have suffered from the wounded foot. That night I found an asylum in a cow-house in a suburb of Belfast, and the next morning I was off by day-light for Donaghadee. My reason for going there was that it was the port I landed at when first coming to Ireland. On my way I called at a farm-house and begged a little food. I reached Donaghadee about ten o'clock in the morning, and found that the packet was not to sail till late in the evening. For fear I should be discovered, I hid myself among the rocks on the sea-shore until the sailing of the vessel. When that time arrived (which I thought would never come), I stowed myself in the forecastle until the vessel was a good way out to sea. I cannot express the joy I felt when I found myself safe. The captain badgered me when he found I could not pay my fare, but this was soon over. We arrived in Portpatrick harbour, about two o'clock in the morning, where I had the honour of another good blowing up from the boatmen who put me ashore—that, too, passed by without giving me any trouble. I thus landed in Scotland a penniless wanderer, but with a mind full to overflowing, with real joy at my escape from bondage. No officious porter importuned me to carry my luggage; nor did any cringing lodging-house keeper invite me to accept of his hospitality. After looking about me for a few minutes, I observed a gentleman's travelling carriage standing before the head inn; with a light heart I took up my quarters in this comfortable abode, where I slept soundly until I was unceremoniously pulled out by a servant in livery about half-past six in the morning.

You may be curious to learn what were my future plans and prospects when I had got thus far. To tell the truth, I had no definite idea of what was to come of me, only that I was determined to fly to England. All my happiest childish associations were centred in the valley of North Tyne, in Northumberland, and I was, therefore, continually attracted in that direction. The distance from Portpatrick to Bellingham, which I looked upon as my destination, would be about 150 miles. The distance gave me no trouble—indeed, if it had been 1000 miles it would have been all the same to me. I took the road for Dumfries, and travelled about twenty miles the first day. I begged my way with as good a grace as possible; all I required was food and

[48] His natural father's name was McBurney.

lodgings, and I had very little trouble in obtaining either the one or the other. The day after I landed, I went into a farm-house on the way side to solicit a little food. The good woman observing my *bag*, naturally imagined I was one of a family, and kindly gave me a quantity of *raw potatoes*, which I could not refuse. These potatoes gave me no small trouble, as I could not make up my mind to throw them away, so I carried them to the end of my second day's journey, and gave them to an old woman in Ferry Town of Cree, for liberty to lie before her fire all night. Poor old creature! she gave me share of her porridge in the morning, seasoned with sage advice. Next day being Sunday, I took my time on the way, and travelled until nine o'clock in the evening. Seeing a farm-house a little off the road, I went and asked for lodgings. At the time I called the inmates were engaged in family worship, as soon as they had finished I was inundated with a shower of questions, to which I had to reply by a volley of answers. The gudeman *thoucht* I had run *awa'* frae me place, "saying it was an *unca* like thing to see a *laddie* like me *stravaging* about the *kintra* on the Sabbath-day; he was *shere* I belanged to somebody, and it was a pity, for I was a weel-faured callant, he wad warrant I was hungry." After this he ordered the gudewife to gie me some *sipper;* I had, therefore, an excellent supper of sowans[49] with milk, and bread and cheese. After my repast, the good farmer made me up a bed in the barn, with the winnowing sheet for a cover. In the morning I had a good breakfast, and before leaving, the good man gave me a world of advice. Up to this time I had been so elated with my escape that I had not had time to feel the wound on my foot; but the novelty was now beginning to wear away, and my foot began to assert its right to attention as a useful member of the body corporate, and to make me feel smartly for my neglect of it. A great part of the instep was festered, and the pain became so great that my whole limb was affected. I had, therefore, to limp along, and nurse it as I best could.

On the morning of the day I arrived in Dumfries, and just as I was leaving a farm-house where I had lodged all night, in the neighbourhood of Castle Douglas, I fell in with a man who was driving a herd of cattle to Dumfries market, which was held on the following day. Seeing that I was going in the same direction, he invited me to assist him in driving the *nowt*, and *whan* we *gat te* the *town* he *wad gie* me a *saxpence te me sel'!* I was certainly in a bad condition for such a task; the money, however, was a tempting inducement, so I accepted his offer. It would be impossible for me to give you anything like an adequate idea of my sufferings in performing the duty of a dog over eighteen miles of a partially fenced road. When we arrived in Dumfries I was fairly exhausted, and like to faint from sheer pain. To mend the matter, the heartless savage discharged me without a farthing of recompense. The monster excused himself by saying he had *nae bawbees*. There I was; hungry, lame, broken down with fatigue, and without a place to lay my head. The

---

[49] A flummery made from husks or seeds of oats, with fine meal added. It is soaked in water until sour, and then fermented.

toll-keeper, at the entrance of the town, who had witnessed the brutal conduct of the drover, and heard my statement, tried to shame the wretch into
a sense of his duty, but he was just one of those animals, in the form of a man,
who could afford to put up with any amount of abuse if he could save
anything by it.

The toll-keeper being a man who could feel for the sufferings of others,
kindly invited me into his house, where he not only supplied me with a hearty
meal of victuals, but he also got his wife to wash and dress my wounded foot.
This man was a good Samaritan indeed. On leaving him I endeavoured to
express my grateful sense of his kindness in the best manner I could.

I had some idea that there was a person living in Dumfries with whom my
step-father had been on terms of intimacy; I therefore sought this man's
residence, in order that I might obtain a night's lodging. After making
inquiry, however, I found that he had left his country by authority! So I had
to seek quarters elsewhere, and after some little time I got a lair in a hay-loft
belonging to one of the inns.

Letter IV

MY DEAR THOMAS,—The man who has made up his mind to push his way through the world must be content to take men as he finds them. I am glad to say that the conduct of the heartless ruffian I described in my last letter, is an exception to the humanity of my experience. This man's humanity was a thing of pure selfishness, which he could no more help than he could fly. In some natures there is a living feeling of generosity, which is easily called into action at the sight of human misery; and, if it cannot afford relief, it at least sympathises with the sufferings of the victim. While, on the other hand, there are men whose feelings are doomed to dwell in the frozen regions of uncharitableness, and no amount of misery can set them free. Although I have had to fight my way through a busy world, where all classes of society were continually engaged in looking after their own affairs, I am happy to bear my humble testimony to the general diffusion of that god-like feeling which so closely allies man to his Creator.

The next morning after my arrival in the *gude town* o' Dumfries, I went down to the sands, where the cattle-market is held, and I soon got engaged to tent a herd of oxen for the day; my remuneration for this service being two-pence and a *bawbee scone*. In consequence of the restlessness of the animals, I suffered very much with my foot during the day; and as the herd was unsold, I was kept on the sands until late in the evening. When I got my liberty I took the road to Carlisle. As I went limping along numbers of people were returning to their homes from the market, and among the rest, I observed a man with an empty cart, who appeared to be going in my direction. I requested this person to oblige me with a ride, which he readily complied with. After we had travelled a distance of three or four miles, the man stopped his horse and went over a stone fence into a field. I imagined he was going to obey a call of nature: however, I soon observed that he had a very different object in view. In the course of a few minutes he nearly filled his cart with new-cut clover, and there is no doubt that he had made up his mind to the appropriation in the morning. For some time before this, I had been driving the horse: he now took the reins in his own hand and bade me lie down among the clover, which I was very glad to do, and, being much wearied, I was scarcely down before I was sound asleep. When the fellow arrived at home, he left me in the cart all night. In the morning, he invited

me to breakfast, which was by no means unwelcome. On the previous evening, during our journey, he had made himself master of my history, and
therefore knew my condition. This man was a small farmer in Dumfrieshire,
and the greater part of the land he rented was uncultivated moor, while here
and there a patch was being reclaimed. After breakfast, he asked me if I *wad*
bide wi' him and herd the *kye* through the *simmer*. The fact was, that I was
very glad of the offer, and at once made an unconditional tender of my small
services. I had little idea of the nature of my duties: otherwise I should have
walked on.

I have observed that his cultivated plots of land were laid out in patches
on the moors. These little sunny spots were invitingly open to the cattle, as
none of them were fenced. I may observe, that cows are just like other
animals, whether of an inferior or a superior class: when they once taste
forbidden fruit, they are sure to have a desire to repeat the dose. The ground
I had to travel over, in the performance of my duty, was thickly covered
with stunted heath. If I could have carried my unfortunate foot in my
pocket, I might have got on swimmingly; but, as it was, every move I made
was tended with the most excruciating pain, and, while the stolen bites of
green corn were sweet to the cattle—like the story of the boy and the frogs,
the exercise was death to me. Frequently, when I had to run after the beasts,
my very heart was like to break with the painful sensation caused by the
heather rubbing against my wounded foot. After I had been at this place a
few days, the mistress of the house hunted out a pair of old clogs which she
said *wad* keep the heather *frae* my *fit*. These clogs were a world too large for
me, and the very weight of the one on my wounded foot was an aggravation
of the evil I was enduring: I had therefore to dispense with these wooden
understandings. On the eighth or ninth day of my servitude in this place,
when in the act of coming home to dinner, I observed the Dumfries mail
coming up on its way to Carlisle: in an instant I made up my mind to a
second run away. With much difficulty I caught hold of the hind part of the
coach, and hung on by it for a distance of more than a mile: when I let go
my hold I was fairly exhausted, and had to rest a considerable time before I
could resume my journey.

That night I slept in Annan, in a house where there was a beautiful but
heart broken young wife. Her husband was then lying on his death-bed in
the last stage of *delirium tremens*. I have witnessed many cases of human
suffering, but I think this was the saddest and most distressing I ever beheld.
Poor unfortunate fellow! his bed which ought to have been a couch of ease
and a place of comfortable relaxation, was to him a living hell, full of
tormenting devils! I know of no more truly melancholy sight in nature, than
that of seeing a strong man suffering the pains of the damned through his
own folly. I believe this dreadful scourge to be the severest infliction the law
of nature can impose upon those who wantonly violate it. I can never forget
that poor heart-stricken woman: in her sorrow she was willing to forget the

past and cling to hope for the future. The fervour of her love made her oblivious of her own sufferings, and she was willing to go through the world with her wrecked husband in beggary, if he could only be restored to her. God help her poor woman! her hopes were vain, his madness and his pain would soon be over! When I left, he was sinking into the arms of death.

On the evening of that day I had got hirpled[50] as far as Langtown, the first and last town in England: there I had a horse for my bed-fellow—at least, we occupied neighbouring stalls in the same stable. It may well be said, that poverty sometimes gives us strange bed-fellows. The next day I took the road for Newcastleton, and on the way I offered a trifling sacrifice to the god of cleanliness by washing my ragged shirt in the river Liddle, and I had also the pleasure of exchanging my jacket with a customer who gave me all own way in the transaction. The odds were not much on either side; however, the *scarecrow* had the worst of the bargain. That night I travelled until about ten o'clock, when I arrived at one of these old-fashioned feudal keeps, or castellated buildings, which were common on the Border at one time. When I had rapped at the door, a young lady came out whose features were an index to a kind and amiable disposition. After I told her my tale she invited me into the house. The only other inmate was a venerable-looking old man, with hair as white as flax. When she introduced me, the good old gentleman putting a speaking-horn to his ear, heard my tale with much seeming interest. Soliloquising to himself he said, "Poor bairn! Poor bairn! One-half of the world does not know how the other lives!" And looking at me he observed, "*Wha* kens but this poor ragged laddie may be a braw chiel yet?" After this he requested the young lady to prepare me some supper, and while this was being done he addressed me in the most kind and fatherly manner. "Mind, my little *mannie*," said he, "aye put your trust in God, and be sure and keep *yoursel'* honest, and never tell *lees*. If you do these things God will love you, and be your helper and protector, and you will gain the esteem o' a' that ken you." I was served with a really comfortable supper, after which the young woman dressed my foot with as much care and tenderness as if I had been her own brother. How true it is, that in our hours of illness women are our ministering angels. I lay with the old man, and slept as soundly, and rose as happy, as if I had been a lord's son. What a truly happy provision in nature it is that our capacity for the enjoyments of life are to a great extent regulated by our condition. With a little kindness, a belly-full of food, and a good night's rest, my mind was as much at ease as if I had no earthly want to provide for. In the morning I received the same kindly attentions; and when I was preparing for my journey both the old gentleman and his daughter pressed upon me to remain with them for two or three days, until my foot should be healed. I thanked them sincerely, and would gladly have remained, but I knew I could only have a short time to stay with them; so I bade them adieu. As I left, I wished in my heart that the young woman had been my

[50] "Hirple" is to limp.

sister; I thought in my mind how I should have loved both her and her father. The wish was a selfish one; but it must be remembered that many of our best actions spring from selfish motives. The desert of life has many bleak and barren passages, over which numbers of the human family must pass; yet there are many sunny spots, where the virtues spring up like beautiful flowers to make our hearts glad. The gall we drink by the way is too often the produce of our own folly, and the real honey of life is a firm reliance upon the goodness of God, and a kindly regard for all his creatures.

The following night I slept in a farm-house, at the junction of the Liddle with the Hermitage, and the next morning I crossed the ideal line which divides the two kingdoms. The next day was warm, clear and beautiful, and smiling Nature was in her loveliest mood; the sheep were listlessly feeding on the fell, and the vallies below were filled with a thin, transparent haze. The lofty hills of Kielder were standing out in the warm sunshine, and throwing their shadows far over the vallies where the Tyne and the Kielder were creeping along in summer indolence. On a jutting promontory between the Tyne and the Kielder I could see the turrets and embattlements of Kielder Castle[51] peeping out from among the rich foliage of the surrounding trees. As I cast my eyes over the landscape before me, my heart was filled with unspeakable emotions of joy. I knew every hill and dell from this place to Hexham, a distance of about thirty miles. I had enjoyed the hospitality of nearly every house between the one point and the other, and Kielder Castle had always been a kind home to my mother's family. If I had been going to my own home, from which I had been absent for years, my feelings could not have been inspired with a more lively hope in the warmth of my reception. It may be asked what interest these people could have in me, or what claim I could have upon their kindly regard? My answer is, that they could have no interest in me, excepting what was dictated by the innate goodness of their generous natures, and my claim was founded upon the knowledge of such goodness.

During the time that the elder John Dag kept Kielder Castle, there was no house on the Border whose portals were so open to the stranger and the way-farer. There the poor were kindly bid to stay, and the rich man found a congenial home. I drew near to the castle with a palpitating heart and I was full of contending emotions, hope, joy, and fear, alternately filled my breast. Since I had been there before—I had navigated many of the bays and creeks of the stormy sea of life, and I knew the harbour I was sailing into could only be a temporary one, but still I had much cause to hail it with delight. Mr. Dag's family received me with their usual kindness, and their first care was to unrobe me, after which I was put into a full suit of young Mr. Dag's clothes. My old dress even to the shirt was consigned to the dunghill, and my unfortunate foot soon grew well under their tender care. For five weeks I continued a playmate to the younger members of the family, during which

[51] A castellated shooting box built in 1775 by the Earl of Northumberland.

time all my misery was buried in oblivion, and the present time was full of joy with no cankering thoughts for the future. One little incident will prove the familiar terms I was on with the family. One day when I was out in the hay-field, while some of the young men were romping with the girls and bearding their rosy faces, I too held an innocent gambol with one of the Misses Dag, her brother holding her down while I performed the manly operation of bearding her face with a hay wisp in my mouth! Kielder Castle was a paradise to me while I remained, and when I left, it was with a sad and sorrowful heart. I was again lonely in the big world, and as I journeyed on my way, my mind frequently became a mere blank. O! how gladly I could have bid adieu to the busy world, and spent my days in the bosom of that quiet secluded glen. I think if I had been desired to have remained, I would never again have wished to roam beyond its peaceful retirement. I daresay Mr. Dag's people would have willingly given me the home I so ardently desired, but they knew too well the wandering life I had led, and like many others who would gladly have served me, they had no confidence in one who had been tossed about the world under so many changing phases. They imagined that there would be no possibility of taming my wild nature.[52] This impression followed me like an evil genius, and made me the victim of circumstances over which I had no power. It is rather a curious fact, that notwithstanding my lonely condition, I never felt any desire or had a thought of meeting with my mother and step-father; the only reason which I can assign for this want of feeling in their regard is, that when they parted with me I must have been impressed with the idea that it was for life.

On the evening of the day I left Kielder Castle, I arrived at a farm-house in the neighbourhood of Bellingham, called Riding. This place had been one of my mother's friendly places of call, the farm was occupied by a family of the name of Richardson, which was composed of Mr. and Mrs. Richardson, an unmarried son and daughter, and a bachelor brother of Mr. Richardson's. This gentleman was about seventy-six years of age, and must have made a serious mistake in allowing himself to be dragged into the nineteenth century. According to his own ideas of the fitness of things, he had out-lived the age of rationality, and all things were changed for the worse. The new fashions were then *unca* like sights, and the warld was getting fou' o' pride; blacking *shune* was just the way to wear the leather, there was nae *sic'* tomfoolery when he was a young man. Tea and sugar were abominations, and he *couldna'* tell what the warld wad come to! John was not the only man I have known who had the misfortune to live beyond his time. Notwithstanding these peculiarities, few men could button a coat over a better or a kinder heart. The

---

[52] Later in life, during a period of prosperity, he revisited Mr. Dag and greatly enjoyed his reception—"There was nothing wanting in my visit to the Gowanburn to make it all my heart desired. Dormant memories of other days had been awakened by visiting scenes dear to me in my youth. I had been the honoured guest of Mr. Dagg [*sic*.]; one of the dreams of my life had been realised; I had been received upon terms of friendship and equality by a man who knew me in early life". (1882 ed., p. 392).

whole of this family could not have been cast in better moulds for real benevolence of disposition if they had been made to order. Mr. Richardson was one of those men who could do half-a-dozen good actions before he had time to describe one; and his wife was not only a mother to her own family, but she was also one to all who stood in need of her assistance. When I made my case known, I found a welcome home at the Riding, and was employed in doing all the little messages, and such matters as I could manage on the farm. My mind was once more at ease, and I had no longings as to the future; I was also in the only part of the world I had any desire to be in. I may fairly say, that while I was with Richardson's people, my life was like a pleasant dream. I may mention two or three little circumstances which in some measure varied the pleasing routine of my existence. In the first place, I narrowly escaped losing my life by the running away of a young horse, while I was in the act of riding him home after watering. I only missed having my brains knocked out against the stable door, by tumbling off the animal's back the moment before he reached it. My next little escapade was in driving a pair of horses home in an empty cart—the above young horse being the leader,—after passing through a gate-way, I was standing in the cart when the leader suddenly shied off the road, and the counteraction being so quick, the cart was turned upside down, and I was, like the turkey, *whomalled*[53] under a tub. When I was relieved, my memory and senses were in the land of *nod*.

Mr. Richardson's oldest son was the Bellingham carrier, and he went once a week to Newcastle, with three, and sometimes four horses; I was allowed to go with him at his request as an assistant in a small way. During one of these journeys on our way home, we required to come up a very steep bank out of a ravine named Houxsty, and in coming up this ascent the horses had to take the road at angles, and required to rest frequently. Upon this occasion Mr. Richardson had a hogshead of rum for his brother-in-law, a Mr. Charlton, who kept the head inn in Bellingham, and there were several carriers in company belonging to other villages. In sailor phraseology, the admiral was tapped, which was a usual thing when any of them had spirits aboard. After each of the party had a draw through the quill, I was invited to have my share; being green in paying my address to bacchus, either in that or any other form, like paddy at the gallows, I had my whack. Before we got to the top of the hill, we had all three pulls a-piece. After walking about 100 yards after my last draw, I fell down on the road as if I had been shot, and I knew no more about the history of the world for forty-eight hours, and all the parties interested but myself, imagined that my rum-drinking was over. However, the doctor being anxious to prevent a coroner's inquest, pulled me back from the world of spirits.

While I was at Riding, an incident occurred to me which had some little influence over my mind in reference to ghosts. My master's young son

[53] Turned upside down.

who was at home, was very fond of card-playing, which was then one of the leading vices of the country people. Upon the occasion in question, he had been from home much beyond his usual hours, and I was sent down to the village which was distant rather better than a mile, to see if I could find him: I left home about eleven o'clock at night. Before getting into the village, I had to pass through an avenue of trees, whose branches nearly covered the road for about 300 yards. I had called at the various houses where I knew my young master was in the habit of putting up, but was unsuccessful in finding him. The night was both dark and windy, and on leaving the village for home, I felt some symptoms of fear rising about the regions of my stomach. The road I had to pass along was a first-rate place for restless spirits to patrol in. The church, with its grave-yard stood at the entrance of the avenue, the bell hung suspended in a little open arch, and in case of high winds, it did not require the aid of the sexton to bring forth its melancholy notes, and on this eventful night its unmusical tongue was sounding in fitful ding dongs. As I re-entered the avenue, the branches of the trees were lashing each other as if in sport, and the whole covering of the avenue was dancing to the rude music of the gale. The unnatural sound of the bell, the hoarse noise of the wind—the proximity to the grave-yard, and the darkness of the night with the witching hour, were well calculated to inspire me with fear. I endeavoured to keep a good look out, so that I might not be seized unawares, and tried to whistle my waning courage into a feeling of defiance. When I got about half way down the avenue, I became virtually petrified with horror, by seeing the devil standing in the middle of the road. The hair on my head partook of the general alarm of my whole system and stood erect, my knees smote each other, and every part of my body seemed alive and on the watch but one—my heart was drowned in terror. At last when I had power to reflect, my first thought was to run back to the village; my second was, that the devil could beat me at that game; and my third was, the magnanimous resolve to pass on. With a large amount of determination dragging my fears along, I encountered his satanic majesty in the shape of a cow quietly pulverizing her food, and apparently indifferent to the howling of the wind or my fears. As I made the best of my way home with my scattered senses, I gave many a suspicious glance over my shoulder for fear that the cow should assume some other shape. When I came to reflect upon the matter in something like a rational way, I could not help thinking that my conduct was extremely childish in converting a poor innocent cow into the devil. I therefore made up my mind to be very sceptical about seeing the devil in future.[54]

[54] cf. William Lovett's almost identical experience: "I remember one dark winter evening going to meet [my master] in company with a young fellow I had induced to be my companion, and not finding my master at the place appointed, we had to follow him to the next village. Our road to this was up through a long dark lane, in a part of which a monumental stone was erected, on account of a murder having been committed there. Previous to our approach to this dreaded spot our fears had subdued our tongues and quickened our pulse; but conceive our feelings, when we saw through the darkness a

A short time after this I was witness to one of those *serio*-comic circumstances which is sufficient to supply a whole countryside with gossip for at least nine days! ! About three miles from Bellingham, at a place of the name of "The Carritith," lived a person who went by the name of Johny o' the Carritith; this man was a small farmer, and he occasionally employed himself as a common carrier. Report, which is at all times a very reliable authority, said that Johny did a little in the smuggling way. I may mention that smuggling was then a very common practice along the whole of the English Border, and was looked upon as a very venial offence by the people.[55] Salt was then salt indeed, and if the farmers could not obtain the article, their pork and winter's beef would have to go uncured. Some *weel* disposed *freen'* o' Johnie's laid an information against him to the village exciseman. This gentleman made a goodly seizure at the Carritith, and the whole spoil was put on one of John's own carts. While the exciseman and the smuggler were bringing the cargo down to the village in order to have it placed under his Majesty's broad R, they had to ford the river Tyne; before coming to the ford they had to pass down a steep embankment which ran parallel with the river. The road down this bank was composed of a light gravelly soil, and was full of springs. At the time of the occurrence there had been a very severe frost for some weeks, the consequence of which was, that the river had been frozen over, and was at the time sufficient to bear almost any amount of weight. The road down the embankment was also one sheet of ice. Now, the gauger was a man whose height was at least six feet and a half; like one who knew his duty, and was not ashamed to do it, he led the way, and, like a drum-major, walked in front of the horse, while John, with *canny* caution, kept hold of it in order to prevent the animal from slipping. They had only commenced the descent of the hill when the exciseman measured his full length in front of the horse's head, in consequence of which the animal stumbled, and the wheels going of the straight line, the horse and cart and Johny tumbled down over the precipice, a distance of some ninety feet, and

---

monster ghost of about three feet high, with erect horns, and large eyes glaring at us, from immediately opposite the monument. We shrunk back for a moment in great terror, but our presence seems to have alarmed the monster also for it rose up and proved to be a farmer's heifer, which had quietly laid itself down in front of this murderer's monument— which folly had erected in a public highway—doubtless without ever suspecting it would be taken for a demon". (op. cit., p. 9).

[55] See also James Russell's recollections of the same period and area: "Almost fifty years ago, smuggling was carried on to a considerable extent. It was generally counted a very slight offence to defraud the revenue in this form, and the informers were not to be found." ("Reminiscences of Yarrow", op. cit., p. 552). The chief item of contraband was whisky which was smuggled from Scotland to England to avoid duty of 2s. per gallon imposed by the Scotch Distilling Act of 1786 and raised to 2s. 6d. in 1788. The vagrants and pedlars among whom Burn had been brought up were heavily involved in smuggling. See Rev. J. Hudson Barker, "The Gipsy Life of Northumberland" in William Andrews (ed.), *Bygone Northumberland* (Hull, 1899), pp. 238–9.

landed on the ice on the river. In the descent the whisky casks were stove in, and somewhere about 100 gallons of *gude peat reek* was left to find its level on the ice. In the course of ten minutes after the accident taking place, all the shoemakers, cloggers, tailors, blacksmiths, cartwrights, and lazy-corner supporters of the village were on the river. It was seldom that the villagers had such an opportunity of getting a bellyful of whisky at so cheap a rate. Some went upon their knees and lapped the nectar dog-fashion, others shovelled it into them with the palms of their hands, some used the heels of their clogs, and others used such vessels as they could most readily lay their hands on. There was no time for the social ceremony of drinking each other's healths, so they made the most of their time in saving as much of Johny's whisky as the circumstances would admit of. In about half an hour after this exciting event, the little quiet village of Bellingham presented a scene at once ludicrous and disgusting—young and old were rolling about like as many maniacs let loose from some lunatic asylum. If any of the parties who were on the ice had had a particle of common sense, poor John Turnbull might have been saved eighteen months' confinement in Morpeth Jail. Along with the whisky which had been seized there was a large bag of salt; the penalty for smuggling this article was much greater than that on whisky, I suppose the reason of this would be that it was an article of common use. When the cart came in contact with the ice, it made a considerable indentation, and during the whole exciting scene the salt lay upon the very edge of the water, and only required a friendly hand to put it in.

I could almost fill a volume with the numerous smuggling incidents I have witnessed; the following, however, will give a pretty good idea of the dangers consequent upon this calling, and the reckless daring character of those who were engaged in it. When I was in Bellingham there were two families who ostensibly made their living by carrying coals into Scotland from the neighbouring pits, upon pack-horses. One of the parties had as many as thirty of these animals. This business could only be followed in the summer season, in consequence of there being no regular roads; the country over which they had to travel was all moorland, and the horses were allowed to feed by the way. One of the men who followed this business was named Turnbull, and it was pretty well known to the initiated that he made more by smuggling than coal carrying. Mr. Gash, the exciseman, had long had his eye upon this person, but never could catch him in the act. Turnbull knew his kind intentions towards him, and determined to give him an opportunity of serving his master. In order to carry out his laudable purpose, Turnbull got one of his friends to lay an information against him. Upon a specified day and hour Turnbull was to be found in a certain locality, in the act of bringing his cargo into the village. Gash swallowed the bait, and acted upon the information. The place where Turnbull was to be found was in a secluded lane, rather better than two miles from the village. According to the advice in the information, Gash met his man with a five-gallon cask slung over his shoulder in a sack; he made the seizure in due form, after which he invited Turnbull to carry the prize to its destination; the smuggler, however, was too much a man of the world to comply with the exciseman's good intentions; he therefore allowed him the honour of bearing the prize home upon his own herculean shoulders. The day was very warm, and when Gash arrived in the village the perspiration was raining off him. They were met by a number of the inhabitants, who were always ripe for a row. In passing to his own house the exciseman had to go close by the door of Turnbull's; when they arrived at this point Turnbull very civilly requested Gash to prove his prize before giving himself any more trouble; he was morally certain as to the contents of the cask, but as a mere matter of courtesy he laid down his load, and taking a gimblet from his pocket, he spiled the keg; the result of this kindly compliance was perhaps the most mortifying to him of any circumstance during his whole life. Instead of a stream of pure mountain dew following the perforating instrument, one of unreduced buttermilk met his astonished gaze. The laugh and the cheers which followed were loud and long. That stream of buttermilk sealed poor Gash's fate in Bellingham, and I have no doubt but it would cling to him through life.

I remember being witness to a very exciting race between a smuggler and a supervisor. There was a person in Hexham who followed the business as a regular profession. The excise had long watched his movements, but he had always contrived to evade them. This person kept a splendid horse, both strong and fleet of foot. Upon the occasion I allude to, he was coming into town, on a fine summer's evening, with two five-gallon casks slung over his horse's back, and he was snugly seated between them. About half a mile before he came to Tyne Bridge, he observed the supervisor close behind him. The officer was quite sure of his man; however, it will be seen that he calculated without his host. The smuggler gave his horse the spur, and when he crossed the bridge, instead of taking the high road into the town, he turned sharp round to the right and took a footpath along the side of the river. This path led to Hexham Green; but before he could arrive at this place, he required to clear a stone wall and a deep ditch on the other side of it. The officer was a very short distance behind, and he knew the wall would check his career, and he imagined he had his man in a regular *cul de sac*. Never was any man more mistaken in his calculations. The smuggler cleared both the wall and the ditch at a bound. The officer had no alternative but to wheel round and make for the town by the regular road; and he still imagined that it was next to impossible for the smuggler to escape. When he got half way down Gilligate, he met his man riding quietly up the street, as if nothing had occurred in which anybody could be interested. The fellow coolly asked the officer if he was *gaun* to *seek* the *howdie*,[56] he was in *sic'* a hurry? I need not say that the whisky was *non est* by that time! The ride cost the exciseman

[56] Midwife.

many a joke, which he would much rather had been cracked upon anybody else—as he piqued himself upon being a sharp fellow. In these days nothing could please the people better than to see an excise-officer outwitted.

The life of an officer of the Excise on the Border was both precarious and full of danger; as the smugglers were generally a determined set of fellows; the fact was, they cared very little for the value of life. They looked upon their calling, in a moral point of view, as legitimate as any other; and in this they were borne out by the opinions of many who had no interest in the matter. About as smart a trick as any I know of, took place in the neighbour-hood of *Kirkwhelpington*, and not far from *Cambo*. A smuggler was quietly riding along with a load of two ten-gallon casks. Each side of the road was lined with a plantation, and it was quite a lonely place. As he came up to a sharp angle of the road he met an excise officer full in the face. The smuggler was a known fellow: he took the matter quite cool. He observed to the officer that it was the first time he ever met with a loss, and he could *verra weel* afford to let him *tak'* it, an' welcome! The officer lost no time in proving his prize, and when this was done the smuggler requested that he might be allowed to *hae* a *mouthfou'*, as it *wad* be the last he should see o' it. The officer, seeing that he had met with such a condescending sort of a fellow, readily complied. After the smuggler had taken what he wanted, he observed that it was just a *drap* o' as *gude whusky* as ere *cam'* o'er the Border; at the same time, he blandly invited the officer to *tak'* a *sook*, saying it was *na* money o' the trade that bought *whusky* at the price he *gied for't*. The innocent exciseman stooped down to try the flavour of the spirits, but it was late in the evening of that day when he was removed from the spot, and it was more than nine months before he was again fit for duty. The smuggler sold his cargo in Newcastle the same night, and oft related his friendly meeting wi' the exciseman to his companions o'er a wee drappie o't.

There was often a good deal of ingenuity displayed by the smugglers in evading the vigilance of the excise. I have seen a company of melancholy mourners following a rude country hearse, filled with *aqua vitæ* instead of a dead body. I knew a gentleman who carried on a very profitable business in the smuggling line, in the guise of a commercial traveller. His turn-out was really splendid, and he had all the appearance of being the representative of some first-rate London house. His vehicle was so contrived that he could carry forty or fifty gallons, and in order to disarm suspicion he varied his *route* each journey. I believe he carried on this business successfully for several years. At that time Scotch whiskey was not admissible into England under any conditions. This unnatural prohibition was to protect the producers of our colonial rum, which was then made by slaves!

Letter V

My dear Thomas,—Another change is now about taking place in the eventful drama of my chequered life. Shortly after the occasion of my *rum doze*, a Mr. Turnbull, who was then proprietor of Hazelyside Mill,[57] wanted a young lad to ride round the neighbourhood to bring the farmers' *batches* to be ground, and take them home when made into meal. As Richardson's people had no real use for me, they advised me to accept the situation on their recommendation. While I had been with this family I knew no care, and was perfectly happy. Such was the serene state of my mind that I rarely ever thought of the past, unless it was called to my recollection by some joke of my young master, who occasionally made merry at my expense. The future I seldom thought of, and my mind was fairly made up to a country life. I accepted the miller's situation, and left my benefactors with mingled feelings of pleasure and regret. I liked my new berth very well, but as I had not had much experience in the management of horses, I was very likely to get into some awkward dilemmas. The poney I had charge of was both a cunning and a stiff-necked animal. The most of my journies were over moors, and in many places the houses lay very wide apart. About a fortnight after I had entered my situation I was sent to an isolated farm-house for two sacks of corn. In coming home I had to cross a moor, over which there was no road, and the distance was better than four miles. I was seated comfortably on the top of the corn-sacks, and was getting on very quietly, but before I arrived in the middle of the moor, my *Bucephalus* spilled the sacks and myself among the heather. My companion, when he found himself free, kicked up his heels and set off for home. Supposing he had remained I could not have lifted the sacks on his back, so I was forced to follow him home with the tear in my e'e, and get one of the servant men to return with me for the grain. Upon another occasion, my tormentor took it into his head, while fording the Tyne, to lie down with me and his load in the middle of the stream. This brute was my *bublie jock*,[58] and often gave me much annoyance; but on the whole I continued to like my situation, and as I grew stronger I felt better able to manage my companion.

I had only been in my new situation about four months, when on coming

[57] Changed to Hesleyside Mill (its present name) in the 1882 edition.
[58] Literally, turkey-cock; figuratively, cause of difficulty or fear.

home one evening, I was nearly surprised out of a year's growth by the unlooked for appearance of my mother. She was now a widow having buried my step-father about three months before this, in Doncaster, in Yorkshire, she had also the addition to her family of another boy, who was then about nine months old. She had learned where I was when in Bellingham, and could not believe the fact until she could see me with her own eyes. In spite of all I had suffered since she handed me over to the tender mercies of my father, I was much improved. Whether her affection was resuscitated on again seeing her first-born, or whether she thought she could turn me to her advantage, I cannot say, but she strongly pressed me to leave my situation and go with her. At first, I had little notion of leaving, but on being pressed, my heart once more warmed to her and the evil star of my life was again in the ascendant. I was again a vagrant, and continued so against my will for years. When I joined my mother, she had only a few shillings' worth of small-ware, in a basket, for six months after this we lived a sort of a scrambling existence, half begging, half dealing.

The year 1817, was one of peculiar hardship for the lower orders of the people; the cereal crop was a failure over the whole of the United Kingdom.[59] I remember that much of the corn had to be cut in December, and of course was only fit to feed cattle. At this time, and for several years subsequently, the people were in a very uncomfortable state of excitement. The six acts of Sidmouth and Castlereagh, were in full force, and the *Magna Charta* may be said to have been virtually suspended, as far as the rights of the people were concerned.[60] I am firmly convinced, that if the conduct of the British people had not been characterised by the greatest forbearance, this country might have witnessed many of the sanguinary scenes which disgraced the French Revolution. Notwithstanding the rigid character of the laws that were passed to keep down the expression of public opinion, the government did not pass without being exposed. The French war had fairly crippled the energies of the people, and its effects hung like a deadly incubus upon the commerce of the nation. At that time the pension list was filled with the names of both men and women, whose conduct instead of being an honour to the nation, was a disgrace to humanity, and the court of the Prince Regent had become a reproach to the country, in consequence of its licentiousness and brutality.

The *Black Dwarf* was then being published, and widely circulated; this periodical found its way into almost every town, village, and hamlet in the kingdom, laden with the sins of the aristocracy.[61] I cannot give a better

[59] The harvest of 1817 was in fact a good one, particularly in relation to those of the preceding and succeeding years. Between June and September 1817 the price of wheat fell from 111s. 6d. to 75s. a quarter.

[60] Habeas Corpus was suspended between May 1817 and January 1818, and the Six Acts, which included a ban on meetings of more than fifty people, were passed in 1819. For a detailed account of participation in the radical movement of this period see, Samuel Bamford, *Passages in the Life of a Radical* (2 vols., 3rd ed., London, 1844).

[61] Edited by T. J. Wooler, it ran from 29 January 1817 to 21 December 1824 and had a weekly circulation of over 12,000 in 1819.

illustration of the strong antagonistic feelings which then existed between rich and poor, than by relating a little circumstance which came under my own observation:—There was a young man in Bellingham, named George Seaton, who had served his apprenticeship with a Mr. Gibson, a saddler. Seaton was a person of studious habits, and an inquiring turn of mind: he was also a very good public reader. For some time after the *Black Dwarf* made its appearance in the village, Seaton was in the habit of reading it to a few of the more intelligent working people, at the old fashioned cross which stood in the centre of the village. It must be borne in mind that this Seaton was a person of unblemished character, and both sober and industrious in his habits. Notwithstanding these moral qualifications, when it came to be known that he had imbibed a spirit of radicalism, there was scarcely a farmer in the district would employ him. This person was a lineal descendant of Seaton, Earl of Winton, who had to fly his country for his loyalty to *Prince Charlie*, in 1745; and he made some little stir a few years ago in certain circles, when he laid claim to the title and estates of his family, and though he was unsuccessful, I have reason to believe that he was the lawful heir. The title is now in the keeping of the Earl of Eglington.

While my mother and family continued to travel in the vallies of the Tyne and Redwater, we made Hexham our home. We occupied a small house on the Battle-hill, but in consequence of spending so much of our time in the country, we were seldom in Hexham more than a few days at a time. Upon one occasion when we were at home, I accidentally met with a gentleman of colour, called Peters. I believe he was a native of India. He was living at that time in a lonely cottage, rather better than a mile from Hexham. This eccentric gentleman took a fancy to me, and invited me to go and live with him as his servant. There was a novelty about the situation that suited me, so I accepted his offer much against my mother's wishes. Mr. Peters was quite a gentleman, but full of strange eccentricities. I believe Mr. James of Newcastle, was his guardian; whatever property he may have possessed at a former period, he must have got pretty well through it when I went to him. I lived with him in his solitary mansion for nearly six months, and acted the part of cook, slut, butler, page, footman, and *valet de chambre*.

During my stay, we had many strange scenes enacted, some of which caused no little gossip in the neighbourhood. The following incident will give the reader a fair specimen of the peculiar taste, and devil-may-care character of the man:—One day during the harvest of 1818, (I may here notice that our house stood on the side of the road leading from Hexham to the shire of that name), on the morning of the day in question, a large number of reapers passed the house on their way to the harvest-field, but the morning coming on very wet, they shortly returned on their way home again. When the party came opposite the house they made a halt, and sent two of their number to get lights for their pipes, but I should say more for the purpose of seeing how the land lay. Mr. Peters hearing the voice of the party requesting the light,

94

inquired what was the matter? When I informed him, he requested me to give each of them a horn of ale, I therefore brought the whole squad into the kitchen, twenty in number, all of the amiable sex! After I had served them with a pint horn each, Mr. Peters rang his bell, and when I answered it, he gave me a most significant look, as much as to say he expected a Roland for his Oliver. He said, James, do you think you can manage to keep these people all day? Have you plenty of victuals in the larder to give them all a bellyful? I replied, that I thought they would not require much pressing to remain, and that there was plenty of meat ready for cooking. Very well, he replied, go and give them as much ale as they can take, of course I did as I was ordered! The ale we had on tap was both strong and of a good old age, you may therefore imagine that the ladies' tongues did not remain long unoccupied. After they had swallowed three horns each, the place was worse than ever Babel was in its greatest confusion. When the spring-tide of feeling was being unloosed by the maddening influence of alcohol, the various characters, and idiosyncrasies of the dears were brought into bold relief. While I was preparing something in the shape of a dinner, Mr. Peters requested me to send one of the most sober of the ladies to town for a set of musicians. When those who could eat were served, I was ordered to give every one a glass of rum some of the more reckless had two. After the musicians came and mingled the sound of harmony with the universal discord of female voices, it would be impossible to describe the scene that followed. I have witnessed many strange sights in my time, but this was certainly without a parallel. If you can imagine yourself in the hold of an emigrant ship, with one-half of the passengers labouring under sea-sickness and unable to comply with the common decencies of life, and the other half mad with drink, you will be able to form about the most correct idea of this living picture I can think of. One young girl who had made herself conspicuous by her maudling, found her way into the cellar, with the intention of drawing a can of ale, and left the tap running, so that when I had occasion to go into the cellar, I found myself up to the shoe-tops in ale. The majority of the ladies remained with us to ten o'clock at night, and by that time the musicians were fairly floored, their instruments lying in one place and their hapless bodies in another. This truly disgusting scene passed away, and left me a world of trouble in cleaning the place after them. During the accidental visit of these ladies, Mr. Peters made himself at home with some of them in more ways than one.

One fine morning, when I was in the act of making ready to go to town upon some message, a pair of suspicious-looking gentlemen inquired if my master was at home, stating at the same time, that they wanted him upon particular business. I knew the men, and was fully aware that any business they could have with him was sure to be particular! The consequence of this, to me unlooked-for visit, was the loss of my situation and the removal of my strange but really kind master upon a warrant for debt. While I was in his service, I had been much benefited in more ways than one. I was improved in my manners and considerably polished, by having the rusticity rubbed off me, and my clothing was such as I had never worn before. A few days after Mr. Peters' removal, I paid him a visit in gaol, where he received me in the most kindly manner and made inquiry as to my future prospects. His altered condition seemed to make no difference in his general buoyancy of temperament, and he appeared as happy as if he enjoyed the most perfect freedom. Poor fellow! I never learned what became of him. With all his peculiarities, he was really a kind, generous, and warm-hearted man. He was an excellent scholar and a most accomplished gentleman: indeed, there seemed to be nothing wanting to fit him for the highest rank in society, so far as his manners and education were concerned.

When I returned home, I had to begin my old trade of hawking, which I did with much reluctance. Since my mother had settled in the district, she had regularly continued to increase her property, and by this time she possessed a large stock of goods. In the beginning of the year 1819, my mother took it into her head to visit Ireland once more. What were her motives, I never could truly learn; but, in my opinion, it was just one of those false steps frequently taken by people who are well off and don't know it! How long she had been preparing for the journey I cannot say; but there is no doubt she must have been concocting the scheme some considerable time.

I am now about relating another of those mysterious impressments, which were doomed to exercise an extrordinary influence over my life for several years, and, in all probability, over my destiny itself! At this time there was a little girl who resided on the Battle-hill in Hexham, who was somewhere about my own age. She was not pretty, nor was she good-looking, and she had nothing attractive either in shape or dignity of mien: her eyes were inclined more to the grey than the blue, her make was decidedly dumpy, and, to all intents and purposes, she was a very plain and common-place-looking little lassie. No matter, she was perfect mistress of my soul, and what is more, she never knew it. I loved her in all the purity of my young and unsophisticated nature. We had never exchanged words; but, unobserved and in silence, I have looked volumes of my heart's best affections at her. She, too, was in humble circumstances, but her relations were honest working-people, and I was a strolling vagrant. Even then, with our bettered condition, I felt the deep degradation of my condition. My feeling in this girl's regard, which was pure, holy, and lasting, has been to me as great a paradox as my hatred of my father before I knew him. In a psychological view of the case, the subject may be looked upon as a mere matter of human sympathy. I am aware that people are frequently drawn to each other by kindred feelings. But this is one of the common laws of affinity; whereas in my case, the attraction was all on her side, and I have no doubt but that the repulsion would have been in myself, if it had been tested. As to what may have been the cause of the impression I laboured under, I am fairly lost, when I come to reason with myself upon the subject: all I know is, that I was chained by an invisible power, and wherever my destiny led me during three years, her idea never ceased to operate upon my mind, and wherever I wandered her image was with me sustaining me under my trials and attracting me towards her.

In due course of time, everything was prepared for our ill-advised journey. Like Paddy O'Leary in love,

"The place where my heart was you might roll a turnip in!"

we passed many of the scenes of my happiest earthly associations, and, as we travelled on our way, I took many a long lingering look behind. Had my mother continued in Hexham and proceeded with her usual industrious habits, she would soon have been able to have placed both herself and family in really comfortable circumstances. I had often wished her to put me to some trade; but she obstinately refused, nor would she even allow me to go to school. In consequence of her folly, both my brothers and myself were allowed to fit ourselves to play our respective parts on the stage of the world without the incumbrance of education. When we arrived at Portpatrick, my mother took a lodging for us, where she left us in charge of each other while she went over to Ireland. She came back in the course of a fortnight; but after her return, I observed that she was much altered in her conduct to her family and more particularly to myself. I was satisfied in my own mind that I was an uncomfortable inconvenience to her in some way. Six days after her return from Ireland, I made up my mind to leave her, and when I communicated my determination to her, she seemed relieved, as it were, from a heavy burden. If I had had sense, I might have known that a lad of my years could be no pleasant incumbrance to a widow not much past the prime of life. My brother Robert, seeing my determination to leave, requested me to take him along with me; which I readily consented to do. We were fitted out with a few goods from the stock, to the amount of three pounds, and with this little fortune we sallied forth into the world. I would gladly have gone back to Northumberland, but my mother had left a *stigma* behind, in the shape of certain unpaid accounts. We made the best of our way into England, and wandered like a pair of pilgrims following a blind destiny. In the course of about six weeks we arrived in Yorkshire. Robert was not able to lend me any assistance, and I was a very poor man of business; either my pride or my dislike to the trade totally unfitted me for making a living by it; and the consequence was, that our stock of goods became small by degrees and uncomfortably less. At the end of six months our little pack was totally perished. At this crisis of our affairs Robert got home-sick. Seeing, therefore, that he was anxious to return to his mother, I gave him the only money I had, which was three shillings and sixpence; and with this small sum he set out for

Scotland, where he arrived safe, as I learned afterwards. I was once more alone in the world without friends or money. I made application to a gentleman in the hardware business in Beadale, from whom I had made some little purchases while about that place; he very kindly lent me assistance, and employed me to go with him to the fairs and markets in the North Riding of Yorkshire. As this gentleman did not require my services, I was only upon sufferance: however, one day while I was attending Ripon Market, I met with a gentleman who offered me a situation to travel with him at a salary of five shillings a-week and my board and lodgings. No offer could have been more welcome, and I therefore engaged with him on the spot.

I had now entered upon a dangerous career, and had my good fortune not saved me, the consequences might have been of a very serious character. This man's name was John Rooney, but he was better known by the title of Cheap John;[62] he was a native of the north of Ireland, and one of the most consummate vagabonds ever manufactured into the shape of humanity. In height, he stood five feet seven inches, well built, broad shoulders and a little round, strong, well-shaped limbs; his complexion was fair and ruddy, and he was slightly marked with the small-pox. His usual dress was a blue coat with gilt buttons, cord smalls, and quarter boots, and he invariably wore a party-coloured silk handkerchief about his bull-like neck tied in sailor fashion. In temper he was a savage, he knew honesty only by name, and his sensuality amounted to beastliness. He was as illiterate as a boor, but what he wanted in education was fully compensated for in low cunning, and he possessed a most retentive memory. The whole of this man's conduct tended to three points in the compass of human action, namely, fighting, whoring, and roguery! I believe the fellow's nature was such that he would rather be fighting, than taking his supper after a hard day's work. In one sense of the term he was a lady-killer, and he was continually involved in disgraceful intrigues. He seemed to have a feverish desire to ruin married females, and he was continually boasting of the havoc he had made in that line. I have been particular in describing this man in order that you may fully comprehend the danger of my position. When I went into his service, he had a large quantity of goods, chiefly composed of linen and silks. After I had been with him a short time I learned the whole of his history. The fact was, he made no secret of his knavery, and I learned from himself that he had had to flee his country for killing a man in some party row. His assumed title of Cheap John was not without being well founded, inasmuch as he could dispose of his goods at thirty per cent. below cost price, and have the remaining seventy per cent as a small profit to himself. The goods he had on hand

[62] A generic title of fairground traders. For an account of their way of life see William Green, *The Life and Adventures of a Cheap Jack by One of the Fraternity*, edited by Charles Hindley (London, 1876).

when I went to him were the residue of a property he had bolted from Newcastle-upon-Tyne with. His manner of victimising wholesale houses was carried out upon a regular systematic plan; he was never without plenty of cash, and took every opportunity of exposing it to advantage. When he had an intention of honouring a house with his patronage, his first essay was to feel the pulse of the proprietor, and if he found the party suitable to be operated upon, he would make a few goodly purchases from time to time, and after he had disarmed his man of all suspicion, he would write for a small parcel of goods as it were to sort his stock upon credit, the payments for these goods were sure to be punctually made; having paved the way in this manner, he made his final *hawl* and *sloped*.

I believe there are few counties in England where there are so many pickpockets as in Yorkshire; the reason of this, I believe, is, or was to be found in the numerous markets and fairs which are held in the different divisions of the county. Rooney was upon terms of intimacy with a number of these free and easy gentlemen; I remember a very smart trick being done by a highwayman upon one occasion while in Beadle. We were lodging in a house which was a general rendezvous for travellers, and while there three highwaymen made their appearance late one evening; the fellows formed a *trio* of nationalities, one was Yorkshire, another Scotch, and the third Irish. The following morning was Beadle Fair; during the course of the day, these three worthies disagreed about the division of the spoil of a robbery they had committed the day before in Westmoreland; in the arrangement of the booty, the Irishman conceived that he had not had justice done him; the consequence was, that he made up his mind to teach the honest Yorkshireman and the canny Scot a lesson. About eleven o'clock at night, a posse of constables came to the lodging-house with a search-warrant; they walked straight into the bed-room occupied by the highwaymen, and found a large bundle of clothing which had been taken from the head inn a few hours before; the Yorkshireman and the Scotchman were both sent off to York Castle next morning. The Irishman, in order to gratify his revenge, had stolen the articles, and lodged information where they were to be found, and at the same time implicated his two companions as the thieves. What became of them I never learned, but I saw the Irishman afterwards skinning the natives aboard of the Hull and Gainsborough steampacket.

After I had been with Rooney about six weeks, he picked up other two stray sons of misfortune; one of them was a fine intelligent and good-looking young man who had fled from his apprenticeship in a draper's shop, in Shrewsbury; he must have been very respectably brought up, he was an excellent scholar, and in every way a genteel young fellow. From his own statement, he had got into bad company, and in order to keep up his unlawful wants had robbed his employer. The other was in every way a most extraordinary person, his name was Thomas Evans; however, I imagine it was only assumed for the occasion. He was a native of the south of Ireland; in age he might be twenty-four, and in his person he was as fine a looking man as ever I beheld: he must have had a first-rate education, and it was evident from his manner that he was accustomed to society of a very different character to such as he was then in. No one could ever draw from him a single syllable, either about himself or his connexions. There was evidently a mystery about him; when he was in repose he seemed continually talking to himself, as his lips were seen moving rapidly. Immediately after his joining us, I was drawn towards this man as if it were by a spell, and as long as I remained with Rooney we clung to each other like brothers; he was as honest as the day is light, and perfectly sober in his habits, and as simple-minded as a child. Rooney frequently used these young men very badly; when he was in his cups, which was by no means seldom, he was in the habit of giving them practical demonstrations of his pugilistic proficiency. I have often seen him battering them about for his amusement for half an hour at a time, in the most brutal manner. It may be asked why they did not leave him rather than suffer such tyranny; my answer is, that he had them in his toils, and they were both much afraid of him, as they knew his reckless character. I believe my diminutiveness saved me many a beating, for he really never used me ill in this manner, with the exception of twice. The life I was then leading was in every sense repugnant to my feelings: when I had a few shillings due to me in wages, he always contrived to rob me of them by getting me to play at cards with him; the fact was, I had neither taste to learn nor inclination to play, but upon such occasions he forced me into the game, and as a matter of course won my money. I have no doubt he used this policy in order to keep me in his power.

Hand selling was a very common practice at that time, and Rooney was quite a proficient in the business, the fellow could talk a horse blind, and he could string nonsense together by the mile;* but a great portion of his language was highly indecent, and, as he was entirely without shame, he was completely regardless of the consequences of his conduct. The class of hawkers I was in the habit of meeting when I was with Rooney, was very different from the primitive strollers on the Borders. As a specimen of the former, I cannot illustrate their character better than by a little anecdote. One day, after I had been standing in Richmond market, and had just completed the packing of my goods, a fellow came up to me, and in the most bland and familiar manner asked me 'how I was! I had never spoken to the man in my life, but had often seen him with Rooney; he insisted that I should go and have a drop of the *crater*. I did not like to be rude with him, so I went and had a glass of ale, and he had one of rum; after we had finished, he insisted we should have another go, I positively declined having any more; when he found how the land lay, he slapped me on the shoulder in a friendly

* A sort of mock auction, where the auctioneer reduces the price to suit the purchaser.

way, and said, "My boy, you'll have to stand this, for, by jaspers, I hav'nt a *meg*, and I'll stand the next *budge*."[63]

While I was paying for the drink, a number of farmers came into the room, he speedily introduced himself to a group of them, who were seating themselves together in one company. He said his brother was a merchant in India, who occasionally consigned large quantities of rich and costly silks to his care, in order that he might dispose of them. In the meantime he pulled out a five-quarter checked and twilled cotton handkerchief, with gaudy colours, such as were then selling at nine shillings per dozen wholesale. Now, gentlemen, he observed, if any of you wish to have eternal sunshine at home, here is an article whose magic will produce the so much desired effect. You observe these colours, gentlemen, these living shades and glorious tints were produced by the fabric being steeped three months in the Ganges, after which they were passed through a·succession of rainbows! You must remember, gentlemen, that this article cannot be purchased in the regular market, as all such goods are prohibited, of course I have them under the rose! The value of this Thibet shawl in India is ninety *rupees*, which means six pounds in our money. The fact is, gentlemen, I am a wild devil-may-care sort of a fellow, and have been on the fly and am a little short for cash, if, therefore, any of you want a bargain here it is. I have plenty of money, but you know it is not always convenient to be counting the hours in waiting for a remittance from London. After this peroration, he quietly slipped the handkerchief into the hands of one of the gentlemen, telling him at the same time to expose it as little as possible, as he did not wish to come in contact with His Majesty's Exchequer,—and whispering into the gentleman's ear, you can take it for thirty shillings. Suffice it to say, he sold the nine-penny handkerchief for ten shillings. I have frequently seen simple-minded and credulous people done out of their money in this manner. At that time it was a common trick for a fellow dressed as a sea captain to carry a sample bottle of French brandy, passing it off as smuggled, and selling it at a pound a gallon; the article was generally made up in five gallon casks, and when the stock and the sample were compared, the transaction seemed all right; these casks were made with tubes to fit through the centre, and only contained about a quart of brandy— the rest of the contents being water,—and as the buyers were as bad in the eye of the law as the disposers, these acts of swindling were kept pretty quiet.

Rooney had done a good deal of business with base money; however, I never knew anything about this matter, until one day we were standing in Lincoln Market, when we were going home to our lodgings he gave me two shillings to purchase beef steaks with. I thought it somewhat strange at the time that he should give me money when he knew I had plenty of change in my pocket. In paying the butcher, I gave him two shillings which proved to be both bad,—the man looked at the money, and then he carefully examined

[63] *Meg*—counterfeit halfpenny; *budge*—drink.

me from head to heel. I could almost have wished the earth to have swallowed me alive, he sent for a constable immediately, when the officer arrived, I told him what appeared the truth to myself, namely:—that I must have taken the money in the market, and to convince the people of my innocence I turned out all the money I had upon me, which amounted to four pounds some shillings, and all proved to be good; this, with my innocent manner, enabled me to get clear off. Had I been detained, the consequence would have been serious to me, as I would have told who I was with, and I learned that Rooney had a large quantity in his possession, nothing could therefore have saved me from being punished as an accomplice. After this I was in continual dread of some impending evil, he had used all his endeavours to initiate me into his own roguish practices; the reason why I did not comply with his hellish desires was, not that I was so much guided by principle, as that I had a natural dislike to the barefaced character of his dishonesty, and perhaps fear had no little to do with my conduct in the matter; besides this, I hated the man for his blackguardism and open profligacy, and however long I should have remained with him, there never could have been anything like congeniality of feeling between us.

The time I am now writing of was towards the end of the year 1819, during that year the whole country was in a state of feverish excitement. The Prince Regent had used every exertion to blast the character of his wife, and hand down her name to posterity with infamy. This event called forth one universal feeling of indignation in the public mind against the Prince and his sycophantic abettors. I am not aware of any circumstance in my time wherein the English people gave such unequivocal and unanimous proof of their love of justice. The fact was, that the more thoughtful members of the community saw that the national character was being compromised, and I believe their unmistakable protest was the means of saving the honour of the nation. From this date up to the year 1832, the country was in a dangerous state of transition. Commerce was crippled in almost every possible way, and the taxes hung like a dead weight upon the industrial energies of the people. The legislative functions were solely in the hands of men who were wedded to aristocratic notions, and government patronage flowed in one muddy and corrupt channel, while the members of Parliament, instead of representing the feelings of the nation, continued to serve their own sinister ends at the expense of the people.

The introduction of machinery was then creating a panic among the working classes, especially in the manufacturing districts. Men who had spent their time, and wasted their energies in the various occupations, were doomed to see their labour superseded by an entire new power. The working men had not then learnt the science of political economy; and even if they had, it would have afforded them little or no relief. Men with hungry bellies have small thought to spare upon abstract principles of speculative philosophy. Under all circumstances, and in all countries, the necessities of the time

102

among the great industrial masses must produce the ruling feeling of the hour. To live has ever been, and ever will be, the great battle of the people.

In reviewing the critical position of the country at that time, and reflecting upon the severe ordeal through which the people have passed, we have much reason to be thankful that the national barque has weathered the storm. It is true that the people were occasionally guilty of trifling excesses but it must be borne in mind, that in many instances they were goaded into acts of insubordination by the greatness of their sufferings. The manner in which the unoffending and defenceless people were treated at *Peterloo*, in Manchester, in 1819, afforded a melancholy proof of the utter disregard of the men in power to the feelings and wants of the industrious classes. The circumstances connected with this cold-blooded event will remain like so many foul stains upon the page of England's history.

I may observe, that in the early part of the nineteenth century, the middle class element was only in its infancy, and it was not until the wonderful discoveries of Watt, Cartwright and Stephenson were brought into operation that this useful body in the state began to assume its proper position. During the last thirty years, the extraordinary energy and directing power of this body have attained for it a moral force unprecedented in the history of the country; and I think it may be justly said, that whatever social advantages we now enjoy over those of the preceding age, are in a great measure due to the well-timed exertions of this now powerful class. If the signs of the times are to be interpreted by their own manifestations, I certainly think we are upon the eve of one of those social changes which will entirely alter the political aspect of affairs in this country. After repeated trials, the aristocracy have been found wanting in the management of the state; as business men, they are proved to be not up to the mark; and it would appear, from the broad expression of public opinion, that John Bull, while he is both able and willing to pay his servants, is determined to put his affairs into the hands of men who can manage them in a business-like manner. In all cases where men are invested with power, it necessarily follows that a good deal of it must be discretionary and irresponsible; in state affairs this is particularly so, and I think the more such a condition of things can be narrowed within the limits of a responsible system, the better for the nation. A system may be made to approximate perfection, though it be not in the nature of man to arrive at such a state.

103

Letter VI

Alloa, November.

MY DEAR THOMAS,—I have lately seen a speech delivered by Lord John Russell, which was addressed to a meeting, held in Bristol, in the early part of this month.[64] In this speech his Lordship has made a discovery which could only be found out by a man profoundly conversant with all the secret springs and motives which regulate the various actions of human nature. His Lordship deplores the calamity (not of the war, nor of the many evils consequent upon it) that we have not an *impartial* historian! I certainly think if his great mind had not been entirely absorbed by this one grand idea, he might have also discovered our want of an impartial statesman! ! !

Had there been one single man in either of the late Administrations with sufficient energy of mind and honest determination of character, to have boldly taken the helm and cast aside the rubbish of *routine*, which everywhere lumbered the deck of the vessel of State, and called to his assistance a sufficient number of able-bodied men from the ranks of the people, the country would have been saved the disgrace of the disasters which have lately befallen the nation, in consequence of the blundering incapacity of its misrulers. In the speech above alluded to, his Lordship cavils with Mr. Macaulay for a poetical fancy he has indulged in, or rather a philosophical reflection, in his *History of England*. Arguing from analogy, the historian concludes that Great Britain will be subject to the same unerring laws which regulated the destinies of the ancient kingdoms and empires of the world, and he has imagined that the time may come when some American prying Layard will contemplate the ruins of mighty London from the crumbling remains of some of her bridges! ! Lord John's patriotism takes alarm at such an unlikely conclusion. I wonder if his lordship imagines that because we are a great nation, cause and effect will cease to operate upon each other, and that progression with us will only end with time. His Lordship stated that all the great nations of antiquity had the seeds of their own destruction in the nature of their institutions. As the egg holds the germ of animal life, so does it also possess the seeds of its decay. How do we know but that there may have been kingdoms far back beyond the written records whose glory and magnificence were much greater than our own, and that there is really "nothing new under the sun." The limits

---

[64] Russell was in fact speaking at the opening of the Bristol Athenaeum on 25 October 1854.

of men's greatness are marked out by the character of their perishable nature, and we are told in the language of human experience, that "thus far we can go and no further."

In arguing a question of this kind, we should do well to remember that men are fighting animals, and that the love of conquest has not ceased (nor do I believe it ever will) to regulate the conduct of nations towards each other, whether they be civilised or savage. Witness our own conduct in the present unfortunate war, which we have entered into merely to ward off distant contingencies which might never have taken place. If this country had been threatened with an invasion, the feelings of the people could not have evinced a more rancorous hatred, or a more determined hostility towards the enemy than what lately existed throughout the whole kingdom. How is this? Will the merciful appeal of the Cross be always made in vain, when men's passions outrage the best feelings of humanity. I really do not think that either policy or justice can sanction the present war, and I am convinced that the future historian will have a disagreeable task in unfolding our motives to action. In concluding this subject I think it is not very likely that Lord John Russell will ever act the part of a second Marius, seated on the ruins of St. Petersburg, but that is no reason why some of his successors should not become the Cicerone of some scientific stranger of a distant age, in exploring the half-buried ruins of the once Queen of the World! ! !

My time with Rooney is now drawing to a close, the affair at Lincoln caused me to be continually in fear for the ungodly transaction, and from that time I had made up my mind to leave him whenever a fitting opportunity offered. I knew quite well that he was a dangerous fellow to break with. For some time I took the precaution to retain my salary in my own hands. I communicated my purpose to Evans, who warmly entered into my feelings and seconded my views. When we got down to Hull, Rooney got on the fly, and continued so for some days, during which time I made my escape. When I left I had twenty-five shillings to begin the world again with; many a one would have made a fortune out of that sum; the case, however, was very different with me. Although I had been accustomed to a wandering life from my infancy, nobody could more heartily despise the calling than I did. My great desire was to learn a trade, whereby I could be looked upon as an honest member of society, but my great difficulty was to find a person who would venture to take one who had led such a vagrant life.

When I regained my liberty, Kitty Dawson's image invited me to Hexham —but my better feelings opposed my going there, so after much reflection, I made up my mind to visit my mother,—I had neither heard of her, nor my brothers since leaving them. I therefore, purchased a few small articles and set out on my journey. While I travelled on my solitary way, my mind was frequently filled with the most conflicting feelings, longing to see my mother, and my brothers, but having no certainty of finding them where I left them. After an uninteresting journey of some twelve days I arrived in Portpatrick, and had the mortification to find that my mother had removed to Girvan in

Ayrshire; and when I reached that place, I had a second disappointment in being introduced to a second *step-father*. This little family arrangement made me a stranger in what should have been a home to me. I think if ever a poor wretch was the football of crooked circumstances such was my fate, I had been blessed with *three fathers* and two mothers, and I was then as comfortably situated as if I never had either one or the other, excepting that I was a living monument of the folly of both father and mother. I knew little or nothing of Fitzsommons, the name of my new *pa:* from what I could learn *he* was a very decent man, but there was a certain mercenary meanness in the connection which I could not digest, he was then a young man in the prime of life, and my mother had passed the *rubicon* some years. I think there can be nothing more contemptible than that of a young man allying himself by matrimony to a female much above his own years for the sake of her property; the lion and the lamb may lie down together in harmony, but age and youth can never be bound together by affection. My mother was then trading between Ireland and the west of Scotland, and her husband occasionally worked at the hosiery business; I was induced to take two trips to Ireland with the old woman; but I only remained three weeks at home, and when I left, I took my brother Robert with me at his own request.

I am now about being carried along by one of those tidal currents whereon my frail barque was in continual danger of being shipwrecked. You may suppose, that I was impelled by a restless desire for change, such however was not the case, I had already seen too much of that; instead therefore of wishing to see new scenes, I was anxiously looking for a resting place that I might become a recognisable member of society. My brother and myself went to Glasgow where I purchased a few shillings worth of goods to renew our small stock. From this place we travelled to Galashiels, Peebles, Kelso, and on till we crossed the English Border. Our little fortune had vanished a second time, when by good fortune, I got Robert into a situation with a small farmer. Although I was my brother's senior by several years, he was much bigger than I was. After this, I got employment in a coal-pit, during the time a boy who had filled the situation was confined by an injury he had received by the falling in of a part of the roof. My wages for this sub-soil labour was hard work and eightpence a-day. I continued at this employment until I was superseded by the return of the convalescent *putter*. My next employment was hoeing turnips for a farmer in the neighbourhood of Elsdon; I had only been in this place a week, when I met with a most agreeable surprise by meeting in with my old friend Tom Evans. He was still the same quiet, self-communing, and mysterious being I had left him. We were both happy at the meeting. Poor fellow, he was something like myself, as poor as a church-mouse. He said, he could raise twenty-shillings from an acquaintance in Morpeth, and if I would go with him, we would try the smuggling. I agreed to his proposal, and he returned in the course of a few days with the cash for our venture. We went up to Carter Bar,[65] and made a purchase of five gallons of Scotch whisky. We carried this load between us, a distance of forty miles, and as we required to avoid the high roads, we had to travel the whole distance over trackless moors, and a great part of the way by night. Before we could dispose of our mountain dew, we were both heart-sick of it, and all the time we had it in our possession, we continually laboured under the apprehension of capture. If either of us had been known in the places where we offered it for sale, I have no doubt but we could easily have disposed of it: as it was, the people were afraid to buy the article from strangers, who might take their money and lodge an information against them immediately afterwards. I found that Tom's visions of making a fortune were not to be realised; besides, neither of us were fitted for the business. After vainly pressing upon me to give it another trial, I left him and went back to Elsdon, where I got employment in making hay.

Shortly after this, I met with a person, a native of Yorkshire, who was then residing in that part of the country: this man persuaded me to go with him to the harvest, to which I readily agreed; so, when the hay season was finished, I went down with him to see a farmer for whom he had worked the previous season. The farmer engaged Smith (which was the person's name); but he demurred to employing me, as I looked so very unlike the work. However, Smith made this all right, by kindly offering to take me as his partner. Our journey that day was the hardest day's work I ever had in my life: when we got back to Elsdon, we had travelled sixty-two miles. When the grain was ready for reaping, we went to fulfil our engagements. I had never cut corn before, and suffered most dreadfully during the first week: however, with the assistance of my kind and good-natured partner, I managed to give satisfaction. We were employed for three weeks, and had our board and lodging in the house, both of which were excellent in quality. We had each a guinea a-week, and had the good fortune not to have a single broken day.[66] When the harvest was finished, we went to Newcastle, where I spent a good part of my money in clothes. When I went back to Elsdon, I got employment during another week in shearing; after which I went to Hexham, in the expectation of meeting with some tradesman who would take me as an apprentice. On arriving there, I went to a person of the name of Ralph Dodd, whom I had known when we resided in the town. This person allowed me to job about his place of business for a few weeks, for which he gave me my

[65] Carter Bar marked the border between Northumberland and Roxburgh on the road from Jedburgh to Newcastle. It was a well-known centre for smuggling. See Rev. James Christie, *Northumberland: its history, its features, and its people* (London, 1893), pp. 94–5.

[66] There was an established pattern of hiring casual labour to take in the harvest in the Border region. The majority of workers were Irish labourers who came over between August and October. About 6,000 a year were making the journey at this time. Burn was indeed well-paid; 2s. 6d. a day was the usual maximum, and few reapers carried home more than £3 for ten weeks' labour. (James E. Handley, *The Irish in Scotland 1798–1845*, Cork, 1943, pp. 34–49).

victuals. During the time I was with him, I studiously avoided being seen by the little angel of my adoration. I was still ashamed of my position, and was afraid, if she should see me, that I should lose—what I never had, namely—her affections!—a blind, and a stupid fellow is love!

I dare say Dodd would have readily taken me as an apprentice, but he had no confidence in me; he could not bring his mind to believe that I would allow myself to be chained so long to one place. This misfortune of having been kicked about the world was, therefore, held as a reason that, like Van Wooden Block's cork leg, I should continue to wander on.

After I had been in Hexham a few weeks, the Northumberland militia was about being raised. At that time, the men required were ballotted for. Several militia societies were then in existence, and when any of the members were drawn, substitutes were paid for out of the funds. Some of my acquaintances persuaded me to take the bounty, I was then beneath the standard height, which was five feet six inches. This, to me, apparent difficulty, was got over by a young man, a tailor, who made me all right by padding my stocking-soles. I dare say I am not the first who has been elevated to the army by fictitious means. I passed the doctor and was duly attested to serve my king and country according to the conditions. My bounty was nine pounds. The first thing I did was to purchase a few shirts and other necessaries I stood need of. I then laid out six pounds in the purchase of tea: I had been advised to this step by several of my friends With this stock, I was on a fair way to become a regular travelling merchant. I was then certainly in a better position than I had ever been during my whole life: I was full of hope and saw before me a bright future; and in all my calculations my sweet little mistress came in for her ideal share. The fortune and pleasures which I had conjured up in my sanguine imagination were doomed to share the same fate as those of the young man in the *Arabian Nights*. Just as I was about tasting of the sweets of fortune's cup, it was ruthlessly dashed from my lips. I took my cargo of tea upon my back, only dreaming of the pleasant reception I should meet with from my old acquaintances among the country farmers. I was respectably dressed, and was sure of having my honest endeavours well supported. When I had got about two miles on the road, I met a gentleman going into the town. He inquired what I had in my bundle? Without the least suspicion I told him. He then asked me to let him see my *permit*. I did not as much as understand the nature of such a document: so, seeing that I could not oblige him in this matter, he said he would be under the necessity of seizing it in the name of the king. The truth of the matter now flashed upon my mind like a death knell. My poor heart became full; and I felt a choaking sensation about my throat. For some moments I could not speak. When I had time to think I thought I was doomed to misery. Again, desolation stared me in the face. I mentally resolved that I had better been struck dead by some invisible power than be ever thus the sport of a wild and hapless fortune. Whatever I thought I said nothing: the fellow asked me to carry the parcel back into the town, for which act of condescension he gave me a shilling.

Never was there a poor wretch more innocent of the sin of smuggling than I was. I had no idea that tea bought in a regular market required in the first place a permit to remove it, and in the second, that I required a license to be allowed to sell it. I therefore lost my all and had no redress; and was again thrown pennyless upon the world. To console me for my loss, several of my friends said that I must have been informed against, and that the person who sold me the tea knew the necessary conditions, and that if he had been an honest man he would have given me proper information how to act. This of course was making my case no better, and I could not believe that any person could have been so heartless as to do me such a gratuitous wrong: I had never injured any one, and therefore no person could harbour revengeful feelings against me.

Once more I had a stormy pilgrimage before me, and like a vessel at sea without a rudder, I was cast adrift to steer my course upon the ocean of life. I could see nothing before me but a dreary wilderness, nor could I tell which way to fly from my impending doom. It is a fearful thing for a human being to stand alone in the world; cut off from all sympathy and fellowship with his kind. Such was my sad and cheerless condition. I know there have been thousands placed in similar circumstances; but I also know that many have suffered shipwreck under the pressure of their misfortune; while only those who have been buoyed up by hope have been able to weather the storm. If my mind had not continually aspired to something above my lowly condition, I should have sailed down the stream of life in my vagrant craft, until I was eventually brought to in a jail or at the hulks. After this sad misadventure, I could not remain in Hexham; so I made up my mind to push my fortune elsewhere.

A few days after my commercial shipwreck, I went down to Newcastle-upon-Tyne, and offered my services to several tradesmen as an apprentice. I found two parties who would have taken me, if I could have got any person to become security for the faithful discharge of my duties, but this, of course, with me, was out of the question.[67] After wandering about for some days without either food or a resting place, I made application for employment to a gentleman who had charge of a large stone-quarry in the neighbourhood of Bishop Auckland. When I presented myself before this person, he looked at me with a good-natured smile, and asking me a few questions as to my previous employment, he said, "My lad, you look more like standing behind a counter than working in a quarry, you would be no use here!" He gave me sixpence, and advised me to look for employment more suitable to my

---

[67] Normally an apprentice's father paid the necessary premium and guaranteed his son's conduct over the seven-year period. In the case of orphans, the parish would occasionally act *in loco parentis*, but having no parish and effectively no parents, Burn was in a difficult position.

condition. From this place I went down to South Shields, where I called upon a small hat manufacturer, whose relations I knew in Hexham. I found I had no chance there, as he was just parting with a young man who had been some time at the trade. I remained in Shields two days. The young man who was leaving was going to Liverpool, and advised me to go with him, and depend upon the chapter of accidents. This lad was a native of Froome; his father was a retired navy-lieutenant; his name was Bird. He was a very fine young man, but I believe he had been very wild. As drowning men catch at straws, I embraced his offer, and we set out together, like a pair of young pilgrims. We were both without cash, but as my partner had served two years at hat-making, he was enabled to call upon the apprentices in the towns we passed through where the trade was carried on; and we managed to box our way as far as Oldham, in Lancashire, without any mishap. Before going into that town Bird requested me to lend him my bundle, in which were my shirts and other necessaries. These things were tied up in a blue and white spotted silk handkershief. The reason why he wanted my bundle was, because he had nothing but what he stood in, and he remarked, what I knew to be correct, that he would look very unlike being on tramp without some change of clothing. I therefore readily gave him my bundle, and we agreed that I should wait for him at the end of the town leading to Manchester. We parted about ten o'clock in the morning, and neither of us had had any breakfast. I went to the place appointed, fully expecting that he would not be more than two hours. I waited patiently until four o'clock in the afternoon; after that time, the hours crept slowly and sadly away. I lingered on until eleven o'clock at night; hungry in both mind and stomach; still the "Bird" of hope did not arrive. I knew it was of no use to go in search of him; and I had therefore no alternative but to move on. The distance to Manchester was seven miles; and when I got to Market-street it was one o'clock. You may well imagine my situation was not a comfortable one. I really did not know what to do. In going down Market-street, I met with a tradesman who was finding his way home. I inquired of him the road to Liverpool; this person was curious to know what I wanted with the road to Liverpool at such a time of night. I told him my situation, and he kindly took me home with him to his lodging; saying he could give me a share of his bed, but as he had been out of employment for a considerable time, he could afford me nothing more. The fact was, the poor kind-hearted fellow, had no victuals for himself. As it was, I was very grateful for his generous conduct.

Next morning, I took the way for Liverpool. I had not lost hope of meeting with Bird, as I had every confidence in his honesty; and I made up my mind that he had been detained by some circumstance over which he had no power. I therefore lingered the whole of the day between Manchester and Warrington, and enquired of every person I met on the way if they had seen a young man dressed in sailor's clothes with a bundle, which I described. The day was beautiful for the season, but there was a heavy cloud upon my mind, and which ever way I turned my restless thoughts, my prospect for the future was cold and cheerless. Late in the evening as I was going into Warrington, I fell in with four working-men, and as they were going in the same direction with myself, I got into conversation with them, and told them my circumstances. These poor fellows gave me all the money they had upon them, which was two-pence, and told me where I could have supper and a bed free of charge. They directed me to the Mendicity Office, where I was treated as they foretold.

If I had not thought I should meet Bird, either on the road or in Liverpool, I had no business there. Indeed, it was quite immaterial to me where I wandered; for whatever might turn up in my favour, I knew must be a mere matter of accident. However, I made up my mind to push on, and rose early in the morning with the intention of being in Liverpool by mid-day. When I had got about half-a-mile out of Warrington, I observed a cottage in a garden on the wayside, with a sign over the door, on which there was labelled, "Bread and milk sold here." I had the two-pence that the labouring men had given me, and I made up my mind to have a breakfast, if I should never have another. Going into that house proved a fortunate circumstance. The first object which caught my attention, was my bundle lying on a table before me as I went in; and I found my "Bird" making himself comfortable over a breakfast of boiled milk and bread by the fire. Our surprise was mutual, and we were glad to see each other again. He explained the cause of his delay quite satisfactorily to me. *Oudham rough Yeads* had made him drunk, which would not be difficult to do upon an empty stomach, and after leaving there he had used his best endeavours to find me.

Apropos to Oldham. This town was at one time, and that, too, not very long ago, one of the most uncultivated places in England. The following anecdote will give a very fair idea of the character of the town. Upon a certain occasion, a pair of married ladies happened to have a social quarrel, which resulted in their being cited before the sitting magistrate. When the case came on for hearing, the worthy magistrate could not make out which of the dears were in fault; however, one of their husbands being in court, and being known by the bench, the magistrate said, "John, *yaw con* tell us *au abeawt* it." "I," he said, "a *con. Yo segn Jon o'th* Top·*o'th* Loan's wife *thrut* a stone at *ma* wife, and if *oo'd it* hur as *ard* as *oo* it *hur, oo'd other* killed *her,* or hur hur! !" "I," said the magistrate, "that's plain *eneuf.*"

Bird had raised four shillings in Oldham and Manchester, so we set out for Liverpool with light hearts, and we arrived there early in the day. Our four shillings soon found their way into other hands; and we spent several days in searching for employment, but all our endeavours were vain. In the meantime, I had to dispose of the most of my little wardrobe to pay our lodging and keep our jaws in something like healthy exercise. On the morning of the fifth day, Bird was shipped aboard of a vessel bound for New York, and as the vessel was to sail with the afternoon tide, we bid each other adieu. As we

111

parted my heart was full, and the tears started into my eyes. Short as our acquaintance had been, I felt a warm regard for him; he was really a good hearted, amiable, and intelligent lad. He had been at sea before, and I think he was inclined to make the ocean his home, and I have no doubt but he would rise in the profession.

Once more I was alone and in the wilderness of a large town; my case was almost a hopeless one; and I felt the sadness of despair creeping over my feelings. I wandered about for two days after I parted from Bird, with my mind almost a blank. By that time all my little things had been disposed of. About the middle of the third day, I found myself staring at a large handbill posted on a wall somewhere about London-road; and during the time I was gazing at the bill, a soldier came up and tapped me on the shoulder and requested to know if I would list. The friendly voice of any human being was welcome to me. I said I had no objection. This was certainly a cheering ray of hope, from a quarter where I least expected it. I gladly went with my military friend to a public-house. Like a man who knows his duty, he opened up his military budget, and pointed out the fame and fortune which awaited me when I should join the Royal 5th Queen's Own. While he was running over his splendid catalogue of inducements to a life of glory, my mind was with my little angel in Hexham; but I suppose this was in consequence of the connection which has always existed between love and fame. I took the magic shilling which was to cut my civilian tie with a world which had been very uncivil to me. After this I had as much bread and cheese and ale as enabled me to drive the horrors from my empty stomach. Eating is certainly one of the most vulgar occupations in life. But, oh ye gods, what divine luxury there is in even a crust of dry bread to a hungry stomach! Poets have sung of love and glory, and all those feelings which prompt men to noble and generous actions; but I have found that the love of the stomach outlives all other love! Taking the shilling and eating his Majesty's bread and cheese was only a preliminary step to two others—I was taken to pass the doctor. You will see that although I had taken the token, I was not a soldier yet: it so happened at that time, that my skin under my clothes was covered with something like a scorbutic eruption—from what cause I am not aware. After the disciple of Æsculapius had examined me, he quietly put me to one side, while he passed the other three young men. The doctor had made up his mind, that though I could eat bread and cheese and drink beer, I should not do for a fighting man! Since then I have often thought he was a very sensible fellow. The sergeant who listed me was a good deal piqued, as he thought me a very likely lad. Notwithstanding my forlorn condition, I looked upon this escape from the army as a providential interposition in my favour. The food I had got dispelled the gloom from my mind, and lent me fresh energy.

As I found that I would not do for the army, I made up my mind to try the navy; so I went down to the Docks and offered my services to several sea-captains. At last, I was fortunate in finding a vessel bound for London, and the captain agreed to take me on a trial-trip. We cleared out of the port on the afternoon of the following day. In the course of a few days I could make myself pretty useful aboard. We had plain sailing until we were off the Landsend, when a fearful storm set in and continued to blow a very heavy gale, accompanied by thunder, lightning, and rain, and during the night we had our decks nearly swept clear. About midnight, I had a narrow escape from being cut in two: the lightning cut one of the chain topsail sheets, and the loose end, which was attached to the sail, swept past me, so near that I felt the wind from its motion. About daylight, in the morning, I had a hydropathic immersion, which was nearly being my last: the vessel shipped a heavy sea upon her quarter which would have carried me over, had it not been for a counter-plunge that she made. The only injury I sustained was being severely stunned: the mate had me carried below, where I soon recovered. In the morning, the *Fame* was rolling about like a drunken man. As the vessel had sustained a good deal of damage, the captain found it necessary to put into Scilly roads. As we entered the mouth of the bay, we received a pilot on board. The captain of the *Fame*, was a cross-grained, stupid, dogmatical, ruddy-faced old tar, instead of giving the vessel in charge to the pilot, he would not leave the wheel. Headstrong men generally get more than they bargain for, and such was the case in this instance: there were several vessels lying in the roads, that had put in through stress of weather, and as we were making for anchor-ground, our jolly old captain ran the *Fame* foul of a brig carrying away a considerable portion of her running rigging, as well as her jib-boom; our own vessel being nothing the better of the collision. This little act of seamanship cost our self-willed commander more than a month's wages.

After we had got snugly moored, the captain required to go ashore for repairs: he took seven men and myself in the boat with him. We landed at St. John's, and, as the captain had to remain a considerable time, the boat's crew had plenty of time to indulge their curiosity in looking over the island. While in the act of strolling about the town, we came to the garrison gates, at the entrance of which there was a large board of caution, warning strangers not to trespass on the garrison grounds. The place termed "the grounds" was a sort of barren wilderness, mostly covered with furze or whins. Seeing the nature of the ground, we paid no attention to the caution. After we had been strolling about for some time, one of the party required to obey a call of nature: while he was in this act, a duck quietly waddled out of the whin-bush close beside him. As soon as he had an opportunity of examining the place, he found a nest of some fourteen or fifteen eggs. I was the only person near him, but did not pay any attention to what he was about, until he asked me if I had a pocket-handkerchief. I gave him one, and inquired what he wanted with it. He replied that he had found a wild duck's nest. I observed that I thought the wild ducks had more sense than to build their nests within the range of the garrison guns. Immediately above the garrison grounds there were a number of people engaged in planting potatoes. Some of these people observed my companion bagging the eggs, and before we well knew where we were, we had about a hundred of the natives down upon us, like as many Philistines. The poacher was soon made to redeposit the unlucky ducks in embryo. The day was both cold and raw; but before the boat's crew got clear of the garrison yard, we had the satisfaction of being as well warmed as any set of Christians could desire. The rabble pelted us with stones and mud until our personal identity was out of the question: during the whole of the time we were thus doing penance, the mob poured a continual round of the most unmeasured Billingsgate into us. This was the first time I was honoured with Lynch Law, and I assure you I shall never long for a repetition of it. After being shuttlecocked about for some time, we at last found refuge in a public-house. The excitement had been too good for the mob to give us up so easily; so a large number of the more unruly continued to howl before the house we were in.

We remained in the Roads until our repairs were completed, which took us four days. Our voyage to London was now plain sailing, as we had very fine weather. As we were passing through the Downs, one of those little circumstances occurred which is calculated to distinguish individual character. The man who had signalized himself in the egg affair, requested me to put his pannikin on the caboose fire to be ready for his breakfast when he required it—my own breakfast being getting ready at the same time. While the pans were warming I was going about my duty. When I went to see if they were ready, the first salute I got was the contents of my mate's pan on the under part of my face. The fellow when he went into the caboose saw that my pan was boiling, and he imagined that his had not had fair play. The fact was, his was just on the point of boiling, but being covered with fatty matter it kept the steam down. I was very much scalded. This unmanly act of cruelty brought the fellow's vindictive character into bold relief; the crew were indignant at the brutal outrage, and the captain threatened to have him punished when we arrived in London. I would not have noticed this little incident had it not been for this man's previous conduct towards me. I was a sort of a favourite with the whole of the crew, for I had never failed to serve them when desired; but with this man I was a special favourite. I believe he was an excellent seaman, and had seen a good deal of the world, both in the merchant service and the navy, and I had not been aboard of the *Fame* three days, when he seemed to take a strong liking to me; if I had had any education he would have taught me navigation, indeed, there was nothing he knew but he would willingly have taught me. One thing is evident, he must have been a man with a most ungovernable temper; and I have no doubt that if he had had a knife in his hand at the time, instead of the pannikin, he would have used it, even if I had been his own brother. This vindictive spirit may have been a part of his education: he was a native of the North Highlands, where the idea of passing over an injury, or an insult, without being revenged, was looked upon as an unmanly act of cowardice, not so many years ago.

Before we left Liverpool, the captain had picked up a pair of lads who had each been at sea for some considerable time. They were both Tom's by name; the one being a tall red-haired bony rascal, and the other a stiff dumpy little fellow; they were much about the same age, which might be seventeen. I think there never was a pair of more consummate young vagabonds afloat in the same ship. They were both lazy as sloths, and crammed full of every species of blackguardism. When we arrived in London, we were moored alongside of some Wharf in Horsleydown. On the second day, the captain went ashore early in the morning, and did not return until late in the afternoon. After he had been down in the cabin, he inquired for the boys; but no one had seen them since they had left in the morning, on the pretence of going to a washer-woman with some clothes. The mate inquired if there was anything wrong; and the captain answered by saying that the young scoundrels had robbed him of his money, clothing, and ship's papers. Every means was taken to get hold of them, and parties were sent in the evening to the different theatres. On the second day after the robbery, the captain learned that they had booked for Liverpool with one of the heavy coaches. One consideration prevented him from pursuing them, which was, if he should get hold of them through the means of the criminal officers, he would be bound over to prosecute them, and his vessel had to be cleared out in a fortnight. They were, therefore, allowed to escape in consequence of the very law which existed for preventing criminals escaping from justice.

The following day when the captain had had time to cool down, I asked him if he would allow me money for an outfit, as he was going a voyage to the Baltic, and I could not think of going there without at least some clothing fitting for the climate; his answer was, if I thought proper to go, he would allow me ten shillings a month until we came home again; after which, if I behaved myself, he would introduce me to the owners, who would not only give me the necessary outfit, but would also give me an opportunity of learning navigation, and under these conditions he seemed wishful that I should go; but from the state of my clothing I found it would be madness for me to undertake such a voyage. I cannot say that I had any objection to the sea, but I certainly had no predilection for the forecastle. If the sailors who are aboard of the same ship are not agreeable with each other, they are continually in one another's way, and consequently lead a regular dog and cat life as long as they are together. Humble as my own lot was, I possessed a spirit of independence which could not succumb to the unmanly system of repaying one injury by the infliction of another. And although my poverty could scarcely sink me lower without degrading myself by crime my ideas of what I considered right were as dignified as those of any lord, and I think I may safely say that whatever good fortune I have had in life has been entirely owing to this species of manly independence.

115

I left the vessel on the sixth-day after her arrival, with four-pence in my pocket, and two ship biscuits. The captain was ashore at the time, otherwise, I believe he would have given me some small trifle. I remember the answer of the sailor when accosted by a highwayman, as he was crossing Blackheath, on his way to London; the man of the road demanded his money, or he would blow out his brains. "Blow away you lubber," said the tar, "a man may as well be in London without brains as without money!" My case was hopeless enough. It was true I had a small quantity of brains, but the fact was, my head was not *screwed* on right to enable me to turn them to my advantage. The first night after leaving the vessel, I slept in a common lodging-house. When the landlady was showing me to bed, she very kindly cautioned me to take care of my money and clothes, for that a young man who had lodged there the previous night had been stripped to the shirt by his bedfellow. Neither the good woman's caution, nor the occurrence, gave me much trouble: when a man is without property it sometimes saves him a world of anxiety. I soon found out a mystery which has been solved by thousands before me; namely, that London was far too large for me. I was fairly lost in a wilderness of human beings; I was a mere atom in a huge mountain of humanity! and as it were an unclaimed particle of animation—a thing that belonged to nobody. In fact, I looked upon myself as one of the outside links in the chain of civilized society. If I could have become a part of the monument somebody would have looked at me, and have set their wits to work to find out my use.

My remaining biscuit, and the pump, served the second day. As night came on I felt my spirits sinking with the declining day. I seemed to fall into that hopeless state when the mind becomes benumbed, and loses it action over the system. The first houseless night in London passed away, and still I strayed about like a ghost without a home. When the morning was breaking I was wandering along the dull hazy streets. Through the course of the second day, I continued walking on, and sometimes unconsciously found myself at the same place from which I set out. I had no aim, and I must have been looking for a miracle. The second night came, and I shivered along the long, cold, dreary streets. I passed men who were reeling along after having left their senses and their money in the taverns. I saw scores of females who had graduated down to the lowest depths of human misery; and young men, haggard, and prematurely old, creeping along the streets like shadows in genteel rags. No man can form the most distant idea of the misery and human suffering that wanders the streets of London in silence during the cold dark hours when the provident and fortunate members of society are enjoying the sweets of calm repose, unless, like me, he has had to commune with his own feelings while wandering to leave time behind him in the *loud* silence of the night in the largest city of the world!

On the morning of the third day, I made up my mind to leave London. My good mentor seemed to draw me to the north. Kitty Dawson's image

116

came to my relief, and by an invisible power drew me in that direction. Somewhere about ten o'clock I found myself in Islington; I inquired the road for Barnet, and left the huge piles of brick and mortar behind me. When I had got about three miles clear of the town I came to an aqueduct where there was a toll of a penny to pay: when I told the man I had no money he let me pass on; if the fellow had used his eyes, he might have easily seen that I was perfectly valueless in point of cash. After I had passed the toll about a mile, I had the good fortune to meet a miracle at last. There are few men who have passed through life, but have met with some good angel in their dark hours of adversity; and such was my fate upon this, to me, memorable occasion. As I was going along the road, (which was a bye one), I met a clerical-looking gentleman coming in the opposite direction. I inquired if he could oblige me by directing me the nearest way to the Great North Road; he very readily gave me the proper directions, and while doing so seemed to take an interest in me. He inquired where I was going. I told him to Hexham. He then named several gentlemen who lived in the neighbourhood of that place, and asked me if I knew any of them. I informed him that I knew the whole of them by name, and their places of residence. He seemed satisfied with my answers, and as I was leaving he gave me half-a-crown. I expressed my gratitude to him in the fulness of my heart, and with tears in my eyes. As I passed on I inwardly thanked God; for if ever there was an angel of peace came across the path of any human being in distress, that man was one to me. Before I met him I was sinking into despair, I was weak with hunger, and both my mind and body were in a state of miserable dejection. This noble and generous act of an entire stranger dispelled the dark clouds which were brooding over my spirits, and filled me with hope, bright, elastic, and cheering. As I went on my way with renewed vigour, I had only one drawback to my complete happiness, and that was the degradation of my situation, which required to live on the bounty of others instead of my own industry.

I shortly arrived in Barnet, and my first care was to propitiate my gnawing stomach. I bought a twopenny loaf of bread, after which I went into a small public-house, and called for a half a pint of porter, which cost me another penny. While I was feeding in the tap-room, there was a solitary individual seated in a corner opposite to where I was; this man was evidently amused at my industry with the loaf, and my economy with the half-pint. I may observe that I only used the liquid to send down the partially masticated solids in what the Scotch call *bite* and *sup* fashion. Whatever the fellow thought, he had the good sense to remain silent until I finished my labour of love. I really believe that eating is the only positive pleasure a man can enjoy alone, and it is not surprising that it should be so, when we know that the vital part of the food becomes a part of our existence. All other pleasures would seem to require a species of co-partnery, and feed upon sympathy, which makes its way to his heart through some of his greedy feelings. When I had finished my repast, I was as contented in mind as if the house had been my own.

Since then I have had my limbs under mahogany covered with the most delicious viands, and the choicest wines, but the accumulation of three days' *sauce* gave that humble meal a zest I have rarely enjoyed. When my sleeping partner saw that I had finished, he observed that I appeared to have been hungry, and inquired if I was on tramp. I answered him in the affirmative; he then said that he, too, had been on tramp, and that it was no pleasant business, unless a man had sufficient money to make himself comfortable with. I agreed to this proposition; he continued his observations by saying he had been on the *fly* for a fortnight, and had spent all his money, and now the landlord would not trust him a pint of beer; but he said it is the way with the whole of them, when they get your money you may go to the devil! After asking me a number of questions, such as only a half-drunken man would ask, he put his hand into his pocket, and, with a solemnity fitting the greatness of the occasion, he put a good old-fashioned farthing into my hand. "Here," said he, "my lad, take this, it is all I have, but if it had been more you should be welcome to it." I could not help appreciating the man's kindness; his farthing was like the widow's mite—it was his all. I knew a circumstance, wherein a political acquaintance of mine had a five-pound note sent to him while in jail, by a gentleman holding a political creed of an opposite character; he was so much gratified with the generous act, that had his pecuniary wants not been greater than his gratitude, he would have had that note framed. In this instance, the case was similar with myself, if I could have afforded it, I would have retained the farthing as a memorial of the poor fellow's kindness. These two events were the preludes to a turn in my fortune for the better.

When I left Barnet, I had three hundred miles before me, and even when I should arrive at the place I had in view, I had nothing more to depend upon there than any other place in the wide world. My going in that direction was a thing I seemed to have no power over, for I felt as if I were impelled by an irresistible influence; so I allowed myself to drift down the stream of fate. With the two shillings and three-pence farthing in my pocket, my heart was as light as a strolling player's with the proceeds of half a benefit in his possession, and his *bills* unpaid. I went down the country by the way of Cambridge. As I was going into that town, it was on a Sunday evening, and beautiful spring weather, I met a number of young men and their sweethearts enjoying each other's society during their evening's walk. The sight of so much human happiness, which ought to have gladdened my heart, plunged me into profound grief, and I could almost have cursed the mother that bore me; the contrast of my own unhappy condition stared me full in the face, and I felt my mind full of wild thoughts as I hurried on. I was determined to husband my small stock of money; so I found quarters generally in some farmer's out house. I remember the day I passed between Cambridge and Ely. After having crossed one of the Cambridgeshire *flats* or marshes, I observed something like a sign-board fixed on the gable-end of a small cottage; the inscription on this board, instead of being "Licensed to retail tea and tobacco," was, "Therefore the name of this place is called *Golgotha* unto this day." I could not imagine what that little old-fashioned house could have to do with skulls; perhaps some dark deed had given it historical significance.

In Ely I slept in a common lodging-house, and while there I had a very flattering invitation to join two genteel young men in the regular *cadging* trade, both of whom had successfully passed their probation in the profession. After we had gone to bed (there being some fourteen or fifteen persons in the same room, composed of both sexes) the two youths fully initiated me into the mysteries of the business, and each of them told me his history. One had been an apprentice to a cabinet-maker, and having been entrusted by his master to lift a twenty-pound account, he cut with the money, and when it was all spent he took to begging; he had often been in *quod* (gaol), and could make plenty of *tin;* when one *dodge* failed he tried another. This hopeful young man was a native of London, and the son of a respectable tradesman. According to his own showing, he had often skinned the old *cove!* The other young man had robbed his father of thirty pounds, and bolted; he had tried the prigging, and had been *nabbed* four times, and had been twice on the mill: he didn't care anything about it. I have no doubt but both these poor lads had been induced to acts of theft by parties older than themselves.

The second day after this, as I was travelling between Lynn and Boston, I had to cross long *Sutton Wash*. I was told that this place could be forded by foot-passengers at low water. Immediately before I got to the Wash, I met a countryman on horseback, and inquired of him if I could ford it; his answer was, he thought I might. When the tide is in, this place is crossed by a ferry-boat; and at low water, foot passengers are carried over on horseback, the price charged in either case being sixpence. I had no such sum to spare, and therefore tucked up my trowsers and took the water. I got on quite smoothly until I arrived about the middle of the stream, when I was carried away with considerable violence. I thought my journey was about being ended; however, I struck out and swam in a slanting direction with the current. I was swept down the river for a considerable distance, and was pulled out by two of the ferrymen quite exhausted. These men took me up to the ferry-house, and after I got round a little, they gave me a glass of hot brandy and water. After my bath I travelled fourteen miles, and lay in a barn among straw all night.

Before I could get to Hull there was another difficulty before me, I required to cross the Humber from Great Grimsby, and the fare was then two shillings and sixpence. On the morning when the packet was to sail there was not a breath of wind sufficient to fill a lady's glove. The want of *Boreas'* bellows was a god-send to me. I got my passage on the condition that I should assist at the oar; this I gladly embraced. The distance we had to sail was twenty miles, there were several passengers on board, among which there was one gentleman who kindly gave me a shilling, another followed his example and gave me sixpence, and during the time I was aboard the boat, the men supplied me with plenty of food. This was a most timeous and fortunate supply.

Little better than a day's journey from Hull there was a sunny spot before me, where I was sure of a day's rest and good treatment. I therefore lost no time in making for Helmsley. This is a small market town in the East Riding of Yorkshire, about thirteen miles from Malton. At that time there was a Mr. Thomas Corbitt, who was head-gardener to Mr. Duncombe. I was upon most intimate terms with Mr. Corbitt's family, who resided in the neighbourhood of Hexham. When I arrived in Helmsley I was kindly received by Mr. Corbitt, although he had never seen me before. The fact was, he treated me more like a brother than a stranger. I was very badly off for clothing, and my shoes were in the last stage of decrepitude: the latter he kindly replaced by a new pair, and he supplied me with several necessaries I stood most in need of. When he found I had a desire to learn the hat-trade, he introduced me to a gentleman in town, who was then a small manufacturer. Here, then, the dark clouds which hung over me with their depressing influence were dispelled before the rising sun of my new destiny.

My new master was a kind, quiet, and good-hearted man, and while I was with him he treated me more like a father than an employer. I had been in my new situation about five weeks, when one day my master, having occasion to go from home upon business, and as there was not much I could do while he was absent, he said I had better go home and keep his mistress company until his return. My mistress was a young woman, and had one child, a fine boy about twelve months old. Before my master came home I had been as much teazed as ever Joseph was! After this I felt my situation to be painfully uncomfortable; indeed it became so intolerable that I made up my mind to leave. I told my benefactor that I had resolved to leave and go to Hexham, without explaining the cause. I had never been in any place I liked better than Helmsley, nor had I ever been so well treated by strangers. I was extremely sorry in leaving my kind employer without letting him know; indeed it was a poor way of repaying him for his generous conduct. However, I could not do otherwise.

The little insight I got into the business while in Helmsley was sufficient to introduce me into the trade. I took the road for the north, and called upon the trade as I went along. The morning I left Darlington I had a very hard day's work, having travelled fifty-four miles. On the evening of the third day after leaving Helmsley I came in sight of Hexham. I can never forget the thrill of delight which ran through my whole system as I looked down upon the town from a rising ground. I imagined that the dream of my life was about being realized. The only being in the world I cared for was there; for three years her very name had been a charm to me, and her secret influence had never ceased to draw me like a magnet of attraction. The sad history of my past life became a blank, and I looked forward to the future with the high-charged feelings of a slave in the hope of obtaining his liberty. I cannot express how I hated the life I had led. Up to this period I had been the slave of circumstances, and my whole life had been a continual round of strange vicissitudes. The Fates had tossed me about in the blanket of adversity until I was frequently sick of my existence. In my early boyhood I had narrowly escaped going to the other world by water four times. Once I was rescued by a sailor, after having fallen over the quay at Aberdeen. The next was in attempting to ford the Liddle, when I was carried away by the stream, and had the good fortune to be hauled ashore by a good-natured blacksmith. My next watery mishap was in tumbling over one of the dock-walls in Greenock, when I was fished out by a man with a boat-hook. My last was in having fallen from a plank which lay across a stream: on this occasion I was pulled ashore by my step-father, who had a narrow escape with his own life on the occasion. I had also a narrow escape from being killed by a fall from the top of a high laden waggon in crossing *Shap Fell*.

It may appear somewhat strange to those who have not studied human nature, and observed the various *idiosyncracies* of men's minds, when I say that I was often the victim of a natural bashfulness; but such was the case. This feeling has frequently been a serious drawback to me, but I have no doubt that it has also saved me from much evil. My bashfulness was pretty well compensated for in a large stock of pride, and no little ambition: the latter feeling frequently prompted me to action when supineness must otherwise have existed. I had also a sufficient amount of self-esteem to inspire me with a proper regard for my person; and my love of approbation enabled me to value the good opinion of others. I feel satisfied, from my experience of human nature, that men owe much of this to their peculiar organization, as well as the directing influence brought to bear upon their opening passions.

When I was with Rooney, if I had had a strong, or even an ordinary tendency to dishonesty, he would have been the very man to have directed and matured it. If I had been naturally inclined to gambling, he would have drilled me into its mysteries with all the care of a father: and if my combativeness had been large, he would have given me frequent opportunities of exercising myself in the delightful science of pugilism. It was, therefore, so far fortunate that the peculiar combination of my own moral and physical elements saved me from the destruction which otherwise must have been the consequence of my connection with that unmitigated knave! Although I have worked my way up from the substratum of society, and have been enabled to take my place among the industrious members of the community, I know that my life was frequently upon the turning point, when the merest accident would have made me a vagabond without redemption. There are many thousands of human beings in this country whose destinies to all appearance have been cast for them at their births; and I am aware that in numerous instances, if they had had the desire to change their positions, there could scarcely have been a possibility of their being able to effect it. You will therefore observe, that it is an easy thing for men to fall in society, but a very difficult matter to rise!

I may here mention, that I had two little circumstances connected with my person which were often opposed to my interest, whereas they should have been in my favour. I always carried an air of gentility in my personal appearance when I was young; my address was good, and my tongue was free from anything in the shape of provincialism. The consequence was, that these little things, which under different circumstances would have told in my favour, were only calculated to raise an unjust suspicion against me. In many instances, I have been taken for the son of respectable parents, and was supposed to have had a good education, and therefore must have been a *scapegrace*. I need not tell you that we are generally liable to judge from appearances, but in doing so we very frequently make serious mistakes.

Letter VII

My DEAR THOMAS,—I have now arrived at what may be termed the second grand crisis of my life. I had floundered through *nonage* in a manner somewhat strange, and in some instances not without being tinged with a sprinkling of romance. I am now, however, upon the eve of entering upon the real voyage of life with something like a man at the wheel!

The little I learned of the hat-making business in Helmsley I knew would be sure to procure me a situation as an apprentice. When I arrived at Hexham I learned that there was a young man just about out of his apprenticeship: I therefore made immediate application for the opening, and was accepted.[68] I entered upon trial, and remained so for three weeks. My new employer very unfortunately laboured under the *sin* of poverty. By the rules of the trade I required to be bound at the end of a month from my first entering. The stamp for my indenture would cost a guinea, not to mention the filling it up with the conditions! Here, then, was a serious difficulty at the very onset; and if I had been turned inside out I was not worth two shillings in the world. I believe when a man has fairly got into the stream of fortune there is no staying his onward progress. While I was on my probation month there was a young lady, who was then verging into that equivocal age where love lingers between hope and despair. This maiden had formed a sort of forlorn attachment to my humble person. Being a near relative of my master's, she kindly aided me in riveting my chains without compromising her maiden delicacy. Poor girl, I was obliged to her both for her cash and affection; the first, I hoped to be able to repay, but the latter was just one of those things I had no power over.

On the evening when I was bound there was an old lady present, the widow of a late hat-manufacturer. She was then carrying on the business by the assistance of two of her sons. She had known me for a long time, and was therefore fully aware of the sort of life I had led. While my indenture was

[68] Hatting was long established in Hexham and was the second largest industry after tanning and leather. As with the trade in general, the numbers in employment underwent seasonal fluctuation and at this time there were 16 master hatters in the town who employed between 35 and 40 hands in the summer and rarely more than 20 in the winter. The total population of Hexham in 1821 was 4,124. (A. B. Wright, *An Essay towards a History of Hexham*, Alnwick, 1823, pp. 23–7; Allen B. Hinds, *A History of Northumberland*, vol. III, pt. 1, Newcastle, 1896, p. 270).

being filled up she said, "*Noo, Jeamie, ye'r aboot* entering into an engagement *ye'll* never fulfil. *Tak'* my word *for't,* ye'll never see the end of a seven years' apprenticeship, as *shere* as I'm a *leeving* woman! I *ken*," said she, "ye've seen ow'er *muckle* o' the *warld, an'* been ow'er *muckle* your ain master to undergo the drudgery of a hatter's apprentice. But," she continued, "If ye be a *gude* lad, and stick to yer *wark,* I'll do *ony* thing for ye that lies in my power." The good old lady fulfilled this promise whenever I gave her the opportunity of serving me. I had the pleasure of falsifying her predictions, but she did not live to see the end.

I have mentioned that this sort of feeling continually opposed my settling down in life. There was not one in a thousand who knew me but would have expressed the same opinion. This sentiment was strengthened materially by my age; and when you reflect upon the drudgery and menial duties of a hatter's apprentice at that time you cannot feel surprised. Being the only apprentice in the house for two years, I had all the water to carry from a considerable distance. Twice a-week I had to collect stale *lant* (urine), from a number of places where it was preserved for me: I carried this fragrant liquid on my head, and had often the agreeable pleasure of having it streaming down my face. When I was bound I knew all my duties, but I had firmly made up my mind under every trial to conquer, and I may say, that firmness was not the least prominent trait in my character. About a fortnight after I had entered upon my new duties, the harvest set in, and as my master was not busy, I got liberty to spend a fortnight in reaping. The money I earned at this employment enabled me to purchase such clothing as I stood most in need of. When I tell you that my salary, after being boarded and lodged, was only one shilling a-week for the first year, with a rise of an additional sixpence each year, you will agree with me, that the produce of my harvest labour was a very acceptable relief. Small as this sum was, I could have managed with it very well; but poor Rutherford (my master's name) could very seldom afford to allow me to be cashier of my own money.

It was in this year (1822) that that exemplary monarch, George the Fourth, paid his Scotch subjects a royal visit; and while the natives of *Auld Reekie* were bowing their loyal knees before their virtuous king, the unsettled state of the monetary system was crushing and paralyzing both the commerce and industry of the nation. About this time, too, Castlereagh had quietly given himself a passport to the other world; and there were some among the people who thought there was something like retribution in the act. From this date up to 1832, the working men of Great Britain continued to take a lively interest in all the great political questions of the day. George the Fourth had broken faith with his Irish subjects upon the Emancipation question; after which Dan O'Connell formed the Catholic Association. This combination rallied to its standard some of the most brilliant talent which Ireland could boast of, and many of the peals of thunder which shook the walls of Concilia-tion Hall vibrated throughout the length and breadth of the nation. The artillery of the association continued to pour the red-hot balls of its eloquence into the camp of the enemy; and such was the efficiency of its practice, that the Government required, upon more occasions than one, to fortify the State garrison by special Acts of Parliament. Notwithstanding these precautions, O'Connell continued to demolish both the entrenchments and the batteries of the enemy as fast as they were formed. At one time the Government imagined that the wily lawyer was completely hemmed in by a line of *circumvallation:* even then he slipped through their meshes, and set their power at defiance, and, as a consequence, rose higher in the estimation of his countrymen. From this time forward, for many years, Cobbett continued to expose the shortcomings of the Government, and point out to the people the numerous abuses which were allowed to exist. His terse Saxon style of language appealed to the sense and understandings of all classes. *Blackwood*, then in the zenith of its Tory power, tried to put the plebeian down, but the Corinthian lance only "*dirled* on the bane."[69] *The Black Dwarf*, too, thundered away at the state paupers, and made the character and condition of a large portion of the proud aristocracy pass in review before the people. About this time the British press was beginning to assume a tone of something like independence. The trial of *Muir, Palmer* and Skirving,[70] combined with the Peterloo affair in Manchester, had roused a feeling of indignation in the minds of many men who were not of any party or political creed, against the tyrannical conduct of the governing party; indeed, it seemed evident to the minds of a large portion of the thinking community, that corruption and misrule had become intolerable, and that it was time the nation should be allowed to breathe the air of freedom!

So far as my new condition was concerned, I may say that my existence was just as unvaried and monotonous as that of any ploughman. I certainly had to put up with many inconveniences, and suffer much hardship; but I knew that the most of the difficulties I had to encounter were the common lot of all the apprentices in the trade; I knew, too, that the battle of life was before me; and I had firmly made up my mind to overcome every difficulty. My conduct made me many warm and generous friends, who really took a pleasure in serving me; and when I had a holiday to spend, I never wanted a home in the most pleasant meaning of the term.

You will agree with me, that there is something strange and unaccountable in what I am going to relate. After I returned to Hexham, the being who had exercised such a mysterious influence over my life and actions for such a length of time passed from my memory like an indistinct shadow in a dream.

[69] Struck sharply on the bone. The phrase is used by Burns in *Death and Doctor Hornbook* (l. 95).
[70] The trial and transportation of the "Scottish martyrs" took place in Edinburgh back in 1793–94 and Burn's reference here is further evidence of the strong continuity of the radical tradition in the North. Their memory was constantly evoked during the Reform Bill crisis in Scotland; several biographies were published, portraits were issued by the radical press, and subscriptions were collected for a monument.

It seems to me now, when I reflect, that her guardian spirit had fulfilled its mission, and quietly withdrew! When I had frequent opportunities of both seeing and speaking to her, I passed her as I would an utter stranger. How this cold insensibility in regard to her took possession of my mind I never could say. For three years she had held me in the most delightful bondage. For her, I had aspired to the position of a free and independent member of society, and when I was about realizing the glorious dream of my life, the magic of her mysterious power vanished; the sweet spell was broken by some strange power, and she faded from my memory like a thing that had never rested there! Twice I had been the subject of strong embodiments of unaccountable thought: the one was pure and unalloyed hatred, and I never knew the cause! the other seemed love in its most dreamy and holy sense,— indeed, there was not a particle of dross in the desire. Before I had seen my father I knew not what sort of a man he was, either in person or character, and yet I hated him as if he had been my most deadly enemy. It was certainly a strange idea for one so young to have been possessed with an ill-will against a person he never knew, and more particularly when that person was his own father. There was something in my love, too, if I can call it by such a name, which was equally unaccountable; and the vanishing of that feeling without any apparent cause was a crowning mystery. When men begin to analyse their thoughts, I believe they will find many feelings, and even lasting impressions, which are calculated to exercise powerful influence over their actions, baffle all their philosophy to account for them by the ordinary rules of investigation. It may be, that there are certain occasions when we are liable to receive impressions from invisible agencies, or perhaps such things may arise from the peculiar *idiosyncracies* of our nature; there is also a possibility that we are sometimes acted upon by sympathetic susceptibilities, the origin of which lies veiled in the impenetrable *arcana* of the Divine will!

The time is nigh at hand when my suspended affections are again to be brought into action. When I had been in Hexham about twelve months I was accidentally introduced to a young woman whose name was also *Kitty*. We shortly became mutually attached to each other, and all the feeling I had had for the other returned, with its train of pleasing anxieties, and were concentrated in my new love. After this I continued to do my duty, and perform my ordinary avocations, *minus* my heart, for nearly three years. This young woman was a servant to a maiden lady in the same street in which I lived; her parents were honest, industrious people; and as to herself, never a more single-hearted, amiable, and virtuous woman, adorned the home of a working man. The first Kitty may be said to have been an ideal creature of my affections; but in your mother I found the realization of my most sanguine dreams.

After I had been with Rutherford between three and four years, he was compelled to relinquish his business. For some time he had manfully struggled against a strong spring-tide of pecuniary difficulties, and at last was fairly stranded upon the lee shore of insolvency. For about three months before he yielded up the commercial ghost we were frequently without food, or the means of obtaining any, so that we may be said to have been regularly starved out. On leaving, or rather having been left, I obtained another employer in the town without loss of time, and one whose position was very different to that of my late employer's. When I entered upon the duties of my new situation I found my condition materially altered for the better, and I had no cause to complain either of lack of work or scarcity of food.

In the year 1826, the Northumberland militia was called up for a month's drill. Mrs. Ritson (my employer's wife), with the regard and affection of a mother, sent me to my military probation with every necessary, both for my comfort and personal appearance.

My first appearance in the character of a soldier was certainly the most ridiculous you can well imagine. The clothing for the men was served out to them without any regard to the principle of adaptation. At that time I was very slender in form, and of course did not require any great quantity of material to cover my person. I had my wardrobe bundled into my arms *sans* ceremony from the regimental store. The shoes were so capacious that, with a little enlargement, and a *Siamese* union, I might have gone on a voyage of discovery in them! The chapeau, instead of being a *fit*, was an extinguisher, and when I put it on I required to bid the world good night! The longitude of the trowsers was of such a character that I could not find my bearings in them, and the coat was of such ample dimensions that if I had had a family it would have made a cover for the whole of us. I dare say you have some idea how an ordinary sized man requires to be made up for the representation of Sir John Falstaff; my case was something similar. The hat was flattered to remain on my head by being padded to such an extent that it looked like a *capital* accidentally placed on a wrong pillar, and I was obliged to hold my head as if I was balancing a pole on the top of it. The coat required two or three others as companions to keep it from collapsing and burying me in its folds; and the trowsers put me in mind of two respectable towns in France, being *Too-loose* and *Too-long!* The shoes were the only part of my *uniform* I could discard without a violation of military rule, so I studied economy for the state by wearing my own. When I found myself fairly encased in my new military costume, my identity was completely *non est*. In this guise I made my *début* on parade, in the character of a defender of my country. So far as appearance was in question, I think you could almost have made a better looking soldier out of a bundle of party-coloured rags, with a monkey stuffed into the middle of it.

During the first week of my sojourn in Alnwick, nearly the whole of the men might be seen running to and from each others quarters, changing coats in one place, hats in another, and trowsers where counterparts were to be found. On the whole, I never remember to have seen such a set of grotesque figures and truly fantastic looking beings. The tall, raw-boned fellows, were moving about with their wings protruding through the sleeves of their coats, and their legs a full day's march beyond the natural boundaries of their *bitruncated* hose. Many of the stout men were like big boys pressed into little boys' cast-off clothing, and the little fellows were like babies dressed in their father's garments. By the end of the first week most of the men got themselves bartered into something like soldier fashion. I may mention that the summer of 1826 was both the warmest and the dryest in the memory of man. The grain crop was very good; but there was little straw, and in some cases the oats had to be pulled up by the root.

I passed muster as a front-rank man during the four weeks of my peaceable duties, and returned somewhat improved in the use of my *understandings*. During this year one of the severest parliamentary election contests ever witnessed in England took place in Northumberland. The county was then represented by two members, and upon this occasion there were four candidates—two Tory and two Whig. Matthew Bell and the Honourable Thomas Liddle were the exponents of the good old stand-still principle; and the Whig, or liberal creed, was supported by Lord Howick (now Earl Grey) and Thomas Wentworth Beaumont. The election cost the contending parties somewhere about £190,000. Mr. Beaumont's share in the expense of this foolish contest amounted to upwards of £90,000. A very large portion of the money spent upon this memorable occasion was paid to tavern-keepers for brutalizing the people! Many of the bacchanalian scenes I witnessed were a disgrace to all the parties connected with the affair. During the fourteen days which the polling continued the county remained in a state of feverish excitement: the constant and unlimited use of intoxicating liquors kept the mad passions of a great number of the people up to the boiling point. Religion, too, was dragged in to sanctify the unholy proceedings, and strengthen the claims of the two gentlemen who had the honour of supporting the Church and State. This was the good old system by which our virtuous legislators gained the portals of St. Stephen's, through the stomachs of their moral and religious supporters. It is true, we are not much better in the management of these things yet; but it is so far satisfactory to know, that some of our modern legislators have either got ashamed of the beer-barrel, or they have been seized with the "damnation o' the expenses"; so it is just possible we may have our elections conducted upon a more rational principle in future. I sometimes think that nothing could afford a better proof of our real English love of liberty than a contested parliamentary election. During these patriotic occasions the people were allowed the humane privilege of breaking each other's heads to their hearts' content. I have often seen bodies of men as industrious at this sort of employment as if it was the only real concern of their lives. It is true, the opposing parties were paid for their labours. I merely mention this to show, that however *con amore* the unwashed went to their work, the honourable candidates were no less interested in the brutal conduct of their partisans.

At this time the pocket boroughs existed in all their accommodating usefulness, for the special protection of certain landowners, and the support of the Church and glorious Constitution! There were numbers of men in those days who were so innocently green, that they imagined the equilibrium of the world depended upon the inviolability of these sacred vested rights. To have removed one rotten stone from the State, in their estimation would have brought the whole fabric of the Constitution to the ground, and reduced the world to *chaos* once more! Since that time the machinery of the State has been tinkered a good deal, and on the whole I think has been considerably improved. Nevertheless, old Mother Church holds on by her *golden* connection, and the Constitution, though it occasionally requires patching, is something like the Jew's old watch—"Better than new."

When I had been about five years at my trade, I began to have certain notions of manhood. During three years I had been labouring under a continual state of counter-irritation. The fact of the matter was, that I was ten thousand fathoms deep in the indescribable regions of love, and I had some vague idea that matrimony would be the only legitimate cure. My prospects for keeping a wife were certainly of a very hazy character; but I had a world of hope, and my intended had an unlimited confidence in me. My firmness had frequently dragged me through the mire of difficulty, while poor helpless Caution, instead of being a leader, was left to follow in the wake of her more reckless neighbour. Indeed, few men with so much experience could have been blessed with a smaller amount of calculation, or a better stock of real sanguine dreamy speculation. If ever there was a man who should have realized a fortune by building castles in the air, I am that man; but I shall have more to say upon this subject by-and-by. Suffice it to say, that I made up my mind to merge the lover in the responsible character of a husband. For this purpose, I went through the dutiful ordeal of obtaining the consent of all the parties who were interested in the matter, and I became the happy husband of a good and virtuous wife. My employer allowed me ten shillings a week, and with this sum we were "surpassing rich," if not in worldly *gear*, we certainly were in the best affections of the heart. If we could have lived upon love, we could have gladly left the dull insipid world behind us. We soon found out the disagreeable fact, that those who are yoked in the traces of humanity, however much they may seem spiritualized, must continue to draw their earthly vehicles along the highway of time, during which the machinery must be carefully oiled. Love is no doubt a very pretty poetical passion, but unless it be fed upon something more substantial than mere sentiment, and dreamy hope, like a wick without oil, it soon loses its sweet flame. After I had been married a short time, I had a quarrel with my master's son, and having been put on my defence by his unmanly treatment, I returned him payment in kind such as he had not anticipated. Had I remained longer, after having humbled the principal manager in the business, I knew my position would have been anything but comfortable; I therefore demanded my indenture. I never regretted this step, and I was fully borne out in the act by the whole of my friends. The young man I quarrelled with was an ignorant, presuming, petty tyrant, and as long as he kept his hands off me, I could very well afford to put up with his empty declamation.

Up to this time I was not able to write my own name, and while I was serving my apprenticeship in Hexham I had no opportunities to learn. Thanks to my step-father, I could read a little, and never failed to turn it to account when I had the opportunity. During my stay in Hexham I had no means of seeing anything in the shape of literature; neither of the families in which I had lived possessed the most distant taste for reading, and as far as my memory serves me, I am not aware of having seen a book read in either of their houses.[71] In the latter end of the year 1826, a friend made me a present of an old edition of Chevalier Ramsay's *Life of Cyrus*.[72] This little volume opened up to my inquiring mind a rich field of useful knowledge. The appendix to the work contained the *heathen mythology*: this part of the work completely fascinated me, and for a considerable time became my constant companion. I had now a continual craving to pry into the mysteries of literature; heretofore the glorious world of man's thought had been a sealed book to me, and I longed most ardently to hold communion with those master-minds who had scattered the beautiful flowers of their intelligence in the garden of humanity. My mind had a decided intellectual bias, but unfortunately, it was firmly chained down in the dungeon of ignorance, and I had none to assist me in breaking the fetters. I believe there have been many men who have become ornaments to society, and benefactors of their kind, whose difficulties were greater than mine; but if I ever possessed the capacity, it was never properly directed, and, on the whole, I think I had more taste than talent.

After I had made suitable arrangements as to my future line of conduct, I left the home I had so long sighed for. After my wife was properly cared for in my absence, I made up my mind to go to Dublin; so I travelled to White-haven, and took my passage aboard of a collier, and had the pleasure of being tossed about in the Irish channel for seven days, and as many nights. When I arrived in the city where "O'Connell was spouting, and Lady Morgan making tay," I found there was no opening for a turnover apprentice. I spent three days in seeing the Dublin lions, and was much pleased with the public buildings and the general features of the city. The population of

---

71 Wright commented in 1823 that "The lower class of people, even now, may be less civilized than their neighbours, although an amazing improvement has been wrought of late years." The pace of improvement was accelerated in 1825 by the founding of the Hexham Mechanics and Scientific Institution which had 100 members and a library of 691 volumes by 1831. (Wright, op. cit., p. 112; *A Catalogue of the Library of the Hexham Mechanics and Scientific Institution*, Hexham, 1831).

72 Andrew Michael Ramsay's *The Travels of Cyrus* first appeared in English in 1727 and was continuously in print throughout the eighteenth century. The book followed the wanderings of its hero throughout the Ancient world and thereby introduced its readers to a wide range of classical history, mythology and theology.

Dublin was certainly the most extraordinary I had ever witnessed. From the beggar to the peer, all was animation, and I certainly never had been in any place where a piously disposed person could procure blessings at so cheap a rate: a few coppers were sufficient to bring down a shower of the choicest benedictions upon the astonished donor; but on the other hand, a crooked look, or a word of reproach, would be sure to inundate the imprudent wight in a torrent of imprecations! The Dublin beggars, in their unmitigated rags, are a unique specimen of the *genus homo;* amid their mountains of motly rags there is a world of *devil-ma-care*, light-hearted fun and humour, and their ready wit sparkles in exuberance from the fountain of originality.

The cabmen in all countries are a peculiar race of men, but the Dublin carmen exceeded all that I had ever seen, both as to their manners, habits and dress. The furniture of the horses, and the clothing of these fellows, were of such a character that it was really dangerous for a man whose risible faculties were easily excited, to look at them; and their mellifluous brogue and soft blarney were irresistible, when used in pumping the feelings of their patrons.

I remember a very good anecdote of one of these men while driving a gentleman past the Bank; the day was both cold and foggy; the gentleman looked up to the Bank, and observed to the carman that he thought there had been figures on the top of the Bank. "An' sure, your honour, so there are, when the weather is fine; but, bedad," said he, "they would be great fools to come out sich a could day as this is any how." In these times a *tinpinny* piece would bring forth the exclamation of "may your honour *niver doie* until I wish it." While a *fippinny* would produce an arch lear, full of the most bewitching roguery, with an inquiry at the end of it, wishing to know if the donor was the only one of his family, or if it was the first time his honour had "*iver* been in the company of a *gintleman?*" The warmth of Irish feeling is surprising; but it entirely depends upon the direction it takes, whether it be pleasant or otherwise; the difference between a smile of affection and the blow of an enemy is often as transient as a flitting moonbeam.

On the whole, I was delighted with my Dublin trip. On the fourth day I took my passage aboard of a steam vessel for Liverpool. This tub of a ship was freighted with one of the most heterogeneous cargoes of men and brutes I ever witnessed. The evening on which we sailed was cold and somewhat stormy; it was in January, 1828. After we had cleared the bar it came on to blow a heavy gale from the north-east. Among the deck passengers there was a man and his wife with seven children; the whole of this family were like living mummies enveloped in rags. Before the vessel had got out to sea, they had taken up their quarters in the front of the raised quarter-deck, which was nearly amid-ship. When the old lumbering vessel began to smell the strong head wind, she tumbled through the waves as if she *did not care a devil* for them, and she washed her living decks as if delighted at the misery she was causing. I think I shall never forget the truly ludicrous, and at the same time melancholy scene I witnessed with this poor family; the steamer had shipped a heavy sea, which rolled along her deck in all the fury of water seeking its level: when the rolling wave reached the quarter-deck it rebounded with violence, and ingulfed the poor hapless family in its boiling yeast. After the poor man had regained his breath, he addressed himself to some of the sailors, with a look and voice of the most profound melancholy: "Och, boys," said he, "can't ye take this *wather* away from us?" At the time the whole of the family were prostrated in sea-sickness. The sailors were too much accustomed to such scenes of human misery to feel for the sufferings of deck-passengers. Had the family been well dressed there might have been a little commiseration shown them; but as they were in rags, it was quite sufficient to shut the bowels of mercy against them. After some trouble, I got two passengers to lend a hand, and we placed the poor creatures aft the funnel, where they were partially sheltered from the storm.

After I arrived in Liverpool, I continued my journey until I came to Yorkshire. When I got as far as Bradford, I learned that there was an opening for a turnover in Otley. I, therefore, lost no time in making application, and was fortunate in being engaged with a Mr. Edward Walmsley, to complete the remainder of my time. The nature of my engagement gave me strong motives to industry. I was paid half journeyman's wages; and during the remainder of my apprenticeship, I made as much money as any journeyman in the place. Of course I had to work both late and early. I was only in Otley a short time when I was enabled to send for my wife. I may look upon the time I spent in this little town as by far the best applied portion of my whole life. I had a kind and generous master, plenty of employment, good health, and a willing mind; and I was blessed with a loving wife, and was without care or anxiety for the morrow. During the first twelve months I was in Otley, I read all the historical works in the only circulating library in the place, which was then kept by a Mr. Walker. I also greedily devoured all the information I could obtain from the newspapers, by which means I became familiar with the leading topics of the time. On the Saturday evenings, I generally spent an hour or two in the bar-parlour of the New Inn. This room was regularly attended by a number of respectable tradesmen of the town The consequence was, that I became easy in my manners, and improved my conversational powers in no small degree; and I can say without egotism, that while I frequented that house, I was looked up to as an authority upon many of the leading questions of the day. On the last day of 1828, I gave a hostage to the State in your birth, and if anything was calculated to increase my happiness, this event could not fail to do it.

The year 1829 may be looked upon as one of the most eventful in the history of the first half of the nineteenth century. During a great portion of this year, the whole country was in an alarming state of excitement. The labours of the Catholic Association were about producing their desired effect. The Duke of Wellington and Sir Robert Peel had opposed the Catholic claims with all the moral force they could bring to bear upon the question; but at length, seeing those claims could be no longer resisted with safety to the state, they made a virtue of necessity, and carried the measure, in the face of taunts and vollies of abuse from their former colleagues. During six months, the Anti-Catholic spirit was in a continual state of effervescence; and petitions and counter-petitions were poured into the Houses of Parliament in waggon-loads. All the trickery of low cunning, and the malignancy of sectarian zeal, with no small portion of honest hatred, were brought to bear against the passing of this measure.

The first scene in the opening drama of religious toleration and social equality was enacted; and what is worthy of special notice, the leading performers were men who had all their lives strongly opposed everything in the shape of progress. The Test and Corporation Act, as a prelude, had been abrogated, by which means the national stigma was wiped away from the Dissenters, and men once more began to breathe the atmosphere of rational freedom. From this time forward, the Legislature received an infusion of new members,—I mean such as were not bound hand and foot to the aristocracy; but it was not until four years after, that the House of Commons fairly began to be innoculated with the middle-class element. The Reform Bill, although it was only an instalment of the people's rights, produced a new era in our national history. When we take a quiet, retrospective view of the state of affairs in Great Britain in the early part of the present century, and compare it with the present, I think it will be admitted, that as a nation we have much cause to feel grateful. The criminal code, which was a disgrace to us as a Christian people, has been revised and greatly ameliorated, by being purged of its sanguinary character. The fiscal regulations have also been modified, by which means many of the unnatural restrictions which crippled the commerce and industry of the nation, have been wisely removed. It may be remarked, that every step the Legislature has taken in the right direction has resulted in the renewed energy of the people, and the extension of our commercial operations. Of all the men in existence, statesmen are the last to leave the beaten track of *routine;* and it may be affirmed with truth, that our law-givers have been dragged up to their duty, rather than prompted to it by a sense of justice.

Letter VIII

My DEAR THOMAS,—I am now about entering an entire new phase of life. I have broken the chain which bound me for seven years. In the early part of my apprenticeship I had much to suffer; a great deal of which was made more *poignant* by my age. But I bore all without a murmur, and found consolation in hope, and a bright future. After I had been little better than twelve months in my situation, I got my brother Robert bound apprentice to the same business, with a hatter in the same street where I resided. This relieved my mind a good deal, as I considered myself responsible, in a great measure, for his well-being. By that time Robert was a big, raw-boned lad. For some time he continued very diligent and attentive to his work; but after he had served twelve months he left hat-making to those who were more disposed to the business than he was, having enlisted into the Twenty-fifth, or King's Own Borderers. When I learned what he had done, my first impression was, that he had been taken advantage of, and I was determined to have him off. However, when I saw him I found my mistake: he had fully made up his mind to the profession of arms. In the course of a few days, he was sent off to the *Depôt*, which was then in Edinburgh, and I saw no more of him for several years. From the time I left my mother in Girvan, I had never learned whether she, and the rest of the family, were living or dead. I might therefore say, that all my family ties were severed.

My apprenticeship expired in November of 1829, and I remained in Otley until the 3rd of January, 1830, when I removed your mother and yourself to Sandhoe, where she was to remain with her father and mother until I should be able to send for her. I travelled direct to Edinburgh, and reached there in a few days after leaving Hexham. When I arrived in Auld Reekie, business was in a very dull state. However, I obtained employment, and was able to send for my wife in less than six weeks. During the month of May, while in Edinburgh, we had an addition to our family, in the birth of your oldest sister. About this time there were two little circumstances occurred, which were matters of gossip for the time being. The one was the coronation of William the Fourth, and the other was the death of Sandy McKay, in a prize-fight between him and Simon Byrne. Just twelve months after this, Byrne was repaid in the same coin by being killed in a pugilistic encounter with Deaf Burke.

In the early part of the year 1827, I had occasion to go to Morpeth upon business, and while there (which was from Saturday to Monday morning) I put up at a small public-house. I had for a bedfellow a little Scotchman, who was then carrying on business as a draper in a place on the east coast called Bamborough. On the Saturday night I could scarcely get any rest for the loquaciousness of this person; but on the Sunday evening we had a rather warm discussion upon a religious subject. The man was full of strong prejudices, and altogether evinced an unmanly and contracted disposition. During our argument, I had treated him with a feeling of pity for his peculiar littleness of mind. When we went to bed on the Sunday night, he never opened his ungodly jaws; having to rise early in the morning, I bade him farewell, but such was the vindictive character of the creature that he took no notice of me. This person was about the most self-righteous animal I ever met with. I had not long been in Edinburgh, when there was a most brutal murder perpetrated in Haddington. The victims of the murderer were his sister-in-law and his niece. After he had committed the foul deed, he covered the body of the young woman with a carpet, and threw that of her mother into a pig-stye alongside of the swine. The murderer suffered the extreme penalty of the law while I remained in Edinburgh. When *Hemans* came out on the drop, what was my astonishment at recognising, in the condemned felon, my Morpeth bedfellow! He died as he had lived, a canting hypocrite.

I remained in Edinburgh until the first week in August, when I removed to Glasgow, in consequence of the slackness of trade. Those who can remember 1830, will know that commerce was in a miserable state through the whole of the United Kingdom. I obtained employment in Glasgow, where I worked until the 18th of October; having lost my work a second time through the slackness of business, I left my family, and went on tramp in search of employment.[73] I travelled 1400 miles upon this occasion ere I could obtain work.[74] At last I got shopped in Sherborne, in Dorsetshire. I remained in this place for rather better than two months, during which time I sent ten pounds to my family, and purchased myself a suit of clothes. My employer in this place was a very kind gentlemanly person, and was anxious that I should send for my family, and remain with him; however, I had made up my mind to go to London.

[73] The system of going on the "tramp" in the hatting trade at this time was described as follows: "A fair man has the privilege of what is called '*turns upon tramp*,' that is, if he cannot obtain work in the town where he resides, or has an inclination to *travel*, he may journey or *tramp* to the next; should any of the *fraternity* be there, and he wishes to get '*shopped*' he is '*asked for*' by one in that factory, (no man being allowed to ask for himself), if unsuccessful, there are two nights' lodging for him, two pots of strong beer, bread and cheese, and a shilling or two to forward him to the next town. The *money turn* in London is five shillings, but no man is entitled to a *second* turn in one place, until after the expiration of six months from his receiving the first." (R. Lloyd, *Lloyd's Treatise on Hats*, 2nd ed., 1819, p. 32.) See also Anon, *The Hat Maker's Manual* (London, 1829), p. 38; and the introduction, p. 19.

[74] A fairly typical "tramp" for the period. The "tour" of a brushmaker in the 1820s was over 1,200 miles, and for the compositors in the 1850s it was as much as 2,800 miles. (E. J. Hobsbawm, "The Tramping Artisan" in *Labouring Men*, London, 1968, p. 34).

Before I left the west of England, the working classes were in a fearful state of suffering and excitement in that part of the country. During my short sojourn, the condition of the country was alarming in the highest degree; vast numbers of the agricultural labourers were in a state bordering upon starvation. When large bodies of men are reduced to suffering from the want of even common necessaries of life, it cannot be supposed, that they are in a condition to be reasoned with by men whose stomachs are well lined. These poor people had no clear idea of the cause to which they owed their misery; and what was still worse, they did not know where to seek a remedy. The consequence of this unfortunate state of things was, that the people did what they often do under similar circumstances, namely, took revenge upon those who were more comfortably situated than themselves, by destroying their property.

In 1830, a very large quantity of farm produce was destroyed by the torch of the midnight incendiary. Of course, such conduct was worse than madness, and in the end was sure to rebound upon themselves. In passing through Devonshire, Somersetshire, and Dorsetshire, I frequently observed threatening notices posted upon public places. While I was in Sherborne, there was likely to have been a fearful tragedy enacted. An agrarian disturbance had taken place in a neighbouring village about three miles from the town. This village being in Somersetshire, while Sherborne was in Dorsetshire, it required some special *routine* on the part of the authorities of the latter place, ere they could send assistance into a neighbouring county. The road from Sherborne to the village in question, passed through a deep cutting, and left a perpendicular wall of many feet on each side. The rioters had learned the time that a large posse of special constables were to set out, and they made up their minds that not a man of them should return to tell the tale of the result of their expedition. In order to carry their diabolical plan into execution, somewhere about a hundred of them posted themselves upon each side of the embankment with a quantity of large stones ready to hurl down on the heads of the constables. Somehow the infernal plot was discovered in time to save the lives of the men, and prevent the infamy of such a dreadful proceeding. I believe if the matter had not been discovered in time, that it would have been next to impossible for a man to have escaped [75]

These agrarian outrages were a sort of second edition to the disturbances which took place in Yorkshire and Lancashire in 1819, when the poor factory operatives were driven to acts of madness, in destroying the machinery, which was then being introduced into the manufacturing of textile fabrics. Some simple-minded people imagine that such lawless aggression could not take place now, in consequence of the improvement of the moral condition of the working classes. I am free to admit that the people, on the whole, have

[75] There was an outbreak of "illegal assemblies", arson and machine breaking in north-east Dorset in the second half of November 1830. See E. J. Hobsbawm and George Rude, *Captain Swing* (Penguin, 1973), p. 99.

been considerably improved in an intellectual point of view; but it must be remembered that the necessities of human nature are as urgent now as ever they were; and that philosophy and hungry bellies are as uncompanionable as they were at the siege of Jerusalem! Let us suppose either the middle or the upper classes in society exposed to the pangs of hunger, without the means of relief, while surrounded by abundance,—I would ask what would they do? It is the simplest thing in the world for men in comfortable circumstances to moralize upon the sins and weaknesses of human nature,—herein lies the difference between theory and practice. I feel satisfied that man's nature will ever remain the same, and that his conduct will be regulated by the various circumstances of his position. There cannot be a better illustration of this fact than in the aptitude there is now being displayed by our army in the East, for learning the game of wholesale murder. I have no idea that man will ever cease to be a fighting animal, or that the bloody court of war will ever discontinue to be the last court of resort amongst even the most civilised nations.

I left Sherborne with some little reluctance, inasmuch as I both liked the place and my employer; but I found there was no dependence upon a continued regular employment. Immediately on my arrival in London I got shopped in Messrs. Mayhew and White's.[76] After I had been in town a few weeks, I found that either the foggy atmosphere, or the close confinement, did not agree with my health; I therefore only remained between two and three months. The world of London has seen a few changes since then. At that time the new bridge was finished to the approaches, and I believe it was opened to the public about two months after I left. While I was in town, Mr. Hunt, the member for Preston, in Lancashire, had a narrow escape of being lynched by a London mob, for the part he took on the Reform question; his life, however, was saved by the then new police, a body of men he had denounced only a short time before in no very measured language. The poor old Duke of Wellington displayed some uneasy feelings about this time, relative to the active character of the London unwashed, and, for fear they should pay him an unwelcome visit, he had his house ornamented with barricades, which I observe have outlived his Grace.

When I left town, I took my passage in a steam vessel for Leith; after which I went direct to Glasgow. I had been away from my family about eight months, my return had been anxiously looked for, and it was not without feelings of the most profound pleasure that I again returned to the bosom of my family. I have often realized the truth of the sentiment, that "there is no place like home." Since I had become a loyal and independent journeyman hatter, my career up to the time of my arrival at home had only been so-so. Before I went to the trade my life had been like a feather on the stream, and I was being continually whirled along from one eddy to another. My own impulses had little or nothing to do in producing the varied colours

76 A well-known firm, with premises at 128 and 129 Union Street, Borough.

137

in the ever-changing views of my living kaleidoscope. Notwithstanding my altered condition,—when you might suppose that judgment, matured by experience, should have taken the helm, and quietly steered me along the ocean of life, avoiding the quicksands of dissipation, and the misty headlands of speculation,—I am sorry to say you will find that my life still continued to be the mere sport of fate, and instead of regulating my feelings by the rule of reason, my passions dragged me headlong through the by-ways of folly. I do not wish you to understand that I was guilty of such conduct as would affect my character or position in society by indolence, roguery, or dissipation; on the contrary, I was both temperate and industrious, and I can say with the confidence of truth that I never lost half a day from my employment through drink as long as I continued the servant of another man. My follies were of quite a different character, which you will observe as you proceed with my narrative.

I obtained employment as soon as I arrived at home, and for some time diligently applied myself to my work. In this year (1831) the agitation for a reform in the House of Commons was gathering strength over the whole of Great Britain, and the whole of the manufacturing towns were beginning to show unmistakable symptoms of a determination that would not submit to a denial. Meetings were being held in Birmingham, Manchester, Sheffield, Leeds, Glasgow, and Edinburgh. These meetings, though generally composed of the working classes, were supported by several members of the aristocracy, many of the liberal gentlemen, and more especially by large numbers of the influential merchants and manufacturers. Before the passing of the Reform Bill, the country may be said to have been divided into two sections, namely, the Tories and the Whigs. The good old self-willed Tories had long possessed the power and patronage, and the consequence was, that the stream of government favour flowed in one channel, while the power was frequently used to crush the rights and liberties of the people. The liberal party were, therefore, galled by an unjust exclusion from the honours and emoluments of office. The real strength of the Tory party was in the machinery they had been able to keep in motion over the whole of the country. This machinery was composed of all the working elements under Government, from the lord-lieutenants of counties to petty constables. On the other hand, the Whigs were numerically strong, and carried with them a considerable moral power; but their greatest strength lay in the sympathy and hearty support of the working population. The antagonism of party feeling was mixed up with the whole of men's actions, and the nation seemed plunged in the boiling vortex of party strife.

A short time after I returned home, meetings were being held by the working-men in all the districts of Glasgow. The hatters, as a body, had never made themselves conspicuous by identifying themselves with any political movement; however, upon this occasion they became infected with the common feeling, and a general meeting of the trade was held in order to co-operate with the other public bodies. By this time the Radicals of the west of Scotland had appointed a central committee. This body of men had the power of calling general meetings of the combined trades, and also of organising large meetings of the whole working population; they also suggested the rate of the levies, which were made from time to time, in order to carry on the war. At the meeting of my own trade, I was appointed to represent the hatters at the general meetings of the delegates from the various bodies in the west of Scotland. My maiden speech at the first general meeting I attended got me elected a member of the Central Committee.[77] Here, then, I got into the gulf-stream of political agitation, and was carried onward with amazing velocity. I was seized with a wild enthusiasm, and for the time became politically mad; my pride, too, was flattered, by being made a leader in the camp of the people. From this date I took an active part in all the proceedings of both the Whig and the Radical parties in Glasgow for several years.

The Trades' Committee was entirely composed of working-men, and many of them would have done honour to the highest rank in society. Among them were several very excellent public speakers, who could acquit themselves in a becoming manner upon almost any subject. The fact was, the Committee was an excellent school for young beginners in the science of oratory and public debating, and many of the members made no small proficiency in the art. The gentleman who was chairman for this Committee for several years, (Daniel Macaulay,) was a small man with a large mind; he was both fluent in speech and quick in debate; and he possessed most excellent tact in keeping order in public meetings.[78] There was also a Mr. John Tait, brother-in-law to the chairman, who was looked upon as the Moses to the Radical camp. This gentleman drew out all the petitions, attended to the literary department, and exercised a general directing superintendance over the whole business of the Committee. Some of this man's literary compositions were both an honour to his head and his heart. His style was chaste, easy, and fluent, and he was quite at home upon almost every subject within the range of our business. Mr. Tait conducted the *Trades' Advocate* newspaper for many

---

[77] By 1830 the Glasgow trades, which had a tradition of involvement in collective political activity dating back to the 1817–20 period, had formed a United Committee of Trades Delegates which had a dual aim of promoting political reform and organizing a more integrated general trades union, and had close links with the Owenite co-operators in Glasgow. It held regular weekly meetings in the Trades Hall in Hanover Street and was involved in petitioning Parliament and organizing a series of mass meetings in Glasgow from the autumn of 1830 onwards. By November 1830 it claimed to represent 50,056 members. It is not clear exactly when the hatters joined, though they were certainly present in the demonstrations by September 1831. (*Herald to the Trades Advocate, passim; Loyal Reformers' Gazette*, May–September 1831; W. H. Marwick, *A Short History of Labour in Scotland*, Edinburgh, 1967, pp. 16–17; W. H. Marwick, *The Life of Alexander Campbell*, Glasgow, 1964, pp. 7–10; Alexander Wilson, *The Chartist Movement in Scotland*, Manchester, 1970, pp. 25–30.)

[78] Macaulay was a powerloom tenter, and died young on 7 September 1835.

years,[79] and during the whole time he stood deservedly high in the estimation of all classes in the community. The Committee had also its Poet Laureate, in the genial, honest, warm-hearted Sandy Rogers. This gentleman's political squibs frequently went the round of the British press. The social qualities of Mr. Rogers were of the most pleasing nature, and the amiability of his mind was happily reflected in his broad *soncy* face.[80] Though some of his satirical effusions were exceedingly pungent, they were entirely free from the gall of personal bitterness. His well-timed squib upon the Edinburgh gentry, during the visit of George the Fourth, will still live in the memory of those who were in the country at the time. I allude to

> "*Sawny noo* the King's come,
> *Doon* an' kiss his gracious *bum.*"

There was also another gentleman, of no mean poetical talent, a member of the Committee. This person's name was Mr. George Donald. I think it could scarcely be possible for any two men to be more dissimilar in their moral and social characteristics; poor Donald's very soul seemed to dwell in the dark regions of misanthropy, and to look at his doubting, snarling face, one would have imagined that his mind had never been enlivened by a single ray of hope. Poor fellow! he became a moral wreck, and an outcast among his kind. During the time I was a member of the Trades' Committee several highly talented young men became moral shipwrecks; such was the nature of the temptations they were exposed to, that not one in a hundred could bear up against them for any length of time. The social habits of the Scotch people are, in my opinion, much more calculated to lead young men astray than those of the English; and as the general beverage is whisky, it soon makes an inroad upon the nervous system sufficient to unfit men for business. I am not conscious of more than four members, out of all those who were actively engaged as committee-men, who did not become victims to the accursed vice of intemperance.

From the time I became a member of this body, until long after the passing of the Reform Bill, my mind was continually directed to some business connected with it. Indeed, there was rarely a single night in the week that my time was not occupied, either in sub-committees, or on the general

---

[79] The Trades Committee decided to launch the *Trades Advocate* in July 1830 but as a preliminary it published the 2*d*. unstamped *Herald to the Trades Advocate*, edited probably by Tait and possibly also by Alexander Campbell, which ran from 25 September 1830 until its suppression in May 1831. It was one of 34 unstamped periodicals published in Glasgow at this time. Like the Trades Committee it combined a fairly orthodox reformist political outlook with an espousal of ambitious Owenite co-operative and trade union programmes. It had a peak circulation of 4,500. It was succeeded by the *Trades Advocate* which ran until December 1833. No copies survive and it was probably edited not by Tait but by a schoolteacher called Warden. Tait's major enterprise was *The Liberator* which he edited from its foundation in November 1832 until his premature death on 19 October 1836. During this period it was much the most important radical paper with a circulation rivalling that of the *Glasgow Herald*.
[80] Jolly or plump.

140

committee. The most dangerous feature connected with these meetings was the everlasting adjournments to the taverns after business hours. In this little political squad every man was as full of self-consequence and legislative importance as if each were a political Atlas, and the battles of the committee were frequently fought a second time o'er the *gill stoup*. After I had been a member of the Trades' Committee about six months, I was also elected a member of the standing committee of the Reform Association. This body was çomposed of the resident gentry, merchants and manufacturers of the Whig party.[81] You may well imagine, that if I was not a person of importance, I thought myself so. I know that nothing great can be attained by man without the salutary spur of ambition, and that he who would honestly serve his fellow-men must be self-sacrificing. I dare say I was a good deal actuated by a true spirit of patriotism; but if I had done the same duty, with anything like the amount of zeal, to my family, I could now have looked back upon the past with a feeling of satisfaction very different to what I possess. In looking at my political career from my present position, I have reason to be thankful that I passed through the dangerous ordeal without sustaining greater loss. It was so far fortunate for me that I never indulged in drinking habits, and I never lost time from my employment.

During the year 1832, several open-air meetings were held on the Green of Glasgow. Some of these gatherings I believe to have been the largest political meetings ever held in Great Britain. The manifestation of public feeling displayed at some of these meetings produced no small effect upon the Legislature. The meeting which took place during the time the Duke of Wellington held the seals of office, and had the whole of the administrative power vested in his own person, gave such a demonstration of outraged feeling and disappointment, that the country became greatly alarmed, and the Sovereign was obliged to recall Earl Grey. During the whole of my life I never witnessed such a display of self-possessed determination. Many of the flags and emblems indicated the feelings of the people in the most unmistakeable language.[82] The portraits of the King and Queen were turned upside

[81] The Trades Committee made approaches to the Glasgow Reform Association at the beginning of 1831, suggesting the formation of a "Political Union of Scotland", "embracing as far as possible the higher, middle and lower classes." The G.R.A. finally agreed to reduce its 5s. subscription entry fee to 6d. and its quarterly subscription to 6d. and on 17 March elected a Committee of Management which included leading members of the Trades Committee but not, at this point, Burn. Alongside this tactical political alliance the Trades Committee was pursuing its attempt to form a general Trade Union for the Protection of Labour, the main function of which would be the provision of a strike fund to support a union in conflict with the employers. (See *Herald to the Trades Advocate*, January–May 1831.) The Reform Association never succeeded in attracting large numbers of working men, and on 16 November 1831 the Glasgow Political Union was founded in an attempt to create a more permanent alliance. (*Reformers' Gazette*, November, 1831; Peter Mackenzie, *Old Reminiscences of Glasgow and the West of Scotland*, vol. II, Glasgow, 1890, pp. 262–7; Fiona Montgomery, *Glasgow Radicalism* 1830–1848, unpub. Glasgow University Ph.D. thesis, 1974, pp. 70–80.)

[82] The hatters' banners in this period were described as follows: "Flag—White ground—one side, emblem of the trade, motto, 'Love as brethren', crest supported by two beavers; opposite side, Glasgow Arms, motto, 'King and the Rights of the People' Flag—White

down, and burned amid the execrations of above 200,000 people. There was no boisterous mirth among that vast assemblage of human beings; all feeling of levity was checked by the serious symbols which were so numerously displayed. In various parts of the meeting brawny arms were seen to cling to weapons of death, and death's-heads and cross-bones gave the meeting a solemn import. I had the marshalling of the whole of these out-door displays, and in all cases they passed off with the utmost order; but upon the occasion of the one above alluded to, I was somewhat afraid that the leaders had raised a power they could not subdue.[83]

After the battle of the Reform Bill had been fought, the parliamentary elections under the new order of things brought a host of candidates into the field. Here, again, was a fresh cause of excitement for me; and as I imagined that I had been instrumental in carrying Reform, I could not do less than assist in returning proper men. I therefore willingly transferred my services to the field of electioneering strife. I attended district meetings, and boldly expatiated upon the claims of the Honourable Sir D. K. Sandford; I eulogized his talents, his patriotism, and disinterested devotion in the cause of civil and religious liberty. My judgment and discrimination in reference to this gentleman were soon put to the proof. He lost his election for Glasgow; but, being fully determined that the House of Commons should have the benefit of his transcendent talents, he threw himself upon the suffrages of the

---

ground—one side, emblem of the trade, encircled with Rose, Thistle and Shamrock, motto, 'Love as Brethren'; opposite side, inscription, 'Reform', and 'Down with the Buroughmongers'." (*Reformers' Gazette*, 10 September 1831, p. 297). Other banners in this demonstration bore such epithets as "Liberty or Death", "By the bones of our fathers we shall be free", "Better to die in a good cause than live by slavery", "He that hath not a sword let him sell his garment and buy one." (See Thomas Johnston, *The History of the Working Classes in Scotland*, 4th ed., Glasgow, 1846, p. 245).

[83] During the "Days of May" 1832 two mass meetings were held on Glasgow Green, the first, on Saturday, 12 May attracting about 70,000 people, and the second, on the following Thursday, which is the one referred to here, attracting the biggest crowd ever seen in Glasgow, estimated by the *Glasgow Herald* and the *Reformers' Gazette* to number 120,000. It is impossible to verify Burn's claim for his own role, but if it is true his achievement was substantial. For the second meeting bills were posted in all the towns and villages for twenty miles around, and marshalling the contingents as they poured into Glasgow must have been a complex problem. The atmosphere in Glasgow was electric. The radical Peter Mackenzie thought in retrospect that the city was on the verge of revolution, and the whig Lord Cockburn agreed with him: "But for the restraint of the Whigs . . . revolution would unquestionably have broken out . . . I never before actually *felt* the immediate presence of a great popular crisis. I advise nobody to create it. The fearful part of it was the absence of riot. There was nothing to distract the attention, or to break the terrible silence—nothing but grave looks and orderly public proceedings, unconquerable resolution and the absolute certainty that if any accident had made resistance begin anywhere, it would have run like an electric shock in a moment . . . The political atmosphere was calm, but heavy and oppressed with the lurid sulphury feeling of a coming storm". All sides united to congratulate the organizers on the perfect order of the occasion, but had not news of the recall of Earl Grey reached Glasgow on the eve of the meeting, the outcome would probably have been very different. (*Loyal Reformers' Gazette*, 19 May 1832, p. 392; *Glasgow Herald*, 18 May 1832; Peter Mackenzie, op. cit., pp. 340–1; Henry Cockburn, *The Journal of Henry Cockburn*, vol. 1, Edinburgh, 1874, pp. 29–31).

Paisley Tories, who returned him in the face of public opinion in that *ultra-Radical* town.[84] Sandford, on being elected, resigned his situation as professor of Greek in the University of Glasgow, and his first essay in the house was to flash the sword of his maiden speech in the face of Daniel O'Connell. The big Irishman crushed him without an effort, and he never spoke again in the hall of St. Stephen's; his political career was therefore as transient as it was inglorious.[85]

During the latter end of the Reform agitation, Sir D. Sandford had made a favourable impression upon the working classes in the west of Scotland, and the members of my own trade were quite enthusiastic in his regard. In order to give a tangible manifestation of their feeling, the men decreed that he should wear their approbation in the shape of a superfine beaver drab hat. The *chapeau* was made, a committee appointed to wait upon him, and I was selected to present it, in the name of the members of the trade. Upon this mighty small occasion, the expounder of *Thucydides*, like a second *Hannibal*, swore upon the altar of his country never to cease from fighting the battle of liberty as long as a foe should remain. Since then the country has had frequent opportunities of being amused at the *Jim Crow* gyrations of high-sounding politicians.

In the year 1832, I made the acquaintance of a gentleman who had made himself conspicuous during the Reform agitation, and who afterwards obtained no little notoriety from his questionable advocacy of the Charter. This was Dr. John Taylor. The first time I was introduced to him was at a large out-door meeting, held on the green of Glasgow, to receive the late Earl of Durham.[86] There was a considerable degree of eccentricity in the doctor's conduct, which gave him an air of romance. At that time he wore a sailor's dress, with a sort of brigand hat, and the collar of his shirt turned down in the Byron style; in height he stood about five feet ten inches, his complexion was more of the Italian than British, his hair was jet black and hung upon his shoulders in graceful curls, and his eyes were large and dark as coal. On my first acquaintance with Taylor, I was quite charmed with him; indeed, there was a fascination in his manner that was quite irresistible. Few men were better calculated to make a favourable impression upon a

---

[84] In the General Election of December 1832 Sandford came third in the contest for the two Glasgow seats, gaining 2,168 votes to James Ewing's 3,214 and James Oswald's 2,838. He won the single seat Paisley constituency at a by-election on 24 March 1834. Whatever the source of his support he was described in the election returns as a Liberal.

[85] Burn's account of Sandford's rise and fall is confirmed by all other references to him. Following his Parliamentary failure he did not stand in the 1835 election and died of typhus in 1838.

[86] i.e. October 1834. Taylor was born in 1806 and had at various times served as a naval surgeon, mixed in Jacobin and Babeufist circles in France, and is said to have dissipated most of a legacy of £30,000 in fitting out a ship to assist the Greeks in their War of Independence. He had unsuccessfully fought Ayr Burghs as a radical in 1832 and March 1834, and was soon to become chairman of the West of Scotland Radical Association. (See W. H. Marwick, "Dr. John Taylor, 'The Mirabeau of the Chartists'", *Glasgow Herald*, 23 September 1933, p. 4).

public meeting: he was not only a good speaker, but he possessed a large store of general information, and was therefore quite *au fait* upon every subject that came before him as a public man.

In 1833 the hatters of Great Britain found it necessary to remodel the constitution of their association. A delegate meeting of the trade was appointed to be held in Manchester.[87] Scotland was represented by two members, one from Edinburgh and the other from Glasgow. I had the honour of being elected member for the latter place, and acted the part of vice-chairman to the meeting. At that time there were many tyrannical rules in the trade, which I was instrumental in having altered. While I was on this meeting, which lasted fourteen days, I had ten shillings a-day and my expenses paid.

During the time I was in Manchester, acting the part of a legislator upon a small scale, my memory more than once wandered back to my previous visit, when my friend Bird left me to run under the close-hauled topsail sheets of poverty, without a shot in my locker to balance my empty stomach. The difference between prosperity and adversity is only like that of sunshine and shower—the traces of our joys and sorrows are soon swept away by the brush of time and thus the world wags. Men who sail down the ocean of life with their canvas filled before the trade-winds of affluence only know humanity in part. It is true they have their own little demons to battle with, in the character of their perverse passions; but it is very different with the numerous host who have to double the Cape Horn of poverty, in vessels which are scarcely seaworthy at the beginning of the voyage; and it is still worse for those who are sent to sea without chart or compass to guide them on the voyage of life.

In the early part of the following year I was delegated on a similar mission to a meeting which was held in Liverpool. Shortly after this event I commenced business in Glasgow upon my own account.[88] My capital was but small, but I had a large round of acquaintances, and had no fear of not succeeding. Strict application and industry were all I required to insure my getting on in my new calling. For the first two years I did very well, and would have continued to have done so; but I was for ever running in the face of my own interest by dabbling in politics. The fact was, I had been too long a leader in the ranks of radicalism to think of retiring. The consequence of this folly very soon told upon my business, and by my egregious stupidity I allowed dull plodding men to distance me in the race of enterprise; like every other man who is blinded by self-conceit, I was surprised to see men who had neither the energy, talent, nor apparent aptitude I had, succeed in business. It was certainly an uncomfortable reflection to one who was so full

---

[87] For an account of this conference and the circumstances surrounding it, see P. M. Giles, op. cit., pp. 127–8.

[88] In the *Glasgow Post-Office Annual Directory* for 1835–36 (published in 1835) Burn is listed as a hat manufacturer at 67 Trongate, Leigh Kirk, entry. Trongate was one of the principal shopping streets of the city, but it also bordered one of the most densely populated areas of what was the most densely populated city in the United Kingdom.

of self-importance to find that he was awanting in the commonplace ability of conducting his own business—but so it was. In 1836 I opened a retail shop in Nelson Street, and continued to manufacture my own goods.[89] I soon found that this business was totally unsuited for me in more ways than one. I was troubled with a conscientiousness, or what will be looked upon as a false independence. I could not bear the idea of higgling with my customers. At that time it was a general custom in Glasgow for people in the retail trade to ask more for their goods than the legitimate price; such being the case, no one thought of paying the price asked in the first instance. I looked upon this system as not only dishonest, but there appeared to me something in it highly contemptible and unmanly.

In the spring of 1837, I was engaged on Mr. John Dennistoun's committee, while he was standing for the representation of the city. This was the only time I had ever received anything in the shape of remuneration for my political labours: at that time the parliamentary agent made me a very handsome present.[90] As the season advanced I found that I could not proceed with my business; I therefore wound it up and entered upon a new line of life, perhaps the most dangerous of any I had ever been engaged in. I opened a tavern in King Street under the auspices of the "Hatters' Arms."[91] For some time after I opened this business, all "went as merry as a marriage bell."[92] You will shortly see that my want of business habits, and thorough independence of all calculation, made me the scape-goat of my own imprudence as usual. At this time Dr. John Taylor was joint proprietor and editor of *The Liberator* newspaper (formerly *The Trades' Advocate*), and as the country was upon the eve of a general election, the little political bodies and cliques were in a state of lively excitement. The Radical Association held meetings in order to look out for a suitable member to represent their interests. After much canvassing, it was found that that body could not find a man with sufficient funds to come up to the mark. Several gentlemen of well-known liberal opinions were applied to, among whom were Mr. Aytoun, of Edinburgh, and a manufacturer belonging to the town, whose name has

[89] The 1836-7 Directory lists "James Burn & Co., 27 Nelson Street. Hat manufacturers".
[90] The contest was for a single seat at a by-election, on 26 May 1837, caused by the resignation of James Oswald. John Dennistoun, a banker and "radical reformer", defeated the Conservative Robert Monteith by 3,049 votes to 2,298.
[91] He appears in the Directories for 1838-39 and 1839-40 as "hatter and tavern keeper, 27 King Street".
[92] The business will have been sustained by the long-established drinking habits of the hatters. Burn provides a detailed description of the way in which the consumption of alcohol was woven into the working life of the hatter in his *A Glimpse at the Social Condition of the Working Classes of the United Kingdom during the early part of the present century* (London, c. 1868), p. 39-40, and his account is confirmed by the evidence of John Dunlop of Greenock to the 1834 *Select Committee on Inquiry into Drunkenness*, PP 1834, VIII, Q4632. See also Henry Mayhew's retrospective comment in 1850: "These [hatting] operatives used to drink great quantities of beer when at work—two pots or even ten pints, a day being a frequent consumption . . ." (E. P. Thompson and Eileen Yeo, eds., *The Unknown Mayhew*, 1973, p. 538).

escaped my memory. I think Mr. Roebuck was one, and I also wrote to Colonel P. Thompson.* The expense necessarily consequent upon a contest for such a large constituency as Glasgow was sufficient to deter men of small means; but there was a still more formidable obstacle in the pride, self-importance, and petty squeamishness of the Whig body. After the passing of the Reform Bill the Whigs soon assumed all the airs of the old Tory party, and their political conduct was characterized, in many instances, by greater deception and tergiversation than ever marked the conduct of their opponents.

When the time for the general election arrived, there were five candidates in the field, one of whom was Dr. John Taylor: I was a good deal surprised when I learned the circumstance. At that time the poor Doctor was bankrupt in fortune and character; I knew that he had no means of paying the election expenses; however, I soon found out where the money came from. Among the rest of the candidates there was Mr. Monteith, younger, of Carstairs, who came into the field under Conservative colours. This gentleman's friends, who were aware of the nakedness of the Radical land, and the hungry condition of some of the leaders, had made overtures to the Doctor, to cause a diversion in the Liberal camp by his standing, and procuring all the votes he could, which were ultimately to be handed over to Monteith. On the evening when this *ruse* was concocted, there was a meeting of the Radical Association, held to learn the result of the Election Inquiry Committee, and during the meeting there was a motion passed that the Radical Association should not lend its support to either of the Liberal members. As I was secretary *pro tem.* at the meeting, of course I was required to insert the motion.

I know you cannot find much interest in this matter, nor would I have noticed it, if it had not been for the after consequences. The gentlemen who had entered into the dishonourable plot to play into the hands of the Tories by a side wind, on learning that I had declared in favour of the Liberal candidates, had my name posted over the whole of Glasgow, coupled with the resolution which was passed at the meeting above alluded to. Both my pride and honesty were at stake; I therefore lost no time in calling a meeting of the Liberal party for the following evening. This meeting was held in the Bazaar; I got a gentleman to preside who was well-known to all those in the Liberal interest, both for his sterling honesty and straightforward character.† When Dr. Taylor had learned that I had called this meeting, he called upon me and endeavoured to persuade me from attending; he laid much stress upon the consequence which would result to my business, and when he found he could not move me, he appealed to my wife. I attended the meeting, where there were upwards of 5000 people, and cleared my character from the aspersion intended in the broadsides which had been so freely circulated. I also damned the Taylor party, and such was the indignant feeling of the

* Now Lieut.-General Perronett Thompson, the prime mover in the repeal of the Corn Laws.
† David Walker, Esq.

meeting after my explanation, that neither the Doctor nor any of his party were allowed a hearing. On the following morning Dr. Taylor was taken upon a warrant for debt, and lodged in jail, where he remained until some short time after the election.[93] I certainly was sorry for the Doctor; for I was aware that he was made the victim to the cupidity of a set of cormorants who had long lived upon the public. On the third day of his incarceration I went down to see him, and as I was entering the prison I met Dr. Bowring coming out from paying him a visit. During the time I was in Mr. Taylor's room a little circumstance occurred which is worthy of notice. A messenger delivered a small packet to him, and after he had examined its contents he unfolded a five-pound Bank of England note. "Here," said he, "gentlemen," (there were three of us present,) "you see I am not altogether forsaken by the world!" The gentleman who sent that note was a Mr. Samuel Hunter, who was then, and had been for many years, editor of the *Glasgow Herald*, and, of course, was a decided opponent to the Doctor in politics. The delicate manner in which he sent it, requesting Mr. Taylor to drink his health during his short captivity, was both honourable to his feelings as a man and a Christian.

Now again comes the winter of my discontent. The very party I had quarrelled with had been my principal supporters in my new business. Instead of the turmoil, noise, and bustle of a busy tavern, my house became as quiet and orderly as any private establishment in the town. By this time my family had increased to a goodly responsible charge, being five in number, which was composed of three boys and two girls. The old adage was being verified in my experience, that misfortunes never come single. My wife was seized with typhus fever, and in the short space of seven days she left myself and young family to mourn her loss.[94] This was both a serious and unlooked-for calamity. In her I lost a faithful and affectionate wife. In her temper she was quiet and gentle; she possessed a very passive character, with a very small amount of energy; but no woman could have a greater reliance upon a husband than she had upon me, and while we lived together I never abused her confidence. At the time of her death my youngest child was only eight

[93] The election took place at the end of July 1837. Burn's account is the most detailed extant, but is confirmed in outline by Marwick (*Dr. John Taylor*, op. cit.), L. C. Wright (*Scottish Chartism*, Edinburgh, 1953, pp. 219–21) and by the *Reformer's Gazette*, edited by Peter Mackenzie, a personal enemy of Taylor, which claimed that Taylor was prepared to sell out to the Tories for £1,000 (29 July 1837, p. 147). Despite these setbacks, Taylor soon recaptured the limelight with his resolute defence of the Glasgow cotton spinners later in the year, and went on to become the leader of the physical force Chartists in Scotland. He retired from politics in 1840 and died from consumption on 4 December 1842.

[94] The death rate in Glasgow was rising rapidly throughout the 1830s and reached a peak of 1 in 24.63 in 1837 (the national average was about 1 in 45). A series of escalating typhus epidemics was a significant factor, and in 1837 a quarter of all deaths were from the disease. In 1837, 1,187 men and 993 women died from typhus, and as it was estimated that the rate of mortality was about 1 in 10, the total number attacked may have been as high as almost 22,000. (See Robert Cowan, *Vital Statistics of Glasgow*, Glasgow, 1838, p. 37). A contributory cause of the epidemics was poverty, and by the beginning of the summer of 1837 Glasgow was entering a slump and, to quote a contemporary report, "a large number of the working classes in Glasgow were reduced to very necessitous circumstances." (*Observations upon the Poorest Class of Operatives in Glasgow in 1837*, Glasgow, 1838).

months old, I had therefore to send it to nurse; the loss of its mother's breast, and probably the change of milk, so far affected its health, that in little more than two months he followed his mother to his silent home. The dark clouds of my fortune still lowered upon my devoted head. My brother Robert had returned from Demerara, and shortly after he came home he took the same trouble of which his father died. Poor fellow! he lingered only a short time upon the threshold of death, until he too paid the debt of nature. Of course I had the whole of the expenses to sustain. These successive shocks rapidly altered my position, and cast a gloom over my hope for the time being.

My brother Robert's career was full of uncomfortable incidents. It was his misfortune to be ruined by kindness. Before he was nineteen years of age he was made sergeant, and intrusted with the charge of a recruiting party. While on this duty he was quartered at Banff, in Aberdeenshire, where he became acquainted with a young woman; shortly after which he deserted, and appropriated the money with which he should have paid the men in his charge. He was only absent about a fortnight when he was retaken; all the punishment he received for such a glaring breach of discipline was being confined to barracks for a month. He had no sooner regained his liberty than he repeated the misconduct in a second desertion; he was again brought up, and received similar punishment; and repeated the same conduct a third time, with the same result as to punishment. The reason why he was treated in this lenient manner was in consequence of Colonel Chambers having taken a stong liking to him. I certainly never saw a finer looking soldier; in height he was fully six feet, he was also well-made, and possessed a thorough military bearing. After all his wild escapades, his wife was allowed to go out to Demerara with the regiment. After they had been out about twelve months, upon an occasion of his coming off duty, he had the mortification of finding an officer with his wife. He took summary revenge upon the man on the spot. After some little time he was brought to a court martial; the case was so fully brought home to the officer that he was cashiered. Colonel Chambers knew that Robert would not have much peace in the regiment after such an event, he therefore purchased his discharge; after which he paid both his and his wife's passage, and sent them home. I never knew an instance where a young man had such a bright future opened up to him in the army, and sure I am it was not possible for any person to take more effectual means to damn his prospects. In every particular he was a *fac simile* of his father; he was a creature of impulse, and allowed his passions to hurl him headlong to destruction. Such was his life and such was his end.

By this time my brothers Thomas and William, whom I had not seen since they were mere boys, had got tired of living with my mother, and both enlisted into the Twenty-fifth. Thomas died while the regiment was at the Cape of Good Hope; and the other fell a victim to the cholera in India. They were both fine young men, and good soldiers. Thus, out of the whole of my mother's family, I am the only one left to toil on in the journey of life.

Letter IX

My dear Thomas.—I dare say you will wonder in what new phase of existence you will find me next. You will see that my lot is somewhat like that of the Wandering Jew—doomed to wander on through continual changes. It is written, that "Man never continueth in one stay;" and that he is "born to trouble as the sparks fly·upwards." I know not whether I have had my full share of these accompaniments to frail humanity, but in my own mind I think I could have spared some of my sorrows, to help to balance the joys of others who have not been similarly tried with adversity.

In the year 1838 I again bound myself in the hymeneal noose. The young woman I married was a native of Carlisle, and was of a highly respectable family. I think no man was ever more fortunate in the choice of his partners. In marrying the second time I felt the emotions of love even stronger than the first; and this case, as in the first, I was perfectly free from any mercenary feeling. In the whole of my experience I never knew a single instance where a young woman was brought in to do the duties of a mother to another woman's children, who so faithfully, so ardently, and so affectionately performed her part. The fact was, the children never knew what it was to have lost a mother. I was fully aware of my wife's warmth of affection for myself; but she bound me to her by the double ties of love and gratitude. I am aware that many of the discomforts of married life entirely arise from the imprudence of the men. When a man allies himself to a wife, it is both his duty and interest to make her condition as comfortable as his circumstances will admit of. When a married woman sees her husband begin to treat her with coldness and neglect, she must necessarily feel, that if ever her husband had any affection for her, it has ceased to live in her regard; if, therefore, she forgets the duties of her position he has himself to blame. I have frequently observed that many men, after being married some time, have the misfortune to find that their wives are not quite the *angels* they thought them, and they have neither the sense nor the good feeling to put up with their little weaknesses. This is a grievous error in more ways than one. There is no human being free from imperfections; and those men who are the first to discover sore spots upon the character of their wives, are generally the last who should "cast the first stone." One of the most common causes of matrimonial unhappiness in this country, arises from great numbers of men spending their time in public-houses, instead of their

149

own homes. When the society of pipe-and-pot-companions is preferred to the sacred comforts of the home fireside, there can be no such thing as matrimonial happiness; and, as Huddleson Wynn says, such marriages are "not matches, but bundles of matches, filled with claws and scratches." I hold the man who spends his money and time in a public-house instead of his own, to be one of the most selfish animals in existence, and unworthy the holy name of either husband or father.

I continued to struggle on in the Hatter's Arms until 1839, when I found that my business had become so hopelessly irredeemable that I was obliged to give it up. At that time I had some political acquaintances in Greenock, who got me persuaded to hang out my sign in that amphibious town. This was another of my false steps, which was purely caused by want of calculation. I removed my family to that place, after having taken a spirit-cellar in one of the low streets in the town. I very soon found that I had made a serious blunder in coming to this town. I know of no business in the whole catalogue of commerce, so utterly contemptible and truly degrading as that of keeping a spirit cellar in a poor locality; and before I had been in this place a month I was heartily sick of it, and felt myself humbled in the lowest degree. The tavern business is sufficiently bad in all conscience; but when compared with the other, in a moral point of view, it is immeasurably superior. There is something truly revolting to every right feeling of humanity, to live, as it were, upon the degradation of the unfortunate members of society. It is true that this infamous traffic is legalized by the law of the country; but it is equally true, that the law is one of blood, murder, and crime, which stains the black catalogue of our social condition. I could not for the soul within me apply myself to this loathsome business; and in my endeavour to make it somewhat select, I tried to weed the wheat from the chaff of my customers, but in doing so ruined the business entirely.

While I was in Greenock I had in some measure identified myself with the Charter movement, but up to that time the agitation had been conducted upon something like rational principles, if I except the mad conduct of a few of the leaders. About this time, the People's Parliament was holding its sittings, and its sage members, in the abundance of their wisdom, had propounded the sacred month.[95] If the devil had been legislating for the people, his satanic majesty could not have devised a better plan for their destruction. A meeting was held in Greenock, in order to carry this hellish suggestion into execution; and I was not only invited to attend, but was pressed to take the chair. At this meeting I told the working men of Greenock that if they wished to cover themselves with infamy, by assisting in bringing

[95] The Convention met in London, Birmingham and London again from 4 Feb.–Sept. 1839. Following the rejection of the first National Petition on 12 July the dispirited and severely depleted Convention voted by 13 votes to 5 for a 'Sacred Month' to begin on 12 August. The intention was to bring down the Government by a month long general strike, but the proposal received little serious support except in some parts of Lancashire, and in the end the strike was called off before it was due to begin. See Introduction, pp. 21–3.

the industry of the nation to a stand, they would do well to proceed. I told them also that one of the immediate consequences of their conduct would be, to let loose the whole vagabondage of the country, who would rob, plunder, and murder the innocent and defenceless members of society, and that the honest and well-conducted would have the credit of it. Such, however, was the infatuation of the more unthinking, that I had the pleasure of being branded with the character of a renegade and a traitor to the cause. I did not blame the working classes, who were then paying men to think for them, and in whose wisdom and prudence they had trusted the management of their affairs; but I certainly felt disgusted with the mercenary horde, who were not only deceiving them, but were also guilty of the treachery of misleading them. Perhaps there never was a greater farce played off upon the credulity of the working classes of Great Britain than that of the People's Parliament. I grant that there were a few honest men among the members of that august body, but I certainly think their judgment was of a very questionable character. On the other hand, the great majority of the members were a set of hungry knaves, who embraced the opportunity of turning their spouting qualifications to their own mercenary account. From what I knew of the character of some of these would-be leaders of the people, I have always been impressed with the idea, that poor John Frost was a victim of treachery! !

I was personally acquainted with many of the men whose names figured in these exciting times. My friend Dr. John Taylor, whether from some infatuation or design, identified himself with all the madness of the Chartist movement, and was among those emissaries who endeavoured to get the people to rise, and rush upon their own destruction. When these men were in Manchester and Birmingham, they told the people that the men of the west of Scotland were all armed and ready to rise in rebellion, and only waited the co-operation of their brethren in the south; and while in Glasgow the same story was told of the people in the manufacturing districts south of the Tweed! ! All I can say is, if these men were honest they must have been mad, and if not mad, no conduct could have been more infamous.

While Julian Harney, Bronterre O'Brien, M'Dowall, Taylor, and others, were inflaming the minds of the people, Feargus O'Connor was amusing the world, disgusting sensible men, and bringing scores of poor people to misery by his memorable land scheme! I am convinced that O'Connor was perfectly honest in his intentions, and that he was sanguine of the entire success of his strange abortion of a plan for the redemption of the people; and there can be no doubt, that if he could have made his scheme a practicable one, it would have been the means of bettering the condition of a large portion of the population. The idea of possessing land, if it were only six feet by three, is a pleasing one. When we know that Sir Walter Scott plunged both himself and others into irredeemable difficulties from an insane desire to possess landed property, we cannot wonder at the alacrity with which numbers of the people seized upon the agrarian bauble, and it is well known how many of them have suffered for their honest credulity.[96] I think I may affirm without fear of contradiction, that not one in ten of the Chartist leaders escaped moral shipwreck. It is only a very short time ago that one of these gentlemen, whose matrimonial connection was surrounded with a tinge of romance, left his wife and family in a state of helpless destitution, and made his way to the diggings, where I believe he is existing as a wandering outcast. The great misfortune which befell many of these men was their falling into intemperate habits. Besides this, some of them, after leading lives of indolence, and assuming the character of gentlemen, could not lower their pride, nor allow themselves to return to their ordinary avocations. I believe John Collins of Birmingham, and Lovett of London, to have been two well-meaning honest men, and with them I may class Mr. Vincent: the two latter I knew more by report than experience, but I was intimately acquainted with Mr. Collins. Like every other respectable man who had passed through the trying ordeal of public agitation, he was a decided loser, both in a pecuniary point of view, and in his domestic comforts. After John had retired into private life, and was succeeding to make a comfortable living for his family, some of his foolish friends carried him into the Birmingham town council, where he had not been long until he became divested of his reason![97]

The intended *emute* of 1848, is scarcely worth a passing notice, were it not that the Government made such a fuss about it. The leaders upon that occasion were utterly contemptible, and are not worthy a place in the history of small political events, or even to be named with the insane but honest leaders at *Bonny Muir*. At all events, they were not like *Ossian's* heroes,

"Who never court the battle, nor shun it when it comes."

I had only been about eight months in Greenock, when I was fairly stranded on the lee-shore of poverty; and to crown my misfortunes I was afflicted with a most terrible malady in the shape of *sciatica*. My family, which had increased by one in Greenock, I now removed back to Glasgow; when I got there I intended applying myself to my trade. I knew I never could be badly off while I could work at my business. This hope soon vanished, and left myself and family in desolation. I got employment with Mr. Thomas M'Gregor. When I went to make an essay at my work, I utterly broke down, and was not able to stand on my limbs five minutes at a time. I shall never forget the crushed state of my feelings on leaving the shop, with the assistance of a staff; I had the greatest possible difficulty in getting along the street. While I was in the act of limping along, and enduring the most intense suffering, I met a gentleman with whom I had been on

[96] For a detailed account of the Land Plan see Mary Hadfield, *The Chartist Land Company* (Newton Abbot, 1970). Scott's financial collapse in 1826 was partly due to the cost of purchasing and extending his estate at Abbotsford.

[97] According to Gammage, he "sank into physical weakness and imbecility", and died in 1850. See R. G. Gammage, *History of the Chartist Movement* (1894), p. 401.

terms of intimacy, who on seeing my unfortunate condition, exclaimed, "My God, Mack, what is the matter with you?" I told him I was like to faint with pain; he took hold of my arm, and assisted me into a public-house close by. Before we left, I had buried all my infirmities and the cares of life in whisky. My friend and I had finished our imperial pint each; and I went home in a state of comfortable oblivion, and my sufferings were *non est* until the following morning. You may imagine that my prospects were sufficiently gloomy for any Christian man. However, my hopes became brightened once more; for while I was in the act of sinking, a friendly hand was extended to me. Several of my old acquaintances, when they learned my circumstances, subscribed the sum of twenty pounds, and made me a present of the money at a dinner-party. With this sum I bought the license of a public-house from a person who was leaving town. This transaction turned out very unfortunate. When I obtained the license, I found it was not worth a farthing, in consequence of the previous holder not having procured a magistrate's certificate for the current year, I purchased the license in May, and the certificate should have been renewed in April, in order to make it available. Here, again, I was in a dilemma, of a very uncomfortable character, and I did not know which way to turn for relief. I was obliged to leave the house, where I was not allowed to carry on the business. I therefore took a couple of rooms for my family; and as I was totally unfit for any employment, in consequence of my disordered limb, I made up my mind to go into the infirmary, where I was sure to have the first-class medical assistance. The superintending physician ordered me to be put under a course of mercury, by which means he anticipated a cure from a change in the system. In the course of little more than a week I was reduced to the weakness of an infant; after this I was plied with *neuralgic* medicines. I remained in the house for five weeks, and came out no better than when I went in. At this time no man with his neck clear of a halter could have been in a more uncomfortable position. If my own fate had only been at stake, it would scarcely have given me a thought, but the idea of the condition of my wife and family pierced my heart with the daggers of burning reflection.

Before I had left the "Hatter's Arms," a lodge of Odd Fellows of the Independent Order of the Manchester Unity was opened in my house.[98] This was the first introduction of the society into the west of Scotland, and in a short time it spread its branches over the whole of that part of the country, which was in a great measure owing to my labours, as you will learn by and by. I had paid a good deal of attention to the character of this institution, and was satisfied that if it was conducted properly it would be of signal service to the working classes, as it offered them the advantages of mutual assistance in case of sickness or death. I knew that many futile attempts had been made during the whole of the beginning of the nineteenth century, by the working

[98] On 22 May 1838. There were initially 20 members.

men of Great Britain, to institute Friendly Societies, whereby they could make suitable provision against the hour of trouble. In nine cases out of every ten, these praiseworthy efforts ended in failure, in consequence of the societies being founded upon a wrong basis. The fact was, that in all these attempts the men were working in the dark, inasmuch as they had no data to direct them. Indeed, it is only within the last thirty years that public attention has been directed to this branch of political economy. During that time the labours of Neisom, and other actuaries, have furnished statistical tables, which are now used as infallible charts both for Friendly Societies and Insurance Companies. I took it into my head to give a lecture upon the character and objects of Odd Fellowship. After having arranged the heads of my subject, I delivered a lecture both in Glasgow and Greenock; after which I published it in the form of a pamphlet.[99] I realized a few pounds from this labour, but during the whole time I suffered the most excruciating pain, so much so, that in a very short time the hair of my head had changed from black to gray.

In the latter end of the year 1839, I was sent for by the Odd Fellows of Edinburgh, to deliver a lecture in the Freemason's Hall there. I went as requested, but owing to my trouble it was with the greatest possible difficulty I was enabled to perform the duties of my mission. When I returned home, I was seized with typhus fever of the most virulent character; and to fill the cup of my bitter sorrow, my whole family, with the exception of my wife, were prostrated at the same time.

I never was the man to repine under afflction. The difference between life and death with me has always been a thing of small moment, inasmuch as I have always had an unlimited confidence in the goodness of God, and a just appreciation of my own infinite littleness. Upon this occasion, I owed my life to the medical skill, and unwearied attention, of my friend Dr. Archibald Johnston; and while I am writing this, I feel an inward satisfaction in thus giving expression to the lasting and grateful sense I feel of his never-to-be-forgotten kindness.

I have often had opportunities of witnessing the untiring zeal, anxious solicitude, love, and devotion of women, when ministering at the couch of sickness. But in all my experience I never knew a case of so much heroic devotion, self-abnegation, unwearied attention, and self-sustaining love, as that exhibited by my own wife upon this occasion. During nine days and nights she never had her clothes off, and she was the only nurse we had to wait upon six patients. The younger members of the family soon recovered, but I lingered for two months. When I was just sufficiently recovered to move about the house, the over-strained system of my wife gave way, and she, too,

---

[99] It was published in Glasgow in 1840 as a 28-page pamphlet entitled "Lecture on the Moral, Social and Friendly Character of Odd-Fellowship of the Manchester Unity, delivered by James Burn (of the Loyal Banks of Clyde Lodge, Greenock) in the Mason Hall on Wednesday Evening, July 21, 1840."

became prostrated. It certainly was a very fortunate circumstance, that she was blessed with strength and courage to see us all through our illness, before she was seized with the disease herself. I feel called upon in this place, both as an act of duty and gratitude, to state, that as soon as my calamity became known to the Odd Fellows' Lodges, several of them sent me various sums of money. "The Banks of Clyde," in Greenock, of which I was a member, cleared me on their books, and sent me three pounds ten shillings. I may here remark, that I had long been out of benefit in consequence of not being able to pay my contribution. One of the lodges in Edinburgh sent two pounds. One of the country lodges also sent the same sum; and two of the town lodges sent five pounds between them. My sufferings, and those of my family, are very common-place things in the abodes of poverty. My condition was therefore by no means singular; but the manifestation of generous feeling, and the substantial proof of friendly regard I received from a large body of my fellow-men was certainly something to feel proud of. You will therefore perceive, that though I have had my small troubles in passing along the rugged highway of the world, I have frequently had my path smoothed by the generous conduct of my fellow-men. Believe me, Dear Thomas, the choicest blessing of heaven to man is the truly godlike feeling of kindness. However unbounded our knowledge, the magnitude of our thoughts, or the profundity of our genius, if we have not the electricity of love in our hearts, sufficient to make us feel for the sufferings of others, the chief end of our creation is unfulfilled. The man who dries the tears of sorrow, and relieves the wants of suffering humanity with acts of charity, is the greatest among the sons of men.

After I had sufficiently recovered from my weakness, I was engaged as foreman to Mr. Robertson, hat-manufacturer in Paisley. It is a matter worthy of note to mention, that when I recovered from the fever my sciatica had made its escape; and the hair on my head, which had been bleached grey with pain, came forth on my recovery in all its pristine blackness! The fever had, therefore, produced the effect which the medical men in the Infirmary failed in doing; and I can assure you that I was much obliged to it for its valuable service. Ever since, my right limb has been a *pedesternating* monument to its profound skill in the healing art. It is said, that there can be no positive good without a partial evil. I am of the opinion that the axiom might be reversed, and be equally true.

I found my situation in Paisley very comfortable; and my family were as pleasantly settled as any working man could wish. While I was with Mr. Robertson, numbers of my old associates from Glasgow were in the habit of calling upon me; among the rest, there was one very intimate acquaintance, who was a dashing, dare-devil, good-hearted fellow; when he came to Paisley I had much difficulty in being able to mind my employment for him, for he sometimes remained four or five days at a time. After I had been in Paisley eight months, my friend offered to lend me money to go into business in Glasgow. After some reflection I accepted of his generous offer.[100] This little step once more altered the future tenor of my life, and plunged me into a train of circumstances as varied as it is almost possible to imagine. When I went into business upon this occasion, the commercial affairs of the country were in a critical state, and business in general was extremely dull. I therefore soon found that the capital I had borrowed was not sufficient to carry me through the difficult season. In the meantime my kind and generous friend had unfortunately got involved in a serious law-suit, the result of which completely changed his position in society. Seeing, therefore, that it was a very doubtful question whether I should be able to weather the storm if I should proceed, I concluded under the circumstances, that it would be better to retire from the dubious contest. I at once sold off the property, and turned the proceeds over to my friend; and after our account was balanced, his loss amounted to about twenty pounds.

At this time my circumstances were again down to the freezing point of poverty, and the trade to which I had served my time was in process of being virtually changed into a new business, so far as the workmanship was concerned. Since that time the whole character of the business has been transformed, and as it exists at the present time, is as unlike the old stuff-hat system as the difference between making wigs and ladies' bonnets. I must say that the public have got the only advantage by the change. Hats are not only much cheaper, as well as better in point of durability, but they are infinitely superior in the look as an article of dress; and what is a matter of no small consequence, the silk hat will retain its colour, which is more than can be said of the stuff one. I think the revolution which has been effected in the hat trade has tended in a great measure to diffuse it among a much greater number of manufacturers; by which means the respectability of the profession has been greatly reduced. For instance, large numbers of men are continually getting into the business who possess little or no capital; and the consequence is, that so soon as they are enabled to get goods ready for the market, they must be sold at whatever price can be got for them. Of course, when men do a business with the profits on the wrong side of the ledger, somebody is sure to be the loser! In consequence of this state of affairs, many of the *wee* manufacturers are continually passing through the insolvent courts, where they are enabled to obtain absolution from their commercial sins.[101] One anomaly has arisen out of the change in the trade, which is, that the journeymen are not able (I speak generally) to make half the wages they could do in the good old fuddling times of *short turns, maiden garnishes,* and a hundred other little imposts; and yet they are now decidedly a more respectable body of men than formerly in their general conduct! ! During my apprenticeship, many of the elder journeymen were little better than half savages; one part

[100] He set up business as James Burn & Co., hat manufacturers, at Old Post-Office Court, 114 Trongate.
[101] For the decline of the felt-hatting industry see introduction, p. 19.

156

of their time was spent in working like slaves, and the other in drinking like madmen.[102] I have seen as many as seven stand-up fights among a shop of men before noon in one day.

After I wound up my short-lived business, I scarcely knew what to do; and I was reduced to that state of lethargy that I depended more upon the accident of chance than on my own energy. I had been going about in this truly uncomfortable condition for nearly three weeks, when I met an old acquaintance, who offered to give me the chance of a new trial in the world by again furnishing me with the means of going into the tavern business. This gentleman thought that I had been the victim of circumstances, and he imagined that I had all the elements of success in my character and capabilities; with the folly of self-conceit I was of the same opinion, but you will see how egregiously we were both disappointed. I accepted of my friend's generous and truly disinterested offer, and readily obtained a house in the Trongate, which I opened under the sign of the "Manchester Tavern."[103] This place was favoured with no very happy *prestige*, inasmuch as the three previous occupants had been starved out, merely for the want of customers. This little matter did not deter me from the venture. The day before I went into this house I did not possess a sixpence in the world, and the only decent coat I had was in the care of *mine* uncle.

Before I had left Greenock I had run the gauntlet of political folly, and while in that town I had got completely cured of my *monomania*. I was now on the eve of being infected with another species of insanity, in the shape of Odd-fellow-phobia.[104] When I was in private life the members of the order did not trouble me much; but the case was now very different, inasmuch as my business made me patent to all. I was delegated to all the grand quarterly committees of the district, was appealed to in all cases of dispute, either between members or members and their lodges. I became Grand Master of the district, and was required to superintend the opening of all new lodges, and the formation of new districts. I believe many of the members in the country thought I had nothing else to do, while others conceived I was making a fortune. At that time there was a wild enthusiasm among the whole of the members both in town and country, and there was a considerable rivalship among the lodges as to which should have the greater number of members.[105] In consequence of this peculiar state of excitement

[102] For a detailed account of the extensive drinking rituals within the hatting trade at the time of his apprenticeship, see R. Lloyd, *Lloyd's Treatise on Hats* (1819), pp. 31–5.

[103] He appears in the 1843–44 and 1844–45 Directories at the Manchester Tavern, 49 Trongate.

[104] A rare misuse of language. He may have been thinking of terms such as hydrophobia and claustrophobia and assuming that the word simply meant madness.

[105] Although it is not possible to confirm the precise role played by Burn, this was certainly the period in which the Oddfellows movement took root in Scotland. The oldest of the surviving Scottish lodges all date back to this period, viz. Denny (1838), City of Glasgow (1838), Banks of Clyde, Glasgow (1841), Kilmarnock (1841) and Thornhill (1841). Burn claimed that by 1845 "the number of members which Glasgow has given birth to is now

my small services were constantly in requisition: I was sent for to all parts of the country, to lecture upon Odd Fellowship. The following list of towns will give you a good idea of my labours in this way: Kilmarnock, Troon, Stranraer, Maryhill, Kirkintilloch, Greenock, Dunfermline, Edinburgh, Crieff, Auchterarder, Dunning, Perth, Dunkeld, Stanley, Blairgowrie, Cupar Angus, &c. In the end you will see to what advantage I turned all this popularity.

The members of the Odd Fellows lodges in the Perth district had frequently written to me, requesting that I would go down and give a lecture upon the character and objects of the institution. At last, when I found leisure to comply with their desire, I went, and was not a little surprised on my arrival to find that the Committee of Management had planned work for me which would have detained me at least fourteen days. In going for only two or three days I had put myself to a good deal of inconvenience; it was therefore quite out of the question for me to remain so long from my place of business; however, I met the committee half-way, and continued with them a week. I went down in the second week in June, when lovely nature was decked out in all her luxuriance; the season of the year was therefore the most pleasant for enjoying the varied beauties of that really delightful district. "The fair city" is charmingly situate on the southern banks of the river Tay, between her two *Inches*, which form, as it were, a pair of lungs, thereby contributing both to the health and recreation of the inhabitants. The bold and rugged scenery round *Kinfauns* forms a really beautiful and romantic landscape to the background of the view from the southern side of the city; while a little to the north-west, the royal palace of *Scone* is seen sweetly situate in its quiet sylvan retreat, amid its wide-spreading lawns. The road from Perth to Dunkeld leads through a most delightful country. About two miles before the stranger arrives at Dunkeld, the character of the scenery changes, as if by magic, from that of an undulating and highly cultivated country, to one of bold romantic grandeur. On the right-hand side of the road the clear winding Tay rolls along over precipitous rocks, or quietly meanders beneath a number of umbrageous arcades. The scenery in this locality is historically associated with many stirring events in Scottish lore. It was here that the "*Thane* of Cawdor" learned the truth of the prediction of the "coming wood." The last tree of "*Birnam* wood" may still be seen, like the last rose of summer, alone; and as the "Fairies dance o'er heroes graves" in the *mirk*[106] hour, the lonely traveller may hear the wind sighing through its branches, and keeping time to the murmuring of the

---

about 12,000." (*An Historical Sketch of the Independent Order of Oddfellows, Manchester Unity*, Manchester, 1845, p. 118. See pp. 116–9 for a slightly fuller account af his activities in this period.) The movement as a whole grew from 90,000 to 220,000 members between 1838 and 1842.

[106] Dark.

stream below. On the left-hand side of the way a mountain rises in lofty grandeur, and as the stranger winds along the road, its geological formation is frequently brought to view in a series of huge quarries of blue slate, which have been worked since heather went out of fashion as a covering for houses in that part of the world.

The town of Dunkeld is delightfully situate in the loving embrace of the surrounding mountains, and when viewed from any of the neighbouring heights, appears like a fairy town in the arms of its guardians. The principal objects of attraction to the stranger in Dunkeld are the church, the residence of the Duke of Athol, the pleasure-grounds belonging to his Grace, the hermitage—a delightful romantic retreat, embosomed in the deep recesses of the forest, above the town about a mile—the inns, and last, though not least, the auld half-ruined cottage where *Neil Gow* was born,

> "The man that played the fiddle weel."

I should think from the style of architecture that the church is at least seven hundred years old: much of the ornamental work is yet in good keeping, and I believe that there are few better specimens of the florid style of architecture to be found amid the Gothic remains in the kingdom. Dunkeld is divided into the *auld* and new *touns*. The new town stands on the north side of the river; nearly all the buildings in this place are of modern date, and of course in keeping with the taste and requirements of the age. On the other hand, the Old Town, with the exception of Birnam Inn, is composed of a few heather-thatched cottages, which seem struggling with Time, and scowling upon the innovations of modern improvement. The road through the Old Town leads to the Hermitage and the North *Hielands*. As the stranger wends his way up the hill in the direction of the Hermitage, he is sure to be solicited by a number of persons of both sexes, who keep stalls by the way-side, to purchase a *bicker*,[107] a *quaigh*,[108] a drinking *caup*, or *twa* three horn *spunes* as *souvenirs* of his visit to Dunkeld. The grounds belonging to the Duke of Athol are well worthy of being seen by strangers, and are, like Mr. Wyld's great Globe, open to all who can afford to pay. Every visitor to these grounds must have the attendance of a guide, for which he must pay—the demand made upon me when there was one shilling. It is said that his Grace has the lion's share of the money obtained by his showmen. Dunkeld stands in the mouth of the North Highlands, and I know of no more delightful place in Scotland for those who can appreciate the beauties of nature, where rude grandeur revels in wildness blended with the improvements made by the genius and industry of man, to spend a few days in. For my own part, I am not aware that I was ever in any place which appeared to me so full of poetical objects. The variety and sublimity of nature in this sequestered vale are well calculated to fill the mind with the most pleasing emotions. Burns's description of

[107] A wooden bowl for holding liquor.
[108] A small and shallow cup with two ears for handles.

Aberfeldy seems to be peculiarly applicable to much of the scenery round Dunkeld, where he says—

> "The hoary cliffs are crowned wi' flowers,
> While o'er the linns the burnie pours,
> And rising weets wi' misty showers
> The birks of Aberfeldy."[109]

The whole of this district is full of historical associations. Dunkeld formed at one time the ancient barrier to the Roman army under Agricola; beyond this mountain pass the daring and hardy Gael was safe in the fastness of his Alpine retreat. Between Perth and *Auchterarder* there is still to be seen a Roman fortification which must have been next to impregnable; its form is that of a crescent, and the rear is protected by the Ochill Hills; the name of this place is *Auchtertyre*. A few miles to the south of *Crieff*, there is the most entire Roman encampment in the kingdom;* and between this place and Dunblane, to the left hand coming south, lies the battle-field of the *Shirra* Muir. This memorable battle was fought between the Earl of Mar for the Chevalier, and the Duke of Argyle for the Government, in 1715. The contest seems to have been of a rather dubious character, which is pretty well described in the old song *Shirra Muir*,—

> "There's some say that we wan,
> Some say that they wan,
> Some say that nane wan at a', man;
> But one thing I'm sure,
> That at the Shirra Muir,
> A battle there was, which I saw, man;
> And we ran, and they ran, and they ran, and we ran,
> And we ran, and they ran awa, man."

After I had done the duties assigned me by the committee, the members of the Order of Odd Fellows of the Manchester Unity in Perth district did me the honour of presenting me with a very handsome purse, in which were deposited a goodly number of sovereigns, at a public dinner given upon the occasion. My first visit to Perth was in the character of a *wee* ragged beggar laddie, on which occasion I lodged in a common *Padden Kane*,† in a dirty close in the High; after the lapse of nearly forty years, I was the honoured guest of some of the first men of the city, when I put up at one of the first-class inns, and was lionized as a person of no small consequence! Such are the ups and downs of life.

* Ardagh.
† Common Lodging-house.

---

[109] From Burns's poem, *The Birks of Aberfeldy*, lines 17–20. "While" should read "White". Birks are beeches.

I remained in my new place of business for two years, when I removed to a larger house.[110] After I had been in this place about twelve months, the Odd Fellows of Glasgow were honoured with the meeting of the Grand Annual Moveable Committee being held there.[111] Upon the occasion of this meeting, I furnished another convincing proof of my great capacity for making blunders. It has always been the practice at these meetings that the members of the district in which they are held should have the opportunity of meeting the officers of the order at a public dinner. The Committee of Management for the district did me the honour of proposing that I should provide the dinner; the charge was to be five shillings each for dinner, including a pint of wine. I was requested to prepare accommodation for 600. Now you will mark my simplicity. The providing for such a large number of people involved not only a considerable outlay of cash, but also a great deal of personal labour; and, instead of acting as any man with his head screwed on in a proper manner would have done, I proved that my credulity was a long way in advance of my judgment, in acting on the advice of the committee without requesting any security for the fulfilment of their part of the engagement. In order that the dinner should pass off with *eclat*, I waited upon Sheriff Alison (now Sir Archibald Alison), to request that he would do the members of the Order the honour of presiding at the dinner, which he very readily consented to do. I may mention that while the meeting lasted, I performed the duties of a delegate as well as having the business of my house to attend to. The dinner came off with much credit to the Society, and a clear loss of thirty pounds to me, with all my labour as a set off! ! The following year I was elected to attend the G.A.M.C. which was held in Bristol, at which meeting I was elected a member of the board to superintend the general business of the Society for the ensuing year.[112] The meetings of this body were held in Manchester four times a year. I am almost sick of relating my own folly; but the record of my strange life would not be complete if I withheld it.

My new place of business was a very out-of-the-way sort of a house, and therefore only fitted for a sort of customer trade. Now this, above all others in the profession, is the most dangerous. If a man would succeed in this business, he would require an indestructible stomach, in the first place; and in the second, he should be able to put up with any amount of insolence, bullying, blackguardism, and insult, which men in the act of ruining them-

[110] He took the name "Manchester Tavern" with him to the new premises at 4 Dunlop Street. He appears at that address in the Directories of 1845/6, '46/7, '47/8 and '48/9.
[111] The G.A.M.C. was composed of delegates from all the "districts" in the organization and was responsible for electing the governing Board of Directors and deciding general policy. It met in Glasgow between 12 and 17 May 1845 at the Trades' Hall. An attempt was made at the conference to impose more central discipline and this led to the secession of a group of lodges containing over 16,000 members which set up the "National Independent Order of Oddfellows".
[112] A James Burns (Glasgow) appears in the list of directors elected in 1846.

selves at their own expense think they are entitled to confer upon the person they patronise. This characteristic of the business is decidedly worse in Scotland than in England, in consequence of the difference in the social habits of the people. If two or three Scotchmen go into a public-house to have a social glass together, one of the party is sure to pay for what has been called; the consequence is, that the rest stand treat as a matter of course, and thus they injure themselves through their mistaken kindness. Whereas in England each man calls for what he drinks, and pays for what he calls. You can well imagine the case of a poor landlord who has the smallest possible respect for his health. The first customer who makes his appearance *speers* for the *gude* man, and if he is in, "Send him *ben*,"[113] says he. Now this person in all probability is some neighbouring tavern-keeper, who has made this call in order to relieve himself of the *dry bock*[114] before he can meet his own customers; one glass, however, is not sufficient to bring his relaxed nerves into working order, so the two have a pair of gills. In a few minutes some other flying customer pops in, and as he is by far too independent to call for a glass for himself, he tells the *lassie* to bring a *bit gill*. These flying shots very likely continue the whole day, and when the evening arrives the landlord's face is distorted by Mr. Alcohol pulling the muscles in different directions, so he is ripe for anything except attending to his own business, and if he be a married man the duties fall upon his wife, where she becomes exposed to every species of licentiousness.

While I was in this business I knew many well-meaning and sensible men, who were imperceptibly led away by moderate indulgence in the first instance, which gradually increased upon them until premature death was the result; and I have known scores of my own immediate acquaintances become the victims of *delirium tremens*, and tumble over the edge of the world, in all the appalling horrors of that sad disease. So far as I am concerned, it was a very fortunate thing that I had a constitutional dislike to taking spirits in a morning, and I also flattered myself that I had an excellent command over my feelings in reference to improper indulgence in drink; however, I am bound to confess that for some short time before I left the business, I began to feel an uneasy sensation about the stomach when I was not getting whisky regularly. I looked upon this as the most uncomfortable symptom I had ever laboured under, as it was most assuredly the forerunner of destruction if not arrested in time.

Since I had commenced the tavern a second time, my business had never been what may be called a paying one, inasmuch as it was full of uncertainty. Occasionally I was as busy as it was possible to be, and at others in the dead calm of neglect. But the truth of the matter is, I was not fitted for the calling. In the first place, I was above it, and hated it for its debasing character. In the second, I could not bear to see my friends franking themselves to ruin,

[113] Inside.
[114] Retching on an empty stomach.

without remonstrating with them for their imprudence. Had I been made of suitable materials for the profession, I would have acted differently, and my wife might have been a widow and my children fatherless.

I think it was in the year 1848 when Mr. John Dixon stood for the representation of Glasgow. At that time there were four candidates, viz., Messrs. Dixon, Dennistoun, McGregor and Hastie. The two first of these gentlemen occupied my house for their committee-rooms for the district in which it was situated.[115] When I made the agreement with the agents, they requested me to give the committee all suitable refreshments, and when the committees were in active operation, the agents dined at my house daily. Mr. Dennistoun's account was paid as soon as it was presented; on the other hand, Mr. Dixon's agent offered me thirty pounds for my forty-one pound bill. I was so incensed at the insult offered to my honesty, that I immediately put the account into the hands of an agent. About this time I borrowed eleven pounds from an acquaintance, a gold-beater in Glasgow, and handed over Mr. Dixon's account to him; he was to sue for it in his own name, and pay me the balance when he brought the suit to a close. Mr. Dixon's agent litigated the suit as long as he could make a single reply. In the meantime the gold-beater had purchased a large quantity of stolen property, which had been taken from a jeweller's shop in the Arcade, twelve months before. The gold-beater was incarcerated, but got out upon bail to the amount of two hundred pounds. Shortly after which he became a fugitive, and fled to the United States. Two days after he left, my lawyer brought the suit to a favourable issue; but as the person in whose name it was prosecuted had become an outlaw, I lost the whole amount. This would have been a matter of little consequence had my business been in a healthy condition; but unfortunately it was just the reverse: so my reign as a publican came to a close, I was going to say an inglorious one. But this was one of my seeming misfortunes, which I now look upon as one of the most fortunate events in my life; and I think you will agree with me in the expression, when you know of my improved condition.

[115] "John Dixon" was in fact William Dickson and the election took place on 31 July 1847. Dickson and Dennistoun came third and fourth in the contest for the two-member constituency.

Letter X

Edinburgh.

MY DEAR THOMAS,—I am now writing from modern Athens, where the philosophy of Dr. Chalmers in some measure smoothed down the savage theology of John Knox. I am not far from the apartments where the *Noctes Ambrosianæ* was manufactured, amid the exhilarating fumes of *mountain dew*, vulgarly called whisky toddy. A short distance from where I am located, the printer's devils handled the doubly interlined proof-sheets of the Great Magician of the North, who amused the present generations of the world by the resurrection of their forefathers, whom he commanded to act and speak in the language of ages long gone by. If I cannot see *Habbie's Howe*, I can observe the hill above it made warm by the rays of the sun. Down beneath me Sir Walter Scott sits in marble glory, under his canopy of pinnacled flying buttresses; and above me are the pedestrian statues of two men who hold very different positions in history—the one is that of William Pitt, and the other George the Fourth of blessed memory. Auld Reekie has been the home of the muses from the time that George Buchanan offered false incense before their holy shrine, until Wilson turned his lyre in "The Isle of Palms." It was here too that Hogg had his small ambition and smaller egotism flattered by two of the literary lions of the day; and it was here that the immortal ploughman bard, like a rustic meteor, became the observed of all observers for the time being. Poor fellow, like *Fabius*, he stripped himself of the gown of his living fame, and went back to his plough; but since the days of old Homer no man has ever found a more lasting monument in the hearts and sympathies of his countrymen. In looking to the South, I can observe the building where the Messrs. Chambers throw off weekly their tens of thousands of sheets of cheap literature, by which means they amuse and instruct hundreds of thousands of human beings in all parts of the civilized world. I think it is more than probable that I was in Edinburgh at the time when these enterprising publishers must have received the first idea of commencing their glorious career. In the year 1829, or early in 1030, a small periodical made its appearance in Edinburgh, under the very pretty and appropriate name of the *Cornucopia*, it was printed in a folio size, being the same as Messrs. Chambers' first series of *Information for the People*, and it was also the same in price. This little pioneer in the field of cheap literature contained many excellent original articles both in prose and verse; there was, however, one serious drawback to its success—it was printed by some person who was only possessed of old worn-out founts of type, and the impression was sometimes so bad that it was unreadable; besides this, it was printed upon wretched bad paper. I cannot vouch for the fact that the Messrs. Chambers took the idea from this work, but I do think it was very likely to have suggested it.[116] I may mention, however, that the *Cornucopia* was not the first attempt made to supply the people with cheap and useful literature. As far back as 1827 there was a very neat little publication, octavo size, brought out in Newcastle-upon-Tyne, and if my memory is not at fault, I believe it was published by McKinzie and Dent, of that place: the price was two-pence.[117] Since Chambers' people have been in the market, there have been many attempts to divide the public favour, or perhaps it may be more correct to say, to speculate in the same useful field of labour with themselves. In my opinion, the *Dublin Journal* was the only weekly publication that at all came up to their standard of excellence, either as to talent in the general character of the articles, or its high tone of morality; of course, I except *Dickens' Household Words*, this speculation, however, turned out a dead failure. Since then the only successful competitors in this line are the *London Journal* and the *Family Herald.*

Edinburgh has long held the proud position of being the first literary city in the United Kingdom, and her press continually sends forth to the world the living thoughts of men upon every conceivable subject in the round of human knowledge.

The first half of the nineteenth century has just passed away, and with it a whole host of men whose genius shed a *halo* of glory round their native land. When Walter Scott was composing his *Lay of the Last Minstrel*, Jeffrey and others were lashing poor Byron into poetical madness; but since the time Pope first steeped his pen in gall, never were critics more cruelly flogged with the instruments of their own punishment, and instead of crushing the rising genius, they called forth the latent powers of his mastermind. The muses have now to mourn the men who erewhile scattered their beautiful flowers in the paths of humanity, and offered their acceptable incense before the shrine of intellectuality. He who tuned his lyre to the *Pleasures of Hope*, is gone to realize its blessings in another world. The bards of the lake have crossed the dark ferry, and the bright scintillating author of *Lalla Rookh* has hung his harp on "Tara's walls." The author of the *Isle of Palms*[118] has thrown off his *humanity*, and left his chair to put on immortality. The border minstrel has left his *Legendary Lore* to amuse succeeding generations of men; Hogg, too, has laid aside his moorland reed, and Rogers's lyre is unstrung.

To-day I have had a stroll through Holyrood Palace, once the seat of Scottish royalty. I passed through the suite of rooms which were occupied by poor Mary, and looked upon the bed where her repose must oft have been

---

[116] William Chambers later confirmed that *Cornucopia*, a 1½*d.* unstamped weekly, published and edited by William Mudie in 1831, served as a model for the *Chambers' Edinburgh Journal* which first appeared on 4 Feb. 1832. See William Chambers, *Memoir of Robert Chambers* (7th ed., Edinburgh, 1873), pp. 236–8.

[117] *The Selector: a Cabinet of Prose and Poetry* (Newcastle-upon-Tyne, 1827–28).

[118] The author of *Pleasures of Hope* was Thomas Campbell (1717–1844); *Lalla Rookh* was by Thomas Moore (1779–1852); and *Isle of Palms* was by the Professor of Moral Philosophy at Edinburgh University, John Wilson (1785–1854).

165

disturbed by the midnight visions of her sad fate. Poor Mary! I cannot help opening the fountains of my heart to shed a tear to thy unfortunate memory. Thou wert cast among thy countrymen when their little civilization was all but extinguished in the madness of religious zeal, and there was not a man in all Scotland to be found that could pilot thee through the storm; and he who should have been thy protector was the miserable creature of an imbecile mind. Thy dear royal cousin was like the Turkish monarch—she could bear none other near her throne. She ended thy suffering career by murder, and covered the sin with the mantle of hypocrisy! The dilapidated state of those rooms, with their decayed memorials of an unfortunate family, forcibly impresses the mind with the truth, that man's power and greatness is all a dream.

I remember very little of my first visit to Edinburgh; but it is now a quarter of a century since I worked in it as a journeyman hatter. Since then the sweeping power of progress has made a complete transformation in several parts of the *Auld Town*. The West Bow, with its oak-ribbed buildings, pro-jecting gables and overhanging attics, quaint devices and curious designs, have all been swept away. The Canongate has also been much modernized; here and there a new building has been introduced between a pair of old tenements, like a young man supporting two old ones. The Grass Market is still honoured with the quaint architecture of three hundred years. Some of these old veteran houses look down upon their modern compeers as if in scorn at their upstart presumption. The *Tolbooth* yet graces the [*Coo*] Cowgate with a few frowning bars, which here and there ornament its gloomy front.

Amongst the various towns in Great Britain that have gone through a rapid state of change within the last forty years, I think Glasgow may be placed at the head of the list. I remember quite well when the High-street, and the Salt-market, with a part of the Trongate, were embellished with *piazzas* and pillars, half gothic and half Norman. The town was then bounded on the east by the Cattle Market, on the west by Jamaica-street, on the north by the Old Thorn-tree, and Laurieston and Hutchieston were all green fields. The miles of splendid quays which have been erected of late, were then sleeping quietly in their quarries. In my time there are several towns in Scotland which have now become places of consequence that were mere villages. When I passed through Galashiels in 1821, it was then, in Scotch phraseology, a mere *clachan*, in which there were a few small makers of coarse *wad*, blue dyed cloth. Since then it has become one of the most thriving manufacturing towns in the country. Thirty years ago Hawick was a place of note for its hosiery; it is now a first-class manufacturing town for shawls and tweeds. When I knew Langholm first, the only manufacturing done there was in a paper-mill, about a quarter of a mile below the town. This building is now a whisky distillery, and the town is kept alive by several large manufactories of shawls, tweeds and hosiery. Forty years ago the Prince's Dock in Liverpool was its boundary on the west. I should think there are docks now extending two miles below it. How many new ones there are on the upper side of George's Dock I cannot say. In my time Birkenhead has been conjured into a stately town by the magic of progress, and the town of Liverpool has swelled itself into more than double its former size. Manchester, too, has kept pace in the race of commercial enterprize. In 1822, when I wandered in loneliness, and almost in despair, down Market-street, it was then only a narrow lane, full of old Elizabethan buildings, and the town was not then half its present size. When I was in Bradford, in 1819, it was little better than a village. It is now a second-class town; and Leeds, too, has greatly extended itself. And such is the case with several other towns in the manufacturing districts.

In my opinion there is a comfortable idea in again renewing an acquaintance with an old town after the lapse of forty years, and finding it unchanged. One of the beauties of this *statu quo* state of things is, that you are sure to find the people equally primitive as their dwellings. By this means you are enabled to consult the living history of a by-gone age, in the manners and habits of a people, who quietly allow the rest of the world to leave them nearly half a century behind. For my own part, I am always pleased when I can visit the little by-nooks of the world, where the people live, as it were, out of the stream of revolution. In 1854 I visited Dumfries, and had it not been for the innovation of the Railway-station, and the removal of the saw-pits from the sands, I should have found the town as unchanged, in all its physical aspects, after fifty years, as it was possible for a good old-fashioned people to have kept it. Carlisle, too, retains a good many of its old characteristics; but the stream of humanity has been turned from the centre of the town to the west side of the Castle, where the railway forms the means of transit between the two divisions of the kingdom. The Watling-street of the Romans is fast becoming obsolete as a highway of commerce, and ere long it will bloom as verdant as the surrounding hills.

There are very few towns that have undergone a more complete transformation in character than Newcastle-upon-Tyne. It is true that "Pandon" still graces the under part of the town with its amphibious charms and muddy fragrance. The sand-hill is yet the emporium of the *piscatory* tribute of the ocean, and the *rendezvous* of the "Cullercoats" ladies, whose *understandings* are of the first-class order! The "Side," too, remains in all its ancient glory, being the most *upright* street in Europe. The Castle continues to frown like a hoary-headed cynic upon the surrounding innovations, and the *lang* stairs yet try the *puff* of many a valetudinarian. Mr. Grainger, up to 1848, had nearly modernized the whole of the upper part of Newcastle; new streets were laid out in all directions, and he designed and built one of the most splendid and capacious Market-places in the United Kingdom. The new Corn-Exchange was without a rival; this building has been converted into a Reading-room and a Commercial Exchange. But the railway acted the part of the great magician in its wonderful transformations. The high level bridge which spans the Tyne, in the novel character of a pair of bridges, is one of the greatest undertakings of the age. The old *brig*, which unites Newcastle and Gateshead, looks like an ancient pigmy beneath its modern rival. The fearful explosion which took place in Gateshead in 1854, has been the means of opening up Pipergate and Millgate; these two streets were called into existence before carts and carriages were fashionable. On the whole, the Newcastle of 1855 is a very different place to what it was in 1809, when I was in it for the first time. Middlesborough, in the neighbourhood of Stockton-upon-Tees, has been conjured into a thriving commercial town within the last thirty-five years. Whitby remains in *statu quo;* but Scarborough has more than doubled its old proportions. Leamington is the production of the go-ahead principle, and though an infant it has attained the proportions of townhood. The Cliff at Bristol was ornamented with a few straggling man-sions forty-five years ago; it is now a magnificent town, with streets, squares, and crescents, all laid out in accordance with the taste of the age. If Clifton continues to progress as it has done during the last twenty-five years, *Durdom* Downs will be a place only to be found in history, and the old *Folly* on the cliff will have given place to some new one, without a *legend.** The members of the old corporation of Bristol had grown so great, in their own estimation, over the slave-trade, that they imagined Bristol would continue to keep the lead as a maritime port; but while they flattered themselves in their power, the glory of their ancient city was transferred to Liverpool, where commerce flourished under more liberal treatment. During the time some of our large commercial towns were opening up their improvements, the old-fashioned stand-still corporation of Bristol commenced a splendid chain-bridge; two towers, partially finished, remain as monuments of the industry and enter-prise of the projectors of this wonderful undertaking. Malvern, with sunny slopes, isolated mountain in miniature, and hydropathic establishments, is fast rising into a goodly town. This is one of those delightful places where the dilapidated in health can be washed, dried and mangled at pleasure, and returned to their friends regenerated members of society. The Harrogate of my young days, though it stood *A*1 in the world of fashion, was only a fraction of what it is now.

I remember a very good anecdote connected with this little quiet watering place. In the early part of the present century there was a gentleman who had long represented a Newcastle house of first-class standing in the iron trade, as *bagman* or traveller. The circumstance I am about to relate occurred while the worthy gentleman was on his last journey. Having the stirring memories of many happy days on the road in his mind, and being a sincere lover of number one, he had made up his mind to throw all his importance into this his farewell journey; he put up at the head inn, and gave his orders with the air and manner of a person accustomed to command. After being

* "Cook's Folly" is a tower built on the top of the cliff, with a very pretty improbable Legend attached to it.

seated in his room, he rang the bell for the landlord, and ordered a pair of the best ducks in the house to be roasted immediately, and to be served up with green peas. While his glorious feed was being prepared, he assisted his cogitations with sundry goes of brandy. During the time his dinner was getting ready, a carriage and four drove up to the door of the inn; the fresh arrival consisted of a lady and gentleman, who, after being ushered into a room, demanded to know if mine host had anything in the shape of dinner ready? The landlord's answer was, that he really had nothing he could set before them, but he would lose no time in preparing anything they might order. The lady inquired if he could oblige them with a roast duck? His answer was, that he was really sorry he could not comply with her ladyship's request, as a gentleman, who had just arrived, had ordered a pair of ducks for dinner, and these were all he had. Now it so happened that the lady was in that state when her smallest desires required to be attended to, and she had set her mind on a roast duck! which, if not procured, might produce the most serious consequences. In this state of matters her husband suggested that the landlord should request the gentleman, as a particular favour, to allow the lady to share his dinner, as he thought two ducks were certainly too much for one person, he would therefore agree the more readily to such an act of courtesy. The host waited upon the gentleman, and related his message, to which he was answered, that he ordered the ducks for himself, and that neither lady nor gentleman in Christendom should partake of them. This answer only served to whet her Ladyship's duckish desire. A second message was therefore agreed upon, and the landlord was desired to mention the delicate condition of the lady: in the mean time, her husband observed, that if the gentleman was a gentleman, and possessed the least spark of the gallantry of a gentleman, he could not refuse! When the landlord communicated his second message, the bagman nearly kicked him out of the room, and told him, that if she were the Queen of England, she should not partake of his dinner. Both the lady and gentleman were more astonished than disappointed at this last refusal, and they imagined the fellow must be either mad or a bear. When the dinner was being served up, the gentleman requested that the landlord should leave the door of the bagman's room partially open, that he might see what sort of an animal he was. When the gentleman had an opportunity of looking into the room, he had the pleasure of discovering his own traveller. I need not say that the ducks and peas were readily divided, and the lady was preserved from the serious consequences which otherwise might have ensued! !119

In the march of improvement, Nottingham has been transformed in no small degree. Forty years ago, the business of this place was solely confined

119 The review of the *Autobiography* in *Tait's Edinburgh Magazine* (November 1855, pp. 700–1) quotes the whole of this anecdote, commenting that "The reader will perceive that this story is told with all conceivable clumsiness; but he will have the kindness to attribute the verbiage and confusion of syntax to the writer's antecedents".

to lace-making by hand. Since the introduction of machinery to the purpose of manufacturing textile fabrics, the character of Nottingham has undergone an entire change. In almost every department of the lace business, the article can now be purchased at considerably less than the price formerly paid for the labour. Several new branches of industry have been added, such as hosiery, gloves, shoes, and a variety of fancy trades. The town has expanded in its physical aspect greatly beyond its old proportions. The park has lately been laid out upon a modern plan for a new town; and within the last five years, a splendid pleasure-ground has been added to the town where the inhabitants can both find health and pleasant recreation. Derby has also been much improved both in its social and physical character. This town was once famed for its manufacture of fancy articles in alabaster, the material for which is found in abundance in the neighbourhood. This business has been superseded to a great extent by the introduction of ornaments in Parian marble, or rather an imitation of that article. The leading business in Derby is now, and has been for some years, the manufacture of silk in various articles. This place has also greatly extended its ancient boundary, and the town has been embellished with a beautiful *Arboretum*. When I was in this part of the country first, there was a great number of houses both in Nottingham and Mansfield excavated out of the sand-stone rock, and it was no unusual thing to see cows feeding on the tops of the houses. These primitive habitations have all been swept away by the rolling flood of modern progress.

In my recollection, Aberdeen has been ornamented with one of the most handsome streets in the United Kingdom, and I am certain that it will be the most durable, as all the houses are built of granite.* During the last forty-five years, Birmingham has undergone the process of an entire change in its physical aspect: the railways have disembowelled it with their subterranean passages and gigantic stations; while its proportions as a town have been more than doubled. During the last twelve years towns have been springing into existence at intervals along the whole of the trunk-lines, and the old towns and villages along the great highways of the nation are crumbling into decay. The great north road is becoming an elongated desert, and the glory of Leaming-lane is now no more. There is one class of towns which seem to set the laws of progress at defiance. Time may crumble them into decay, and their inhabitants may succeed each other like vegetables in their seasons; but the innovation of what is called modern improvement can never reach them. I mean the cathedral towns. How these relics of antiquity are preserved from the inroads of modern Vandalism I cannot say; but I am glad they are allowed to remain: in my mind they are invested with a melancholy grandeur, and as they battle with old time, they increase my veneration. I have always observed that there is a coincidence between the inhabitants of these towns and the sombre character of their old temples, which form, as it were, a bond of sympathy. It may be that these venerable piles, with their gloomy

* Union Street.

magnificence and stately grandeur, exercise a species of tranquil contentment over the minds of the inhabitants, that bids defiance to all ideas of change in their notions of the order of things. As the headlong current of change rushes on, and the mania of progress rages in its thousand forms, these old towns will continue to stand like as many castles seated on rocks in the ocean, defying the winds and waves. I would ask, who is there that has any feeling or respect for the memorials of the past, that would wish to see the old piazzas and the galleries "above the rows" removed in the venerable city of Chester, or the old "gates" in York or Norwich substituted by modern streets? In my mind, the modern wise men of Carlisle have destroyed one of the principal beauties of that ancient city, by removing the north or Scotch gate, which in my time stood like a landmark between civilization and barbarism. In the language of one of our *beautiful modern poets*, I would say—

> "Let trade and commerce die;
> But may no Vandal hand destroy
> The monuments of ages long gone by! !"*

When I retired from business, it was into the private life of poverty. After having disposed of the tavern-property, and paid my debts as far as the proceeds would admit of, I was left without a shilling to commence the world in some new line. The poet has sung "that man ever is but to be blest;"[120] if rapid changes in condition of life, and strange transformations in my social position were at all conducive to such a happy state of existence, I should have been doubly blest. However, I have proved the falsehood of poor Burns's misanthropical idea, "that man was made to mourn."[121] My hope has at all times been greater than my misfortunes, and in my storms I have cheerfully anticipated the coming calms. A few days after descending from my inglorious throne in the unhallowed temple of Bacchus, I obtained a temporary engagement with an old friend, who carried on the business of an engraver and lithographer. I remained with this gentleman for twelve months, at the expiration of which time, in consequence of a number of unfortunate circumstances, his business had all but bid him adieu. Shortly after this, I entered into an agreement with another person in the engraving business who was bringing out a system of book-keeping for the use of schools; he wished me to introduce his new work in the midland counties of England, and to be in keeping with myself, I undertook to push an untried article into the market at my own expense, by taking the business on commission! If I had had the sense of the merest tyro in business affairs, I would certainly have allowed the person who was likely to have received the benefit of the speculation the honour of paying for its introduction. You will therefore see,

* Lord Somebody!

---

[120] i.e. Pope, in the *Essay on Man*: "Man never is, but always to be blessed".
[121] The title of a poem written by Burns in 1784.

171

that this engagement is another of my blunders, and one which completely turned the future current of my life into new channels.

During the time I was in Glasgow, which was close upon twenty years, I can confidently affirm that no man was ever blessed with a larger round of friends, and what is of still greater importance, they were not of that class of people who will eat a man's dinner, drink his wine, and give him the cold shoulder when he is without a dinner himself. I know it is impossible for a man in comfortable circumstances to steer clear of sycophants, who, as long as the sun of prosperity shines upon him, will ply him with the base coin of friendship, and when the tide of fortune ebbs, will fly from him like rats from a falling house. This class of people have their use in the social economy, and when fortune changes their conduct carries with it a useful moral lesson. I could name many gentlemen whose generous and disinterested conduct to me will hold a fresh place in my memory as long as that index of the past continues to exist. I do believe that no man ever disappointed his friends more than I have. I have always been an intelligent man, but my friends took me for what neither God or nature intended me to be, namely, a clever one. This is the very subject upon which I mislead my own feelings. I really imagined that I was a clever man! I may, therefore, say that my character through the best part of my life has been a living lie, and at the end of fifty years, I am more disappointed in myself than I have been in all the world beside. I never had any trouble in analyzing my own mind, and could therefore put my hand on my weak points; but strange as it may appear, I have ever allowed my *pride* and *confidence* to retain the whip hand of my judgment. With all my numerous imperfections, I know that I am not without many of those feelings and virtues which lend a charm to our nature. Few men have a better appreciation of right and wrong, more enlarged views of the god-like principles of civil and religious liberty, a greater toleration for the weaknesses of other men, or can feel for the sufferings and misfortunes of their fellows more sensitively. This may be called egotism, but you will remember, that I am endeavouring to give you a true history of my life; and if I did not show you the numerous springs in the machinery of my mind, which have from time to time prompted me to action, you might frequently arrive at wrong conclusions. I am aware that the great bulk of men give themselves no trouble in inquiring into their peculiar organizations, or the causes of their various impulses, and therefore they leave themselves as they are; but I certainly think it is a wise proceeding, for a man frequently to examine the state of his own mind, and balance his little accounts; he will find, in commercial phraseology, that short reckonings make long friends.

I am now about entering upon an entire new career, and the next five years became, perhaps, the most eventful in the whole of my chequered life. The gentleman I had entered into the engagement with, buoyed me up with the flattering expectation that the commission on his business would be worth at least three hundred pounds a-year. "*The gude forgie me to believe him.*" I therefore sold off my household furniture, and removed my family direct to York, where I took a house with the laudable intention of making that city the centre of my operations. I went to work like a man who had made up his mind to be in earnest. I was full of hope, notwithstanding the advice and prognostications of many of my friends before I left Glasgow. My first essay was a failure, but that did not dishearten me; I imagined that I had not got on the right ground. I then swept the country in a goodly circle, when I had the cheering satisfaction to find, that my undertaking was a dead failure. I had spent all my money in removing my family and paying railway fares, and in the course of two months, I was brought to a dead lock. In the latter end of April, 1850, I removed my family to Leeds, where I took a small unfurnished room, and all we had to put in it was our bedding. The first night we occupied this place was during a severe frost, and as our bed-clothes had not arrived, having been sent by rail, we were obliged to lie upon the bare floor, and to make the matter worse, my wife was within a short time of her confinement. For some days after being in Leeds, I really did not know what to do, there were five pair of jaws to find employment for, and I could see no possible way in which it could be done. In my worst times I have generally found something to fall back upon in my own resources; so after steeping my brains in reflection, I hit upon a scheme which relieved us for the time being. I remembered that I had an old friend in Bradford, so after I had arranged the heads of a lecture upon the character and poetry of Robert Burns, I went over to that place, and got my friend to lend me his assistance in disposing of a number of tickets, which he readily complied with. With his assistance, too, I took a hall for the purpose of delivering my lecture. The event came off at the appointed time, and I realized four pounds after paying the expenses. While in Glasgow I had published a small volume, being "A Historical Sketch of the Independent Order of Odd-fellowship of the Manchester Unity." At this time I had one hundred copies of the work in my possession. I was personally known to most of the leading men in Leeds connected with the society; so I made application to the district officer to purchase my stock of books. This gentleman brought the subject before the district committee, who readily agreed to give me one shilling a-copy for the whole I had on hand.[122] I was therefore in clover once more.

After this I spent a few days in Leeds, in an endeavour to find some employment, but was unsuccessful. I left Leeds, and took my family with me to Liverpool. I had no more business in going there, than to other places I could have made choice of; and I can scarcely say now what motive prompted me in the selection of that place, in preference to others more comeatable. Whatever we may think of our free-will, there can be no doubt, but we are often impelled forward in our careers by a directing power over which we have no control; and such seems to have been my case in this instance. I was

[122] The original retail price was three shillings a copy. For the composition and publication of the *Sketch*, see the Introduction, p. 26.

therefore carried headlong into a stream of contending circumstances, and like a chip of wood amid the boisterous waves of a stormy sea, I was dashed hither and thither without any controlling power of my own. I knew several people in Liverpool who were in comfortable circumstances, but as they were only holiday acquaintances I did not make my case known to any of them. There was one gentleman, however, to whom I had rendered some little services while he resided in Glasgow. He was then holding the situation of a warehouseman to a large shipping firm, and he had the employing of the men who were required to do the work of the establishment as daily labourers. This gentleman offered me employment upon the same condition as others, which was, to take my chance for the work when there was any to do. This offer was crippled with a condition that I could scarcely ever account for, namely, that I should never speak back to him! Before he left Glasgow, he held a very comfortable, and at the same time a somewhat responsible situation, but like many others he had committed himself by abusing the trust reposed in him. The matter, however, was not serious, but being humbled in his own estimation he left the town. Like every other man who had not been used to hard labour, and unencumbered with a character, he had to pass through a severe ordeal before he could obtain a fresh standing in the world. This, however, he accomplished by dint of industry and steadiness. I am therefore led to suppose, that he was afraid that I might expose his previous conduct, which certainly would have been the last thought in my head. I was too glad to know that he had recovered his character to think of doing him an injury; indeed, I looked upon his conduct as worthy of all praise. I was well-pleased to accept his offer, as my finances were again exhausted, and my wife on the eve of her confinement.

The first work I was put to was that of turning grain, and I was kept at this for four weeks in succession. Now, turning grain, like any other manual labour which a man may be accustomed to, is very simple work. With me it was anything but simple. During the first three weeks I was at it I thought I should have virtually fallen in pieces. My loins and back were in a state of open rebellion, and every muscle in my body was in arms against the employment, and my spirits required to exert all their influence to keep the mutinous crew in order. During the first week I could not sleep in my bed at night, in consequence of a legion of aches and pains pulling at me in all directions. If I could have thrown off twenty years, which I found an actual incumbrance to me, I dare say I should have felt no inconvenience after the first few days. Age certainly has its advantages, but I found by experience, that they were not to be realised in turning corn. It is one of the misfortunes of humanity, that men cannot keep the barometer of their minds up to the degree of equanimity under the pressure of different circumstances. One evening, as I was shuffling home, with spirits almost crushed, and my body in the most intense state of suffering, while I was passing along Lord-street, and going through a passage where there was a scaffold, erected for the repair of some house, I felt an irresistible desire that it should fall upon me and bury me in the ruins. I have more than once felt life a burden, but I never knew the desire to shuffle off the mortal coil so strong, as upon this occasion. A few minutes brought a holier reflection; I knew that there were more deserving men than myself exposed to sufferings much greater than mine, and a hasty examination soon proved to me my own littleness, and I went home with the gloom off my mind. The second evening after this, on my way home, I met a gentleman I had known intimately while in Glasgow. This person had been the shuttlecock of the fates to a surprising degree; a few years before this time, he was lessee and proprietor of the Adelphi Theatre in that place, and had been favoured while there, with the sunshine of popularity in no small degree. It was nothing strange to see Mr. David Prince Millar at one time bounding over the waves of fortune, in all the buoyancy of happiness, comfort, and affluence, as if he were in his usual element; and at another, holding on by some wreck in the stormy sea of poverty. His difficulty in life was precisely that of my own, he had talent for everything but business! and carried on his shoulders a world of experience, which was the same to him as a miser's gold, being neither of use to himself nor anybody else. Men seem to be created for all kinds of pursuits, but it frequently happens, that great numbers of them get into the wrong places, and therefore lose the opportunities of turning their peculiar talents to advantage. A short time before I met Mr. Millar, he had made a successful hit in Liverpool, by giving a series of entertainments in the Music Hall, in reciting "The ups and downs in the life of a showman." With the money he realized upon that occasion, he went a starring into the surrounding villages, and, as usual with him, he came back to town penniless. We made mutual inquiries concerning each other's condition and prospects, and at the same time, neither of us were blessed with the most humble representation of majesty!

It would appear that Mr. Millar was cast upon the world when he was a mere boy, the consequence of which was, that he had to struggle through it as best he could. One little anecdote will suffice to show how the lives of certain classes of people hang upon the chapter of accident. During his early peregrinations, while putting up at a common lodging-house in the city of Norwich, he met in with a man who was making an excellent living by one of those little fortunate secrets which men occasionally get hold of who exist by their wits. This man's secret was the precursor of the now universal lucifer match; he dealt in little boxes filled with a composition of phosphorus and resin, which, by a little friction, produced an illuminating effect; these boxes he sold at two shillings and half-a-crown each. Millar, although only a boy, was sharp enough to know that the material of which these boxes were made could only be trifling, he therefore made up his mind to obtain the secret. With this idea in his head, he watched the man when he was going to purchase his materials at a chemist's shop, and shortly after he called at the same shop, as if he had been sent by that person to purchase a shilling's worth of the stuff, stating the he had forgotten the name; the material was readily supplied, and without further instructions he commenced operations in his new business. Not having the means to purchase tin boxes, he procured wooden ones, and he disposed of his new unpatented illuminators for two-pence each. It happened, as he was hawking his boxes through the public-houses one evening, he met in with a person who belonged to that nondescript class of men who live by the honourable profession of assisting the magistrate in suppressing vagrancy, and otherwise supporting the laws. This gentleman made an attempt to pilfer one of Mr. Millar's boxes, but being caught in the act, he immediately had the lad up before a magistrate on a charge of selling a highly dangerous article; he affirmed that the illuminating boxes were made for the express purpose of house-breaking, and other midnight robberies. The sapient magistrate required no further proof of Millar's guilt, and he characterized the crime as being one of a most heinous nature, and to mark his sense of it, and at the same time vindicate the outraged laws of his country, he sent poor Millar to improve his morals and his muscles on the tread-mill for fourteen days. In those days, common jails and houses of correction were the best of all possible schools for improving the morals of young men, and expanding their ideas in the principles of professional roguery! If Millar was not benefited by his fourteen days' training, it was no fault of the worthy magistrate.

I have often observed that there is a species of old *womanism* about many of the provincial magistrates that is really quite refreshing. In the discharge of their very important duties, they wisely take care never to err on the side of mercy! The peculiar happy manner in which some of these gentlemen frequently apportion the punishment to the offence, is a proof that their virtuous feelings are more in keeping with the letter than the spirit of the law! ! I have frequently been puzzled, while listening to some of these sage dispensers of justice, and have been confounded by their matchless wisdom, when moralizing upon some two-penny crime against property, by a juvenile tyro in roguery. Men who are filled with the importance of their office have a right to expose their dignity to the best advantage, whether they are adjudicating upon large or small matters; with them it is of the utmost consequence that *their own feelings should be satisfied in vindicating the law.* I have no doubt but the worthy Mr. Shallow, of Norwich, went home after consigning Millar to the house of correction with the self-satisfaction of a man who had performed a highly meritorious action! ! ! I have introduced this little incident to show you how much some men are the mere sport of fortune; if Mr. Millar had not been fully initiated in the principles of roguery before he was sent to the *mill*, I certainly think it must have been his own fault, if he did not learn many useful lessons while there; and there can be no doubt but he returned to the world with pleasant notions of magisterial justice!

In reference to the phosphorescent boxes above alluded to, I have no doubt but the idea of our present lucifer match may have had its origin in that simple contrivance. I have heard it asserted, that Jonathan Martin was the first who conceived the idea of a metallic pen, by having used a piece of tin instead of a quil. By-the-bye, I had the honour of being acquainted with this gentleman. My first introduction to him was in 1825, shortly after he had made his escape from a lunatic asylum in or near Bishop Auckland; at that time he was selling an historical Sketch of his life. Four years after this, I was a witness to the conflagration that immortalizes his name, and consigned his diminutive person to St. Luke's Hospital, where he ended his career.*

A few evenings after this, I met another old Glasgow acquaintance, who had jumped the Jim Crow of life under a number of phases; poor fellow, at that time he was cultivating an acquaintance with the last friend to suffering humanity! About five years before this occasion, he had gone out to the United States upon a commercial speculation, and while in that country, he had the sad misfortune of nearly losing his eyesight; and, after spending all his money in an endeavour to have his vision restored, he returned to his native country, bankrupt in both health and fortune. Mr. Barlow was one of those men who carried with him a large amount of individuality; he possessed a bundle of the most kindly feelings imaginable, and his heart had room in it for any amount of affection, but I never knew a man who could hate with such an amazing number of horsepower. He possessed two ideas, which were to him the Alpha, and Omega of his inborn affection,—his country had no equal, and his religion was without a rival! Like Paddy with his honour, a person might as well touch his life as disparage either of these subjects. We were equally surprised, and, after condoling each other for our misfortunes, in parting, his last words were—"Keep up your heart, my boy, 'the darkest hour is nearest the light.' "

Before the end of the month, I had got pretty well inured to my new employment, but I found that my friend was anything but easy with me in the situation. I could understand that he was afraid of me as a rival; he knew that I was a steady man, and he took it into his head that if I were continued in the employment that I might supplant him. This was just the very last idea in my mind; moreover, if I had been desirous of doing so, I had not the capacity to fill his situation; and under any circumstances, I only looked upon my situation as one of a temporary character; however, he had become thoroughly imbued with the thought. When the first month passed, instead of employing me regular, he only gave me a day or two occasionally. Three weeks after we arrived in Liverpool my wife was confined, and having caught cold, she was unfortunately afflicted with gathered breasts. This circumstance entailed upon us an amount of misery which it would be impossible for me to describe.

* Jonathan Martin imagined that he was deputed by Almighty God to pull down the Established Church, and reform the religion of the country. In order to carry out these views, he set fire to York Minster, in 1829, by which a great portion of the building was destroyed. He was brother to the late celebrated Mr. Martin, the engraver.

There are a number of circumstances connected with the life of working men, which people in an independent sphere cannot feel—the smallest accident in the machinery of a family dependent upon labour, is frequently sufficient to turn the current of life from one of comparative happiness to irredeemable misery. I have often seen the truth of this observation confirmed in others, and I had also felt the serious consequences of having my own resources dried up under the hand of affliction, which was laid heavy upon me. My wife daily became worse, and her breasts continuing to gather and burst in painful succession. Seeing we could not afford a nurse, I had to do the duties of one myself. There were six of us, and out of this number I was the only one that could wait upon myself. During eight weeks, I had to nurse my wife, who was as helpless as an infant, to wash and cook for the family, and, the most difficult task of all, I had to nurse the infant. If we had had wherewithall to obtain the necessaries of life during this time, our case would not have been so entirely hopeless, as my own health was good, but we had nothing to defend us from the overpowering storm, and thus it swept over us in unbroken violence. All our little necessaries of clothing and other things which we could spare, went, one after another, into the hands of the obliging relation of the unfortunate and the improvident. I was often sick to the very soul to behold the sufferings of my prostrate but patient wife; her condition was almost hopeless. When our home was blest with food, the sunshine of happiness was on the innocent faces of my children, but the gloom of melancholy was on my own heart. I did not repine at the fate that had overtaken us—I was satisfied that God knew best what was for our good, and was willing to bear whatever infliction he might send with becoming resignation; but I certainly did repine at my own folly, for having allowed so many opportunities of providing for my family to pass without taking advantage of them.

This dark passage of my existence passed away, and I entered upon life once more with chastened feelings. I may here mention a circumstance connected with the house we occupied in Liverpool. I have been in many places where a colony of bugs held joint possession with the human occupiers, but I never witnessed such innumerable swarms as infested that house; every place was living with them, and the very air was permeated with bug animation—they fell into our food, crawled in lazy indifference over our bodies, and, like vampires, sucked our blood. At night they made processions over our naked faces—travelled upon voyages of discovery round the orbits of our eyes—marched into our ears, and held revel in the groves of our hair, and became joint partners in our clothing. I don't know that I was ever out of temper with any of the lower animals before; but these vile insects certainly did try my patience.

Shortly after I was able to leave my charge, I was so fortunate as to obtain a temporary engagement with a gentleman who was selling off his stock of hats, previous to retiring from business. My salary was only small, but I contented myself with the adage, that "half a loaf was better than no bread." I remained with this gentleman until the expiration of his term with his shop, which was in November, when my small services were again in the market. Before the end of the month, I had the good fortune to be again engaged with a gentleman in Liverpool, who was an agent for a Scotch house in the book-trade. My new duty was that of a deliverer, and the field of my operations was to be in Manchester and the surrounding country. At first I found this work pretty laborious, but I soon became used to it. Delivering serial works is by no means a pleasant business; and a man, to be at all successful in the profession, must be careful, and leave both honour and honesty at home—if he possesses such property. At the end of nine months, I was superseded by a gentleman who was sent up to Manchester by the firm in Scotland. So I was once more shackled with freedom! and to add to the comforts of my position, the addition of another young one to my family.

I dare say you are getting tired in following me through the mazes of my wayward fate. I think you will agree with me, that my journey thus far has been sufficiently varied, even for the most hungry lover of change. You have, however, still a few more milestones to pass with me, ere I can bring you up to my present position. Whether I shall now be allowed to finish my journey on the downhill of life free from the toils and vicissitudes of my past career, is a mystery which time alone can solve.

Letter XI

My dear Thomas.—Being without money in civilized society is just about the same as a man in a savage state of existence being divested of his arms. There certainly are some men who can turn their wits to profitable account; but in nine cases out of ten, their operations tend to the injury of other members of the community. The man who is always on the watch to take advantage of the weakness, credulity or want of attention of his fellow-men, must frequently have opportunities of carrying his plans into action. The class of people, however, who live by chicanery and swindling by profession, are only few, when compared with the entire population of the country, and under any circumstances, their lives never can be happy, inasmuch as they require to be continually on the watch. Morally speaking, I know that such people as these sustain no uneasiness from anything in the shape of conscience. Men who give themselves up to the violation of all principles of right, can have no check from such a monitor, and their lives are in continual antagonism to honour and virtue. Amid the struggle for existence in the ever-changing condition of the commercial population of Great Britain, there are to be found a very numerous class of people who have been plunged into difficulties by those little mishaps, or accidents, which are continually taking place in the social machinery. Many of these people have been accustomed to, not only the comforts, but also the elegancies of life, and when they find their level at the bottom of society, where men elbow each other without the politeness of an apology, in order to live, their condition is melancholy in the extreme. Yet it is pleasing to know, that in humanity there is an energy which accompanies struggling nature, and, as it were, assists the sons and daughters of misfortune to adapt themselves to their new conditions. This is certainly a wise provision in providence; it may be looked upon as suiting the back to the burden.

After I lost my situation as a deliverer, I did not know what to do next, and my late situation was just of that character that I could not save a single shilling; so I was once more steeped to the lips in poverty, while my prospect for the future was full of gloom. With a mind ill at rest, I made application to a Register Office in town, and paid the keeper the only two shillings I possessed. I was requested to call in a few days. In the meantime the wants of my family were beginning to be uncomfortably urgent. I commenced and wrote a series of puffs, and submitted them to a pushing house in Manchester, and was so fortunate as to receive fifteen shillings for them. After this I called several times at the Register Office, and was as often put off with false promises. I would not have ventured my two shillings in this place, had it not been for an advertisement the fellow had upon his board, which I thought would suit me. When I saw that the scoundrel was living upon what he could obtain from the most destitute members of society, I called, and in a very authoritative tone demanded my money back; he tried to shuffle me for a minute or two, but when I threatened a public exposure he returned me my cash. I know the infamous tricks of these leeches, and have not been backward in exposing them, which any one may find in my "Language of the Walls," &c.[123] For the space of two or three months I tried the book-canvassing business. This trade may be looked upon as the last resource of fallen gentility. The man who embarks in it should have the following requisites, namely, a clean face, a suit of clothes sufficiently respectable to insure the wearer a passport into a tradesman's counting-house, an amount of cool confidence that will take no denial, a temper which can put up with any amount of insult, and the smaller the stock of honesty the better. I am aware that if I could have given my mind to this business, I could have made a comfortable living by it, but I candidly confess, that I never went out to do a day's work in it, but I felt myself degraded by the occupation. Although turning grain was a very laborious business, I certainly preferred it a thousand times to the other.

On the 7th of January, 1852, I was introduced to another new trade. I dare say you will think by this time that I have been Jack of all professions and master of none. Should you do so, you are not far wrong in the conclusion. My pliability, I can assure you, was so far in my favour. If I had adopted the motto of *Ne sutor ultra crepidam*, I should certainly have stuck fast in the world, and you would not have had the benefit of my enlarged experience. My next essay in the battle of life was in assisting in making a Commercial Directory for the good people of Manchester. I was employed at this business from January until September, with the exception of one month in the interval, during which I was employed upon Mr. John Bright's Parliamentary Election Committee, for which service I was both complimented and well paid.[124] In September, 1852, I was sent up to Guildford, in Surrey, upon another Directory-making expedition, in order to assist in taking the home counties. This speculation, however, turned out a failure, in consequence of Mr. Kelly, of London, having just completed and delivered a Directory for these counties. When the mistake was found out, I got the *route*, with seven others, for Hull, in Yorkshire.

I remained in this business until January, 1853, when I was fairly starved

[123] See introduction, pp. 26–7.
[124] Bright came second in a four-cornered contest for the two-member Manchester constituency in the general election of 9 July 1852.

out. My wages were so small that I could not manage to maintain myself and family. And what was still worse, I could not get my money when it was due. Having made myself *au fait* in this business to a certain extent, I felt pretty confident of meeting with a better engagement in some other house in the line. At the time I was leaving my Directory situation, there was a gentleman in Leeds upon the eve of bringing out a commercial magazine. I got the offer of an engagement with this person to assist in obtaining subscribers for the work among the commercial and manufacturing community. My first journey in this new business was down to Glasgow. From January to May, I had introduced the magazine into all the principal towns in Scotland, and the Midland counties of England.

I am now about introducing you to the last scene in the shifting drama of my truly chequered life, up to the present time. In the month of May, 1853, I was offered employment from a gentleman to whom I had been recommended by a mutual friend. The conditions of the engagement offered were more liberal than I had been accustomed to for some time; I was therefore not slow in accepting the offer. The character of the business was perfectly new to me; but I had every confidence in being equal to it, and have since both justified my own anticipations, and the expectations of my employer.[125] Since I have been in my present business, I have travelled over the most of England and Scotland, and have therefore passed over many of those scenes that were once familiar to me; and have had many opportunities of comparing the past with the present state of things.

In September of 1854 I travelled from Newton-stewart to Dumfries. This was within a few months of forty years after my runaway exploit. The old widow's house that sheltered me at the ferry-town of Cree had disappeared; but the farm-house on the way-side where I slept on the Sunday evening was still unchanged. In several places, as I passed along, I found that the highway had been completely altered. Modern improvement was everywhere visible. I found villages where formerly there was not the vestige of a house; and in other places ruins, where I had formerly seen cheerful dwellings. I could see no greater change in that part of the country than what was observable in the condition of the soil; everywhere the hand of industry was abundantly visible in the improved state of the land. In one place, hundreds of acres of moorland was reclaimed; and in another, what had been a deep bog was drained, and bearing a rich harvest of grain. The character of the modern dwellings in all the country districts is highly indicative of the improved taste and condition of the people. When I was journeying from Lockerby to Langholm, I saw several relics of a primitive age. Amid the ruins of one old moorland farm-house I found an old corn-mill in a state of excellent preservation. I allude to the hand-mill, which, I believe, was used in Scotland within

---

[125] In the 1882 ed. he is more open about his new profession. He is in fact working for Rev. William Hill, ex-proprietor of the *Northern Star*, as a debt collector. (1882 ed., pp. 220, 25, 54). See also introduction, p. 29.

the last hundred years. I also observed several spinning-wheels, both great and small: the large wheel was used for making yarn for stockings, blankets, plaids, &c., while the small one was used for producing yarn for the *sarks*[126] and sheets.

A great change has come over Hawick, since poor McNamee and myself were inmates of the Tolbooth, between forty and fifty years ago. At that time there were a number of French officers (prisoners of war) quartered in Hawick and its neighbourhood. The *Rubers Law*, and the *Eildon Hills* cast their deep shadows over the adjacent landscapes, as they did fifty years ago; but the physical aspect of their respective localities is strangely altered. The sweet little town of Melrose, in consequence of the beauty of its position, the salubrity of its air, and the magnificence of its abbey in ruins, has become a summer haunt of the invalid, and a place of attraction to the student of nature. Abbotsford has become a shrine before which the lovers of genius delight to bend the knee. This strange conglomoration of all the real and imaginary stiles of architecture is shaded in eternal gloom, inasmuch as the Eildon Hills stand like three giants between it and the sun. The din of machinery now resounds by Galla's stream, where erewhile all was still, save the murmuring of the limpid brook. Selkirk, too, has gone with the age, and become a manufacturing town. I observed when there, that Mr. Brown has erected one of the most splendid woollen mills in Scotland. When I was a boy, these valleys were as quiet as seclusion from the busy haunts of men could make them, and it was then an *unca'* thing to see a stranger within their border. How true it is that "time works wonders."

On my journey from Gallashiels to Lauder, I crossed Watling-street, the old Roman road, which formed the line of communication from London to the wall which divided the Friths of Forth and Clyde. Before steamboats and railways came into use, this road formed the common highway for the numerous herds of cattle which were then sent in droves to England. From my own experience and observation, I would say that the progress of transition has been more rapid in Scotland than in any other part of the United Kingdom. The social condition of the people is as different from what it was fifty years ago, as it is possible to imagine. The annual visits of Her Majesty within the last fourteen years has made that part of her kingdom the regular resort of a large portion of the higher and middle class English. At one time, I could flatter myself that I was one in five hundred thousand, if not a million, of old George the Third's subjects who had made the grand tour of England and Scotland!! Fifty years ago, a journey from Scotland to London, was a very important undertaking, and the preparation for such an event was greater than would be now necessary for a journey to Hong Kong. I dispute that your modern traveller would manifest so much curiosity on witnessing the frowning batteries of Malta, the heterogeneous mixture of Eastern races in the dark dingy streets of Grand Cairo, the little old fashioned

[126] Shirts.

dirty town of Aden, with its noise and bustle of landing and embarking passengers, or the tropical luxurance of Ceylon with its herds of hill coolies,— as your traveller of fifty years ago, would have done upon his first visit to Berwick-upon-Tweed, with its crumbling walls and narrow Gothic bridge;— Newcastle-upon-Tyne, with its side resting on a comfortable travelling declivity, at an angle of forty-five degrees;—the quiet town of Durham, with its zigzag streets and sombre cathedral;—and the good city of York with its narrow street, double-ribbed houses, and splendid minster. But we must remember this is the age of the rail, electric telegraph, and a general desire for everybody to be everywhere. I sometimes feel a melancholy regret at the loss of our old-fashioned method of transit by the stage-coach; there was really something cheerful and exhilarating in seeing a good whip managing his four-in-hand in all the pride of his profession, and listening to a jolly bluff guard, sounding his warning horn. It was pleasant to hear the slang of the clerks of the stable, with their sly observations and rude jests, as they changed the 'osses for the next stage. It was also a pleasant consolation for the hungry traveller, while in the act of masticating a half-crown dinner, to be warned by the guard's horn, that it was time for him to discontinue his knife and fork operations, if he desired to proceed on his journey! A knowing set of fellows were the stage-coach guards, they had a sly look, and a familiar leer, for all the pretty girls on the road, and Dan O'Connell could never beg with more independence than they. A capital race of sportsmen were the guards, and they could bag more game in a season than any lord duke, although they seldom used fowling pieces.

It would be a tedious task to enumerate the many changes which have come over the face of society in my time. The application of steam to machinery has been the means of introducing a great number of new trades. Then came the railways, with their surprising interest and revolutionizing influence, creating a thousand new wants and callings into existence and a great variety of new branches of industry. Electricity, too, has been made subservient to many modern improvements in several of the arts. India-rubber and gutta percha have been turned to a hundred valuable purposes, of both utility and ornament. While new trades and professions have sprung into existence in rapid succession; numbers of old ones have tumbled out of both use and memory; and should the social system progress upon anything like the same ratio during the next fifty years, we will be like Paddy when in love—"Faith, not ourselves at all at all." Fifty years ago, we were the most inartistic people imaginable. The decorations of the cottage, and even the farm-house, were confined to a few stupid prints and rude wood-cuts; a tiger, or a funny looking shepherdess stuck in the centre of a rough and tasteless made tea-tray, and perhaps a few stucco dolls, with a parrot beautifully daubed with green paint on each wing. The old prints and wood-cuts are now displaced by elegant designs, either engraved or lithographed—the ill-informed and badly executed tray has given place to beautiful specimens

184

of art on iron and *papier maché*—the stucco dolls and natural history ornaments of fifty years ago have been superseded by splendid works of art in
bronze and imitation Parian marble. The farmers' wives, in many instances,
make their butter by steam and send it to market by the rail. Fish are now
caught in the Frith of Forth in the morning, and stewed over fires in London
for the next day's dinner. The cheap postage regulation has made men write
who never wrote before; and the steam-press has caused those who read but
little to read the more. The very day-light has found a rival in gas; and our
thoughts are scarcely able to keep up with the ideas we are in the habit of
sending along our magic wires. The dispatch of fifty years ago is the miserable
delay of the present age, and men seem now to be in such haste, that they are
ready to kick both time and space out of the market. I really think that the
only part of our system that lingers with something like reverential fondness
to the good old fashions of fifty years ago, is that of our Government. I do not
know what other people think, but I cannot help respecting men who evince
a veneration for the past. All our antecedents are made up of so many
yesterdays, and the morrow never comes!

Letter XII

London, August 12th, 1855.

MY DEAR THOMAS.—The world is a great school for human education, and the different grades of society we mingle with are our monitors. The methods of instruction may be clearly divided into three classes: the first and most impressive is that which we receive from those we associate with. Our lessons in this department are of a practical character, and embrace the every-day acts of our lives, whether they relate to business or pleasure. The second class of instruction is that which we receive from clergymen and other public instructors, and its object is to impress upon us the beauty and advantage of a correct rule of life. The last source of information is, that which is derived from books, which may be said to embrace the whole round of human knowledge.

My principal object in this chapter is to show you how my own mind and feelings have been acted upon by these different systems of education. During my youthful probation in the school of the busy world, I had ample means of obtaining a rich fund of valuable information, if I had had the power of arranging its various details, and selecting the wheat from the tares; this, however, was above my capacity, my mind, therefore, only received such impressions as it was most susceptible of embracing. The practical lessons men receive in their intercourse with each other, embrace all the various phases of human character, arising from the workings of their passions in their different degrees, modes, and conditions. I may observe, however, that society itself is divided and subdivided into a variety of classes, totally distinct in their character, habits, and conditions from each other. Each of these divisions have their own systems of worldly education. The shepherd, who tends his fleecy flocks far from the busy haunts of the bartering world, requires little learning to enable him to perform his simple round of duty, and his ambition seldom leads his mind beyond the locality where it may be said he vegetates. Transplant this seemingly dull member of the human family into the bustle of the trading world, and you will find that he will soon shake off the rust which the inaction of his former mode of life coated him with. Some men have their education forced upon them by the circumstances of their position in life; others charge their minds with stores of knowledge from the various fields of their observation, and make use of it, either for their own or the advantage of others, as circumstances may demand.

186

During the last fifty years, the field of human knowledge has been opened up in a surprising degree. The development of scientific information, and its application to the improvement of the arts, and the every-day concerns of life, have been the means of changing the whole machinery of social life. From these circumstances, it will be seen that men of inquiring minds have many opportunities of obtaining knowledge, if they will only take the trouble to look for it. Our intercourse with society will necessarily force us to be observers of both men and things. Rubbing against the world is well calculated to sharpen our wits, but in this matter we should be careful lest we allow the kindly feelings of our nature to be blunted. For my part, I have no sympathy with the cold calculating philosophy of the worldly wise, that impresses upon its votaries the heartless adage, of taking every man for a rogue until we have the means of proving him honest! If all men were to act upon this unchristian maxim, the generous impulses of men's nature would be closed up by an eternal barrier of ice. I freely admit that proper caution is highly necessary in our dealings with the world, but I truly detest the mean grovelling principle of such unwarranted suspicion, as is implied in the above doctrine. In my own experience, I have ever found that there is both a noble and generous principle in man, that denies all fellow-feeling with such a mere worldly policy. It is true, that men in their every-day dealings with each other, frequently trespass upon each other's rights and privileges; but it must be borne in mind, that this deviation from the rule of right is often forced upon them from necessity rather than choice. Let it not be supposed that I am an apologist for wrong-doing; my object is rather to prove that our natural impulses, if left free from the influence of pressing circumstances, would lead us in an opposite direction. I think every man who has been brought up under the influence of anything like proper training, must be continually under the control of a regulating monitor; of course much will depend on the susceptibility of this silent prompter. It is true, that certain classes of men are liable to be placed under circumstances which are calculated to blunt their conscientious scruples; but the man who is in this condition demands our pity rather than our hatred.

Every man has a knowledge of his own circumstances and condition in life; but he can only form a very inadequate idea of the influences which regulate the conduct of others. I have frequently been impelled to the performance of actions from the sheer pressure of circumstances, against which my better nature revolted; and such I believe to have been the case with many others who have had to do battle with the world. It must be remembered, that the perfection of our nature is a thing only to be hoped for after we have shuffled off this mortal coil; and when men have time and the will to look into themselves, they will have little room for fault-finding in their neighbours. It is a fact taught by every-day experience, that every state and condition of life has its difficulties, and that wherever humanity exists, it must bear the burden of its infirmities in some degree or other. I have called your attention to this subject, that you may see the danger of the debasing feelings of envy and unmanly repining; and that while you observe the ever active machinery of the social system, you may never fail to act well your own part. Frugality and improvidence may be said to be two of the principal land-marks which lie in the path of working-men; the one should be a continual guide by which we should steer our conduct, and the other should be looked upon as a beacon to apprise us of the rocks and shoals of intemperance, which every way surround us on the journey of life.

Forethought seems to be in a great measure, a characteristic of man; this faculty enables him to look forward to the contingencies which may await him on the morrow. The man who forgets that he owes both himself and society the exercise of such a forethought, is indeed, a very unworthy member of the community. I would, therefore, advise you to use every necessary caution within the limit of your means to provide against future wants. It is a fact in moral science, that every good is liable to abuse by perversion. I know of no feeling so truly grovelling and sordid as that which possesses the *save-all* member of society. The moment a man commences a career of hoarding money merely for its own sake, he snaps asunder the bond of sympathy which connects him with his kind. Money is merely a simple pledge, which men receive in exchange either for their labour or some representation of it. Labour is, therefore, the only true wealth in the world. Money was made to be used as a convenient article of barter; and we use it instead of exchanging the produce of our labour, which would often be both inconvenient and troublesome. The man who saves money for the love of it, is frequently an enemy to himself, by denying himself those necessaries which it was intended to furnish him with. There are two other evils which arise out of this saving propensity; in the first place, he destroys the bartering efficiency of the cash for the time being, and thereby prevents the good its circulation would otherwise produce in society; but the most serious evil is the deadening influence it would exercise over his own character, in steeling his heart against all the kindlier feelings of his nature. A little reflection will convince you, that the proper line of prudence lies between these two extremes. It is a fact, that the standard of men's respectability in all civilized countries, is measured by the amount of wealth he possesses. This estimate of character must have its origin in something like a just appreciation of right, inasmuch as it exists by universal consent. The knowledge of this fact, furnishes an excellent motive to prudent and industrious habits. This state of public feeling has also its dark side, inasmuch as riches frequently gild vice in the false glitter of seeming virtue. The *prestige* of wealth has a still more dangerous consequence to a large portion of the community than what can arise from its immediate corrupting influence. This is to be found in a feeling of exclusiveness which it produces in the minds of its votaries. Strange as it may appear to us, as members of a free country, there exists a very general feeling against men who presume to push themselves upwards upon the scale of society; the opinion both expressed and felt upon this subject, is, that they are acting against a recognised rule. The doctrine is therefore, that if a man should be born a blacksmith, he should remain so. I am aware, that there are hundreds of men, who, although they feel in their hearts the injustice of such a doctrine, are, by the force of public opinion, prevented from avowing the true sentiments of their minds. Whatever men may feel upon this subject, there is one thing certain, that well-directed energy backed by habits of industry and common prudence, will always make way for itself in spite of the cold conventionalisms of the world, or the aristocratic notions of those whom chance has kicked into comfortable berths!

It may be supposed that I have made these observations in a snarling temper; but no, I am arguing this question from the experience of others; for in so far as I am concerned, if any man ever stood between himself and the light of the sun, I am he! It will therefore be seen, that in my own case, I have nothing to complain of. Perhaps, it would be better for society at large, if more respect were paid to character than to the extrinsic trappings of mere wealth; if such were the case, the fortuitous power of riches would stand a chance of being reduced to a more rational standard. From my experience of the social system, I think it is very questionable, whether a more equal distribution of property would be beneficial to the community. Riches furnish an immunity from physical labour; if, therefore, wealth was more equally divided, it is very likely that industry would be cripped in proportion, and as a consequence, society would be a loser; this contingency, however, is amply provided against by the very nature of man's inequality. The knowledge of men's mental and physical disparity, as well as their difference in habits of frugality, must have first dictated the law of primo-geniture, in order to preserve family property by hereditary succession. I think upon the whole, it matters very little whether the riches be held by one class or another, inasmuch as there will always be a select few who will possess great wealth. This unequal state of things has existed in all civilized countries within the range of history; and I am convinced that the same order of things will continue to the end! In a well-regulated condition of society, both men and money are sure to find their level; and I am convinced, that the needy man, who would lend himself as a willing agent to pull down the fabric of the social system, would, in his turn, become a violent con-servator, as soon as he had his share of the spoil! In our experience of all the states and conditions of society, there is one thing which cannot help forcing itself upon our observation, which is simply this—that honesty of character, and kindliness of disposition, form the best passport to the esteem and consideration of those we associate with in our daily transactions. It is a happy consideration, that men of all sorts of temperaments and constitutions are able to find kindred souls and congenial spirits, in which they discover an echo of their own feelings. I think it may be admitted, that nearly all our friendships have their origin in this wise provision of nature. It has been said that friendship is the solder of society, and in my opinion, it is a glorious cement. That condition of existence which is best calculated to bring the generous feelings of our nature into action, is by far the most happy and rational. Men's good actions are the flowers which spring up in the garden of humanity, and make the paths of life delicious with their sweet odours. These flowers spring in every condition of soil, from the lowest to the highest. The friendship of the peasant is as warm and devoted as that of the peer; and the love of the beggar may be as pure and holy as that which charms the soul of royalty. It is a glorious attribute of the divine law, that the measure of our joys is not regulated by our positions in life. Herein lies the whole poetry that surrounds the human family, and lends a charm to the feelings of the humblest as well as the greatest.

Our second source of education, is through the medium of public teachers; these may be divided into three classes. The first of which are the schoolmasters, whose duty it is to prepare the rising generation for the active career of life. The second are the clergy, to whom is entrusted the highest order of human instruction. The duties of these men are of a two-fold character; the first is to teach their flocks the science of revealed religion, in which the rules of faith of the various sects are unfolded. In this department of education, reason is made subservient to belief! The second division of clerical teaching, appertains to moral training; in this department reason is appealed to as the regulating principle of human action. The next source of education is derived from public lecturers. The teaching of this class of men is generally confined to an exposition of the laws of nature, as exemplified in the development of the arts and sciences. In all civilized nations, whether ancient or modern, the clergy have possessed nearly the sole power of directing the public mind. In many instances, this body has been above the civil power; under such circumstances, they possessed the sole directing power over men's consciences; of late years they have been brought within the pale of the civil law. It is a fact worthy of notice, that the generally accepted code of morality among the civilized family of men admits of no dispute. The various classes and denominations of men may have as many standards of faith as they please, but it is a happy consideration that we can only have one standard of morality. Our different weights and measures may vary in their proportions; this we care little for, as long as each denomination is true in itself. I have frequently observed that men are more liable to forget the duty they owe each other, when their notions upon religious subjects are in opposition. It is certainly somewhat strange and anomalous, that when we imagine we have formed correct opinions in regard to abstract ideas or principles, we should take such trouble to force these opinions upon others, whose impressions are different from our own, but whose convictions are equally strong! The law of nature, which prompts men to propagate their opinions and distribute their ideas, is one of those grand conceptions of the Divine will, whereby men are enabled to enlarge each other's views, and contribute to each other's happiness, without any diminution of their own. The manner in which men abuse this heavenly attribute is worthy of notice. When a man is deeply impressed with any principle, or abstract notion of rule of conduct, so that it becomes to him a settled conviction, the very possession of the idea gives him the right to propagate it; but it must be borne in mind, that the moment he interferes with the liberty of his fellow-men, by using coercion in forcing his opinions upon them, he violates the first principle of that liberty which God has decreed to all men. When men use violence in enforcing their religious opinions, they act in opposition to the Divine will; and the only consideration they require to direct them in the matter, is to reflect as to how they would wish to be treated by others! Were it not for the violation of this principle, the teaching of so many conflicting dogmas by the numerous sects, which each sets up as its own standard of perfection, would be comparatively harmless. The fact is, the principle of religious liberty is only beginning to be understood. Even now toleration is looked upon as a charitable license allowed by one class of the community to another! While I am writing, the legislature is engaged in repealing some hundred and twenty old musty penal enactments. Some of these monuments of the wisdom of our forefathers were in active use only a few years ago, and were used for the laudable purpose of preventing the human mind from expanding more rapidly than the time could afford. The country will owe the sweeping away of these legislative deformities in a great measure to my Lord Brougham, whose comprehensive and liberal mind has suggested so many valuable improvements in our legal code during the last forty years.

I think, on the whole, that the great diversity of opinions taught by the different religious denominations in this country, has its value in keeping alive the mental faculties, and acting as a useful spur to honest ambition. As long as men act with charity towards each other, the diversity of their thoughts and opinions constitutes one of the greatest beauties of the social system. In looking at religious associations in a mere wordly point of view, we cannot fail to see their utility. There is an evident wisdom in the frequent meetings of large bodies of the people for the purpose of public instruction; but when we know these gatherings are set apart for the worship of the eternal God, our minds become inspired with a veneration corresponding to such a holy duty. The congregating of men in public places for the service of God, is well calculated to withdraw their minds from the everyday concerns of life, and humble them in their own estimation.

The last member of my proposition, refers to the quiet teaching of books. From my own experience, I would say, that well selected books, not only furnish us with useful instruction, but they also convey to our minds a source of silent pleasure not to be found elsewhere. I well remember when the glowing histories of Greece and Rome opened up to my mind their wondrous treasures, with what avidity I devoured their contents! In my mind, a book is the living depository of the author's feelings and sentiments upon the subject of which he treats; and whether he writes for pay or pleasure, he must leave honest traces of his thoughts upon its pages, whether he will or not. The abstraction from the busy world necessary for reading, is well calculated to enable us to digest the mental food, and thereby assimilate its *chyle* with our previous stock of knowledge. If the subject matter of a book is not directed to vicious purposes, the author is sure to convey, through the medium of his own style, some valuable information or pleasing matter to his readers.

The peculiarities of style is a striking characteristic among authors, and cannot fail to impress us with their varied modes of arranging and classifying their ideas. It is in this strange condition of the human mind, when acted upon by different temperaments, that men's idiosyncrasies are made patent to the world. I cannot do better than give you an illustration of this peculiarity or mannerism among authors. If Mr. Carlisle was requested to describe any common-place occurrence, he would be sure to clothe the subject with the peculiar tints of his own mind. The inverted construction of his sentences would stand out in bold relief, wherein his mind would be labelled in legible characters. While reading his effusions, one is forcibly reminded of travelling upon a rugged road, or of being tossed on a *cross* sea. The lofty and dignified diction of Sir A. Alison contrasts strangely with the terse Saxon of the late William Cobbett. In the latter, we have the plain solid architecture of the ancient Gothic, and in the other, we have all the beauty and elegance of the florid style, with its graceful mouldings, fancy ornaments, flying buttresses, and handsome pinnacles. Each have their beauties. Alison's is well calculated to convey to our minds the majesty and world-wide importance of his subject, while that of the other, is singularly adapted for a slashing onslaught on public abuses. The contrast between Burns and Campbell is equally striking with the above. In Burns, we have the plain Doric, with its simple and homely ornamentation, while in Campbell, we have the Corinthian in all its grandeur and magnificence. Notwithstanding the beauty and elegance of Campbell's style, his poetry wants the magic of that homely feeling which all men claim as a part of themselves. The kindred feelings of humanity are bound together by one simple cord, and this may be looked upon as the electric wire through which the sympathies of our souls are communicated. The man who can successfully cause this cord to vibrate in unison with our thoughts and affections must be inspired with the genius of poetry and such a man was the ploughman bard. I think it will be admitted, that there could scarcely be a greater difference between two men, than that which characterized the minds of Pope and Byron. Both their styles and modes of thinking were of a different caste; yet it is a curious coincidence, that their satires would almost appear to be emanations of the same mind. The bold slashing vigour of some men's writing contrasts strangely with the quiet flow of gentle feeling which characterize that of others: the one puts us in mind of the mountain torrent as it rushes through the vale or breaks in foam over the cataract; while the other reminds us of a smooth running river, on whose surface the moonbeams play amid the gentle ripple of its waters. There is both a grandeur and beauty in the style of Byron peculiarly his own; but, poor fellow! he unfortunately looked down upon the world from a false point of view. Although we are carried away by the magic of his manner, we rise from the perusal of his works with the two-fold feeling of pity and wonder. We pity him for his small estimate of human nature, and his want of faith in the higher characteristics of man; and we are impelled by a sense of justice to acknowledge the surprising majesty of his perverted genius. It has been said that the writings of Voltaire, Paine, and others of the same school, were calculated to unsettle men's minds in reference to the leading principles of religion and morality; but I am fully convinced, that the works of these men never exercised such a demoralising influence over the minds of their readers, as did the works of Byron. He scoffed at the whole family of man from the vantage ground of his great intellect, and treated the highest aspirations of their minds with giant levity.

In speaking of poets, we should bear in mind, that, in an intellectual point of view, they are an exception to the rest of men: the construction of their minds and all their modes of thinking are peculiarly their own, and their happiest home is in the glorious regions of fancy. The temperament of a poet is incased in a framework of keen susceptibilities. There is a spiritualisation in his constitution that is unknown to ordinary mortals: his imagination clothes the humblest objects of his thought in beauty, and he lends a charm to common things which cannot be discovered by vulgar eyes. Love to him is a pure etherial flame, that warms his soul with the fire of heaven. I have ever observed that the genius of poetry loves to dwell where sanity has ceased to wield her sceptre with sovereign sway. Cowper worshipped the muses when reason was tottering on her throne. The mind of Swift often wandered in the mazes of madness. Oliver Goldsmith's life was spent in the fairy land of imagination, where he endeavoured to exist beyond the cold realities of the world. Tannahill, one of the sweetest lyrical poets of Scotland, passed through the valley of life beneath a dark cloud of melancholy. The transient existence of Burns was surrounded with deep shades of mental gloom, and Lord Byron was a victim to the curse of hypochondriaism.

It will be seen, that in criticising the works of poets, we should make allowance for their state of mind. I believe, that the man who devotes the whole energies of his mind to any single pursuit, either in connection with the arts or sciences, is sure to become an enthusiast. It will follow, that the concentration of his faculties to one object will necessarily weaken those powers of his mind that are over-taxed. The nervous system cannot be over-wrought with impunity. It is a curious fact, and one which I have often had occasion to notice, that the class of men employed as clowns in places of public amusement, are invariably the victims of hypochondriaism; and I believe such to be the case with nearly all men who are obliged to tax any particular faculty of the mind beyond the point of endurance. The law of nature, that governs the human system, is always true to itself. We cannot enjoy any great amount of excitement, without suffering a corresponding depression. The madness of poets may thus, in some measure, be accounted for. I am firmly convinced, that no man can be a poet, in the true sense of the term, whose heart and soul is not fairly engaged in it. His imagination must feel the electric influence of creative power, and his fancy must be for ever on the wing. His appreciation of the beauties of nature must be far above that of the common herd; and above all, he must feel within himself those passions that for ever agitate humanity in its tenderest parts. If the poet suffers the depressing consequences of an over-strained mind, he also enjoys the ravishing delights of revelling in his own beautiful creations, and he possesses the balmy pleasure of knowing that he has contributed to the happiness of others. From the time that Homer bowed his knee before the lovely *Nine*, through the succeeding generations of men, poets have been in the van of civilization. Their soft numbers have exalted women, and smoothed the rough asperities of man's rude nature. The glorious firmament of heaven has supplied them with innumerable images, and earth and ocean have furnished them with never-ending subjects. The joys and sorrows of humanity, in the every-changing panorama of life, has been their constant theme. They have played with our feelings like an Indian juggler with his balls, and they have amused us with our follies until we have become our own sport. When they loved, it has been our own, and their patriotism has been our love of fatherland. The "Cottar's Saturday Night," described by Burns, was no ideal picture of a humble but happy home; and we love it the more because of its truthfulness. The meretricious trappings of the sons and daughters of fortune are not the true symbols of poetry; its regions are in the warm affections of humanity, in the homes where peace and contentment love to dwell, whether in the busy town or the peaceful vale. Prattling innocence and venerable age, the *ripening* heart in love's sweet thrall, and the happy union of kindred souls, have ever been welcome food for poetic minds. All men must feel a poetic influence steal over their senses in occasional moments of inspiration; there is a sublimity in a man dividing his crust of bread with a hungry neighbour—in the act he obeys God through his own generous nature; our feelings of admiration may therefore be excited by acts which appear trivial in themselves, but when seen correctly, are matters of deep importance.

It has frequently been asked, What is poetry? My opinion is, that it is merely a truthful picture of nature, wherein the objects are arranged, and garnished according to the fancy of the artist. I cannot illustrate this better than by a quotation from Burns, wherein he says,

> "Gie me a canty hour at e'en,
> My arms about my dearie."[127]

[127] The quotation, from *Green Grow the Rashes* should read, "But gie me a canny hour at e'en,/ My arms about my dearie O;"

You will observe that this is a very homely way of expressing the poet's sense of enjoyment; but its poetic excellence lies in its truth. The desire here expressed is that which all men feel under the influence of love. The following little homely, but beautiful images, are from Tannahill:—

> "Saft the craw-flower's early bell,
>   Deck Gleniffer's dewy dell,
>   Blooming like thy bonnie sel',
>   My ain, my artless dearie, O!
>   Tow'ring o'er the Newton Woods,
>   Laverocks *fan* the snaw-white clouds,
>   Siller saughs wi' downy buts,
>   Fringe the banks fou' breerie, O!"[128]

In these stanzas, we have a beautiful combination of the most homely images; but they are true to nature, and the object of the poet's devotion finds a place in our own affections.

Perhaps the best criterion of measured verse is the power it exercises over our feelings; and this is the simple secret that makes the humblest members of society as good judges of true poetry as the most learned *savans*. I believe there is no better method of finding the social character of a people than through their lyrical poetry. I may mention the fact, that in this department of literature, England is far behind both Scotland and Ireland. The lyrics of both these divisions of the kingdom are full of animation, and they bring before the mind's eye all the leading characteristics of the people. The homely, but expressive vernacular of the Scotch is well suited as a vehicle for their poetic effusions. The Irish lyric poetry is full of broad rollicking humour, and plaintive feeling, while that of England is dull, lifeless, and insipid.

There is one thing strikes me forcibly,—that if we want to find good lyrical poetry, it will not be among the higher orders of civilization. In this case there are certain conditions of life favourable to the outpourings of human passion; and I believe the middle state of a nation's existence to be the one best calculated for such a purpose. The age of superstition is peculiarly one of poetry, when men's minds are kept alive by supernatural agencies.

Few men have possessed the power of lending a charm to instruction in the happy manner exercised by Sir Walter Scott. His style was quiet, natural, easy and playful. The fanciful graces of his truly great mind were scattered like beautiful flowers through the whole of his works. His numerous descriptions were living pictures of nature's scenery; and the personages of his dramas were real human beings, acting, feeling and conversing in accordance with the times and circumstances that surrounded them. He had the honour of making a new discovery in the boundless field of literature, by making

---

[128] Slightly misquoted lines taken from two stanzas of Tannahill's *Gloomy Winter's Now Awa'*. A scattering of spelling errors suggests Burn may only have heard and not read the poem.

195

fiction subservient to history, and no man ever cultivated maiden soil to better advantage.

Books, to me, have ever been welcome companions. Through their pages I have often held converse with the mighty dead. In some, my own thoughts and feelings have been reflected as if in a mirror. In others, I have made new discoveries in the regions of thought, and revelled midst new-born delights. Often have I been carried along the stream of history into the dim vista of time, where men lived in the dream-land of human infancy, and have watched the opening and expanding of the mind of man, until it became like "gods, knowing good and evil." While I was in Otley, my love of reading forced upon me the necessity of learning to write. This I found no easy task; however, I mastered it sufficiently for my purpose, and the possession of this little acquirement has often been of no small value to me.

In scanning these different sources of instruction, you will observe, that each possesses a relative value. The hard, practical lessons of the world are necessary to enable us to perform our respective parts upon its busy stage. Religion is calculated to smooth our paths to heaven, and, if taught in a spirit of love, so much the better. And books give us the experience of thoughtful men, who lay their knowledge before us like so many free-will offerings, and enrich us by the possession of that which taketh nothing from the donor.

In bringing before you the various methods of obtaining instruction, my object is to show you how my own mind and actions have been affected by the unfinished processes through which I have passed. I think I have proved that my experience of the world and its teachings have not been of a very limited character. I am obliged to confess that my education in this department has been a complete failure. Although my teachers have been as various as my different positions, and much of their instructions forced upon me by the necessities of my condition, yet have I always been a dull dog. The materials and advantages of social standing are things that have always passed rapidly through my hands, and I believe, no amount of worldly training could ever have made me otherwise than a temporal custodier of such things. My worldly wisdom has always been confined to acting upon the impulses of my nature, more than any sordid desire to seize hold of the advantages which lay before me. A generous and illiberal view of the character and motives of such members of society as business or pleasure brought me in contact with, have at all times, influenced my conduct in a greater, or lesser degree.

I have ever found, that mere worldly education, when acted upon as a rule of life in business matters, is calculated to produce two results; the one is the saving of money, and the other is the loss of the more generous susceptibilities of our nature. Upon an impartial examination of my own character, I find that I am unfitted for the sharp encounters of commercial warfare. I neither possess the confidence, nor the cunning necessary for such an enterprise, and

I have been personally acquainted with scores of men similarly constituted. It has been well remarked, that "the race is not always to the fleet of foot, or the battle to the strong." The great secret of worldly prosperity is to be found in a *oneness* of thought, or a concentration of the mind to a given purpose. Depend upon it, it is not your clever men who are the best calculated to steer themselves down the stream of worldly prosperity, even though they may be placed in it by fortuitous circumstances; much less are they able to take advantage of the spring tides that lead to fortune. I have found that there are only two classes of men who can appropriate the fruits of their industry and hold them in reserve. The first of these are your plodding men, who have made up their minds to be trustees to society, and who, in the pursuit of their callings neither turn to the right or to the left out of their way, to suit the circumstances or convenience of anybody else. The second class are the men of decided talent, whose genius fits them to play a variety of parts on the stage of life.

In the second department of social instruction, I have received much valuable and pleasing information both from pulpit oratory and public lectures. But I must confess that my most important information has been obtained from books; there is a quiet pleasing enjoyment in lighting up our own knowledge at the torch of another man's genius which we can feel much better than express. Books are the telegraphs by which men's thoughts, feelings, and sentiments are transmitted from one generation of the human family to another. The electric sympathy of mind continually runs through the conductors of the mighty press, and we receive the currents of thought as we are more or less prepared for their reception. The light of knowledge bursts upon some men like the rays of the sun just emerged from behind a dark cloud; while to others it gradually opens up its unfolding beauties like the dawning light of a spring morning. Books are undying monuments of the genius and intellectual greatness of those who have passed over the journey of life, or of others who may yet be wayfarers with ourselves. If the spirit of the Almighty speaks to us through the boundless works of his creation, intellectual natures are the interpreters of his language, and they explain to us the use of all things in the economy of the universe. Books are the repositories of these wonderful translations; by their aid our thoughts expand into the dignity of lofty feeling, which enables us to form a more exalted idea of the sublimity and goodness of the Eternal Fabricator of all things. The choice of books should be made much in the same way a man selects his friends, that is, they should only be valued for the innocent pleasure or good counsel they may afford us. The best aid to religion, I hold, is to be found in the New Testament. Historical books may be fairly placed at the top of all other sources of human knowledge; in this class we have the true character of man in all the phases and conditions of his existence. After history, I would recommend works upon the arts and sciences; these give us an insight into the workings of the human mind, whether directed to the invention of articles for the uses of everyday life, the noble conceptions of the painter, or the divine inspirations of the sculptor; the profound researches of the mathematician or the philosopher, who takes a wider range in the great field of the universe in arranging and classifying the works of creation, and thereby exposing to our admiring senses the beauty and harmony which pervades through all nature, whether in the distribution of plants and minerals, or the order and arrangement of the heavenly bodies. The next useful class of books, after these, may be said to be such as treats of the common humanities. In this walk of literature we have an inexhaustible store, which, if well selected, are calculated to afford a continual source of both pleasure and instruction. I would have you bear in mind that those books that teach us the beauty of kindliness and forbearance in our intercourse with each other are at all times to be preferred. I hold that there is little good to be learned from those men who seat themselves above the common order of humanity for the purpose of finding fault with all who do not come up to the standard of their own assumed excellence. There is a snarling arrogance in the character of such men that is peculiar to themselves. I have no doubt but they have their use in the economy of the world; but one thing is certain, however much we may admire them for their talents and force of genius, we never can love them for that amiable virtue which, while it reproves, commands our affection. The satirist who works with a saw will never correct the follies or vices of men in the same degree with him who wields a razor! There are other two classes of books which I think are perhaps more useful on their shelves than for any other purpose to which they can be turned. The first of these are the works of maudling sentimentalists; these books are full of language without meaning, and pretty flowers without fragrance! Among them are the measured effusions of men who do not possess sufficient specific gravity to keep them on the earth; their works are, therefore, too *starry* for common mortals! ! The second class, comprise the works of authors who manufacture plots and incidents to suit distorted minds; the persons of their little dramas are made up of exaggerated shreds of humanity, who think and act under a lunar influence, and therefore continually outrage all our common notions of congruity!

From the above observations, you must not suppose that I am opposed to all works of fiction; on the contrary, I am of the opinion that some of the best books in the English language are to be found in this class; I need only instance Goldsmith's *Vicar of Wakefield* and Defoe's *Robinson Crusoe*. There is a charm about these books which will always possess a fascinating influence over the minds of their readers. The secret of this charm exists solely in their keeping with our knowledge of right and wrong. Men of lively imagination, and possessing a full command over the language in which they write, may please with peculiar combinations of thought; but it is a fact worthy of notice that only those who are true to nature are able to find an echo in the hearts of all men. It is thus that a "fellow-feeling makes the whole world akin."

Letter XIII

London, September, 1855.

MY DEAR THOMAS.—Like a man that has accomplished a long and arduous journey, and who, while seated on a rising ground, feels a melancholy pleasure in surveying the dangers and difficulties through which he has passed, I cannot help, like Lot's wife, casting one long lingering look behind. The past is fraught with dear-bought lessons of experience; the present only exists in the mind, while the thought rushes through it with the speed of lightning. For aught I know, the future may be to me a dark passage of misery, without the buoyant energy of youth or manhood to spur me in the last battle of life. I think a cursory *resumé* may enable you to seize hold of the salient points in my character, whereby you may take advantage of the lessons it is calculated to impress upon the mind of the thoughtful. During the first twelve years of my life, I was dragged through all the various scenes, and conditions consequent to the *Nomadic* existence of a vagrant. Although this unenviable state was surrounded with innumerable hardships, and even occasional privations, yet it was not without its sunny spots. The storms which passed with even the greatest violence over my head, only lasted for the time being, and after their fury was over, the calm of forgetfulness reigned supreme. The morning of life is the legitimate time for hunting the butterfly on the wing. It is then we pull the beautiful flowers in the very wantonness of thoughtless pleasure, and it is then we follow our untamed *wills* in the madness of delight. Many and many times, the dewy eve has found me wandering by the clear running brook, through some shady dell, or twisting the green rushes into conical hats in some quiet nook, in complete forgetfulness of all the world; while the lash awaited me when night or hunger drove me to my temporary home.

The time I spent under my father's roof was one of continual suffering. Physical hardships were nothing new to me, but I had never before been treated with the freezing coldness of neglect. Had I remained in Ireland, I think my natural energy of mind would have been crushed, and I might have remained a ragged outcast during life. My conduct in leaving under the circumstances gave early proof of my determination of character. Settling down to the business of a country life was indicative of my desire to follow the pursuits of honest industry. During the last two years I was with my mother, I had large sums of money continuously passing through my hands without abusing the trust reposed in me; at such a time, and under such guidance, this was no bad proof of my honesty. During the next three years, I was like a feather on the ocean of life, dashed here and there by the conflicting circumstances of my condition. Although I was an atom in the world of life, I was never without an individuality; in all my miserable littleness, I possessed a mind far above my position; and though I often wandered in the gloomy valley, bordering on despair, the lamp of hope never ceased to burn and light me on my way. My great struggle in the battle of life was to find my proper position in society. You have seen how I suffered, and braved every difficulty in the attainment of my level.

I think I am fairly entitled to credit for one act of wise determination, and that was in serving my apprenticeship to a trade. I look upon this as the grand turning point in my existence; to me it was the half-way house between the desert of my youth, and the sunny lands of my manhood. I have reason to reflect with pleasure upon my conduct as a journeyman; I entirely escaped the leading vice of the profession at the time, which was intemperance. And although I was a young man, when compared to many of my co-mates, who were intelligent, and well conducted, my judgment was uniformly looked up to in almost every case of emergency. My political career was one of pride, folly and stupidity. As a commercial man, I wanted ballast; and my credulity too frequently made me forget my own interest in consideration for the feelings of others. As a publican, I was above the business, and as a necessary consequence it got above me! The next three years of my life, after leaving Glasgow, may be found in the chapter of accidents. When I went to my trade I had all the wild associations of my vagrant existence clinging to my memory; and when I left Glasgow, a ruined man, the flesh-pots of Egypt held their fascinating sway over my feelings, like dreams of past enjoyments. In my moments of sadness, I have had the folly to think that my fall was unmerited; but a little sound reflection would banish the thought, and again and again I have resolved to improve the future by the dear-bought experience of the past.

During my wedded life I have had sixteen births, and twelve deaths to provide for.[129] In the course of events these were things of absorbing interest for the time being, and they have all been surrounded with many feelings of much joy and no little sorrow. I have always been blessed with the enjoyment of domestic love and sincerity; my family and fireside have therefore ever been my first and last consideration. The soothing pleasures and quiet enjoyments of home have always exercised a pleasing influence over my mind, and when the toils, trials, and vexations of the world have pressed upon me with their cankering cares and corroding anxieties, the approving smile of my hoping and confiding wife would chase the melancholy gloom from my heart. The innocent prattle and joyous gambols of my children

---

[129] By the time of the 1882 ed. these figures had become eighteen and thirteen.

have always been a source of real pleasure to me; and now I frequently delight to unbend myself, and occasionally become a part of themselves. In my sad moments, I have sometimes felt my ire kindling at their boisterous mirth, but I have checked the rising spleen, when I reflected that youth is the season when their little laughing batteries should be charged with the electricity of pure hilarity. The wise man hath said, that "there is a time for all things;" and it is surely soon enough to encounter the cares of the world when reason has been assisted to her throne by the experience of years!

You have now before you an honest history of my life up to the present time. I am aware you will find much to blame, but in this respect your censure will not be more severe than my own. You will also find some little to commend; and, on the whole, you will not fail to find much useful matter for reflection. I think you will agree with me, that I have passed through many severe and dangerous trials, and on some occasions suffered no small hardships. The battle of my life is well calculated to prove to young men what energy and determination of character are able to accomplish when rightly directed. It is true that I had frequent opportunities of doing more, and turning my position to a more fortunate account; but in looking at the other side of the picture, if I had gone with the strong tide of my circumstances in early life, I should have remained a vagrant still, if not something worse!

Many of my historical notices will be new to you; and I have necessarily had to speak much about the manners and habits of those who immediately preceded you in the journey of life.

In my little time I have witnessed many strange reverses in the fortunes of others. Upon more occasions than one, I have been enabled to assist in supplying the necessities of those who were once in such a position that I would have been glad of the crumbs that fell from their tables. On the other hand, I have seen scores of men run up the scale of society, some by sheer plodding, some by the force of their genius, and others by less honourable methods. Between forty and fifty years ago, I was a bare-footed and ragged urchin, unworthy of notice, unless I was in somebody's way; like others in the same condition, I was sometimes relieved through a feeling of kindness, and at others to save further importunity!! Like St. Paul, I may therefore be said to have been all things to all men. The ground that I walked over as a beggar, I have also traversed in the character of a gentleman, and upon more occasions than one, at the houses where I once sought alms, I have been saluted with the respect due to rank far above my own. For the last two years, I have held a situation of considerable responsibility, during that time I have come in contact with many of the first-class commercial men in the United Kingdom. And what is of no small importance to myself, I have the entire confidence of my employer. My home is the abode of happiness, and my own, and the lives of my family gently glide down the stream of existence in peace and contentment. Whether the remainder of my journey be rough or smooth, providence alone can decide; and in the language of Jacob on leaving the home of his father, I would say,—"If God shall be with me, and shall keep me in the way by which I shall walk, and shall give me bread to eat and raiment to put on, and I shall return prosperously to my father's house, the Lord shall be my God."[130]

[130] A slight misquotation from *Genesis* 28, vv 20–22.

Index